Dear Brother,

By

Brian Forrest Roberts

© Copyright 2005, Brian Forrest Roberts

For our Family.

Acknowledgements

Through all of the time and effort I've put into this book, I've been consistently reminded of how much I depend on friends and family. It would be a serious error on my part if I didn't take at least a page to thank them. So thanks. All of you. And most importantly, thanks be to God for loving me through such people.

Now for the specifics!

Laura Roberts: My wife, who came into the Church with me and has served as a wonderful partner in the race to Heaven. Thanks for your patience and love, ladybug.
Pat Sullivan: My mentor, who gently and reverently led me to embrace the grace of the Catholic Church. Apologetics without apology and the sweetest, most sincere, child-like faith of anyone I know. Laura and I couldn't have asked for a better sponsor!
Jolene Walker: My mother-in-law. Without her this book would have most certainly been off balance. Sometimes I write like I speak – unfortunately, that can mean a lack of forethought. She ensured that my readers won't put the book down too abruptly.
Geoff Ward: Hanging out with people like Geoff is like taking small vacations. I don't know anyone else who can make people feel so immediately at ease. Geoff, without you I might take life too seriously. Thanks for the friendship and the insights.
Jon Shibata: Good to have a friend from my old community journey home to Rome with me. Thanks for your fellowship, encouragement, and wisdom.
The ROOTS crew and all my friends from the Vineyard: I'll never cease thanking God for the education and example you provided! May your energy and passion for Christ be blessed.
My brother Dave, my uncle Gary, and my Mother: You were the ones I was writing to initially. You've provided the inspiration and motivation for this work. Thank you for your love and I hope you enjoy and are blessed by my book.

Table of Contents

Foreword……………………………………………...…....page i

The First Letter………………………………..………....page 1
The Second Letter…………………………………....…...page 29

The General Councils of the Church

The Council of Jerusalem……………………………….page 34
The Council of Nicea……………………………………..page 37
The First Council of Constantinople……………………....page 40
The First Council of Ephesus……………………………..page 42
The Council of Chalcedon……………………………….page 44
The Second Council of Constantinople……………….page 46
The Third Council of Constantinople………………….page 48
The Second Council of Nicea……………………………page 50
The Fourth Council of Constantinople……………..…….page 52
The First Lateran Council………………………………….page 54
The Second Lateran Council…………………………..page 56
The Third Lateran Council………………………………page 59
The Fourth Lateran Council……………………………page 61
The First Council of Lyons………………………………page 63
The Second Council of Lyons…………………………...page 65
The Council of Vienne……………………………………page 67
The Council of Constance……………………………….page 69
The Council of Florence…………………………………page 73
The Fifth Lateran Council………………………………page 76
The Council of Trent……………………………………....page 78
The First Vatican Council………………………………..page 82
The Second Vatican Council……………………………..page 85

The Third Letter..page 95

The Family on Five Fingers

What is the Church?..page 98
What is the Word of God?....................................page 146
What is the Role of Mary?....................................page 180
What is the Communion of the Saints?...............page 216
What is the Mass?..page 241

The Fourth Letter..page 288

Afterward...page 296

Appendix 1..page 304
Appendix 2..page 322
Appendix 3..page 325

FOREWORD

Isaiah 55:8-9

For my thoughts are not your thoughts, neither are your ways my ways, saith the Lord. For as the heavens are higher than the earth, so are my ways higher than your ways, and my thoughts than your thoughts.

    Though it contains some, this is not a book on philosophy. It was not written by a professor. Nor is it a book devoted solely to theology. It was not written by a famous preacher. It is most likely not going to be the kind of book you would want to put on your mantel as a conversation piece or symbol of sophistication. It may or may not inspire you or convince you of anything.

    What you are now reading was written by a young, married, man who hasn't even finished his college education yet. I've had no intentions of shaking the earth's foundations in my attempts to get this published. In fact, these pages originally were written with a style and intent solely for a few immediate family members – though I quickly discerned the message to be applicable to a much larger Family.

    Nevertheless, these letters are peculiar. The four of them combine into one volume several genres of Christian reading. The first is about my conversion, the second is about the Church's historical struggle to discover herself while fighting heresy, the third is about the greatest blessings of Christ's Mystical Body in Scripture and Tradition, and the fourth is about the cultural relevance of the Church today.

    The whole book has only one principle aim: to arouse an unsettling feeling in you, best expressed by the words, *what if.* Is there a chance that you could misinterpret scripture? Is there a chance you're living in a paradigm? Is there a chance you're putting the philosophy or religion of men above your pursuit of the Truth? Let's be honest: *Is there a chance you could be wrong?*

I've asked myself those questions all my life. That's probably why my favorite fictional reading material has always been fantasy! A good fantasy story can ask "what if" in an infinite number of ways with an infinite number of answers. My own struggles to answer "what if" are most likely why I've devoted so much study to theology and philosophy. And because the one thing I never doubt is that I am not God, nor can I ever hope to know all there is to know, I will continue asking the "what if" questions, even when I *feel* I am completely in the Truth.

Individuals arrive at their own conclusions for a reason (and we would all do well to remind ourselves of this): they sincerely *feel* those conclusions to be the best available to them. The Buddhist who experiences a profound "spiritual" euphoria during meditation. The whirling dervish, drunk on his experience of God's movement within him. The southern Pentecostal who feels the Holy Spirit when speaking in tongues. The Bible-belt Baptist who senses God while memorizing Scripture. All of these people are convinced that their Way is the best way because of a *subjective experience*. They may or may not voice this conviction to people of other religious persuasions, but it is undeniable that their feelings, emotions, and experiences prove to *themselves* that their logic is sound and their beliefs are superior – or they simply wouldn't hold to them.

All that said, I have too much experience in being wrong to claim certainty in being right. That's why so much of life must be taken on *faith*. Now. Faith, I *do* have. I have the most faith I have ever had that what I am writing about in this book is the Truth. I've progressed through many religious modes of thought and many more avenues in my relationship with Christ precisely because I acknowledge that I live by faith. I realize that on any given topic, my logic and reasoning could be affected by my feelings. If the objective facts are manipulated by my subjective intuitions, my logic may be flawed and my conclusions could be wrong. I keep a watchful eye for such errors and misinterpretations.

This approach to life has treated me well. In my pursuit of God's Kingdom (Truth, Beauty, Love, and the Way of Life), I've been willing to let go or grasp hold of anything if it seemed to yield a fuller understanding of – or deeper communion with – God. Throughout my spiritual journey, I've never felt so convinced by logic, persuaded by reason, swayed by emotion, moved by love, or convicted by God that a particular philosophy is the utter Truth as I am of the teachings I now assent to.

So I invite you to step out of the boat and onto the water while you read this book, daring to ask yourself that all important question. Because what if someone you loved already had a personal relationship with Christ, but found *more* from it in an unexpected place? What if the Church you thought you knew had an identity and heritage tracing back much farther than the first Protestants? What if you're missing out on the deepest joys of God's Family? What if you're oblivious to the most culturally relevant aspect of Christianity?

The following four letters challenge you to ask those questions, evaluate your answers, and ultimately decide if you're certain that your thoughts are God's. I wrote them, not to be coldly polemical or to convince you that I'm "more right" than you, but to invite you to an understanding of why I believe the things I do and why those beliefs fill me with such joy. In my most optimistic of hopes, I wrote them so that you might appreciate the way I feel and understand Jesus as I know him – that we might celebrate together in communion with the fullness of all God has to offer.

Throughout this book, I will be quoting from the King James Version of the Bible, unless otherwise noted. I do this because while most Christians don't have a problem with the KJV, there *are* some who have a problem with any other version. So I use the KJV for the sake of the "King James Only" Christians. Also, wherever emphasis or notes appear, they were added by me.

Be sure to keep your Bible readily available while reading this book, so you can look up references as they appear. As you do so, remember that according to our faith, anything that is true is only true through, with, and in the Word of God. Any doctrine pertaining to salvation or the Church must only be efficacious by the blood of Christ. Hence I may say, without hesitation or trickery, that anything conveyed in this book is based upon my belief in the all sufficiency of Christ alone. For if it were not for Christ, everything I say in the pages ahead would be utterly meaningless. Everything. You may need to remind yourself of this by re-reading this paragraph.

    I confess that most, if not all, of the thought in this book is far from original. Indeed, it is nearly 2,000 years old. Even the research, for the most part, was done by other people. I've just taken what they've provided, brought it all together, organized it in my own way and explained it in my own words. In fact, if the only thing this book accomplishes is to get you to read something from the list of my own resources in the first appendix, I will have considered it a success!

    What if...

THE FIRST LETTER

Dear Brother,

I love you. Nevertheless, you may feel these letters are offensive. In retrospect, you may wish you had never read them. It can't be helped. A few short weeks from now, this Easter, I will enter into full communion with the Church of Rome. I am becoming Catholic. And I know because you love *me*, I can count on fears, accusations, even anger in you at this decision – all aimed at the Roman Catholic Church, of course.

But I'm willing to bet most of it is due to misunderstandings based on misrepresentations. Archbishop Fulton J. Sheen once said he didn't think there were 100 people in America who hated the Catholic Church, but millions hated what they *thought* the Catholic Church was! These letters are not principally meant to convince you (although I would praise God if that was the result). They are meant to disarm you. I would like to have a chance to tell you the story of my journey.

You know why I call you brother. More than any other tie that bonds, our mutual faith in the Lord begs us to be called "brothers". We are in a family of people who place their hope in the birth, death, and resurrection of Jesus Christ. Long ago this earned us the nickname, "Christian". Although it was coined to taunt us at first, we embraced it with pride and used it as a base description of ourselves from then on. It is the label on us and all our family members.

It's probable that you don't know the exact circumstances surrounding my conversion. Although I was raised in a King James Bible-believing, Fundamentalist Baptist house, it didn't seem to stick. True, I trusted what my parents taught me and had faith in what the Bible said. I talked with God quite a bit, and believed that Jesus' sacrifice atoned for my sins once I asked God for forgiveness. All I had to do was repentantly ask and He came into my heart. I was baptized at around eleven years of age and every once in awhile (when I felt especially convicted), I would rededicate my life to Christ with the "sinner's prayer". I was even sent to Christian schools! Even so, somewhere in the midst of my teenage years things began to slide downhill and by the time I was off to college you could call me a full blown New Age fanatic.

Eventually, I began to get skeptical of the New Age philosophy. It became apparent that since all the world's religions tell different stories and convey different methods to attain salvation from the burdens of this world (and perhaps the next), they can't all be totally true or inspired by God. So either *none of them* are totally inspired by God and thus, God never cared to be in total, honest, communion with us, or *only one is*. Or God doesn't exist and they don't matter much, anyway. I was swayed to trust the latter opinion more than the others.

My first couple years of college, I became resentful of what I thought was my *brainwashed* youth. I felt people in the world were worse off for being fed "fairy tales" of religion. And since Christianity was the most dominant and evangelistic world religion, I began taking my anger out on it. I devoured anti-Christian articles and essays, feeling I had stumbled across all the secrets my old Sunday school teachers didn't want me to know. When I became editor of my college newspaper, I publicly voiced these opinions.

But I became too cocky. I started challenging the authors of Christian web pages to email debates. One of these people caught more attention than the rest. He was compassionate and sympathetic to my stances, even though he disagreed. He was also knowledgeable and able to defend his faith admirably. Eventually, I was irked enough that I read a book of Christian apologetics that a friend gave me, *The Case for Christ*, by Lee Strobel. In it, I discovered not the blind faith I thought Christianity was, but a reasonable one that stood out among the other religions of the world in its logic and evidence.

This spiked my curiosity enough that I wanted to give Christianity a second chance through other Apologetics related books like Strobel's. Other authors whose works I studied were Josh McDowell, Norman Geisler, and Phillip Yancey, to name a few. Researching Christianity's mounting evidence quickly progressed to seeking the One behind it all.

I remember one evening I cracked open the Bible and began reading the New Testament. It had been ages since I had read the Bible for any other purpose than to point out inconsistencies, contradictions, vulgarities, or atrocities. This time I was reading to hear God's voice. And I read almost all night, picking up right where I left off after some sleep. Eventually, God responded by gracefully opening my eyes to his existence. He did indeed wish to be in total, honest, communion with us – with *me*. And I developed a firm belief that Christianity held the true history of that ongoing communion. It took six months for God to reach my heart through my hard head. But I finally received Him back into my life.

Very quickly I realized where my church home was to be and began attending and serving there regularly. I began fervently praying to the Lord and seeking His response in my Bible studies, devotions, other people, environmental circumstances, etc. I was filled with the Holy Spirit and on fire for God. Over the next two years, I led small groups, performed community services, spoke at church, defended the faith, guided souls to Christ, wrote tracts, grew closer to the Lord, and got engaged along the way.

Everything went well. I held a non-denominational view of the universal Church. It didn't matter what denomination you belonged to – so long as you had a living relationship with Christ. There was no "best truth" – only the Bible. There was no way of telling who was right and who was wrong about the things "nonessential" to salvation. This was why Paul told us not argue about such matters, right? Denominational differences didn't matter much to me.

But I started to wonder who had the authority to dictate what, in God's revealed Word, was "nonessential". Where is the line of unimportance drawn between doctrines like the Trinity or the Atonement and others like Baptism and Justification? At what point is it possible to say, "Okay, this other stuff is pretty much just for theologians or other stuffy headed people – you already know what you *need* to know." After all, disagreements over eating habits are one thing, but disagreements over the literalness of a passage that Christ himself specifically connects to salvation, like John 6:53-55, are quite another:

> *Then Jesus said unto them, "Verily, verily, I say unto you, Except ye eat the flesh of the Son of man, and drink his blood, ye have no life in you. Whoso eateth my flesh, and drinketh my blood, hath eternal life; and I will raise him up at the last day. For my flesh is meat indeed, and my blood is drink indeed."*

I slowly began to realize there had existed an essential flaw in my line of thinking. It was one that, to my discredit, I had experience with. You see, I had abandoned New Age spirituality for the very same reason: not all ways can be best. There can only be one. One Church. One set of beliefs. One set of doctrines.

Even if two people are in the same family, it doesn't automatically mean they are one. Being in a family does not necessarily mean full communion with your father or other family members, as the parable of the prodigal son clearly shows.

I started to wonder who had the authority to dictate what, in God's revealed Word, was "nonessential".

People of different denominations can talk all they want about being "one" through a common relationship with Christ. But that's all it is. Talk.

The very existence of denominations proves otherwise. Christians may be divided on political, cultural, or otherwise secular issues, but *wherever* doctrinal differences occur, spiritual unity ceases to exist. At best, Christians of varying denominations might share a *partial* communion with each other through a few similar beliefs. But since Christ is God's revealed Word, "unity in Christ" means unity in *faith*. And that means a common faith *in its entirety*.

This idea seemed more logical, as I slowly grasped the thread of history. Since the creation of this universe, our God has seen to it that there would be a united front to represent him and guide this world closer to him. True, during every period of time his people have failed him – sometimes horribly so. But he has never abandoned his covenants. Expanded them, made them sweeter, maybe; but abandoned? Never.

And so a Body of witnesses always remained. They must be a kingdom; a city set upon a hill, shining a clear light, which cannot exhibit confusion of sacraments, morals, or doctrine. And after considering that kingdom – that original and legitimate Church – everyone on the planet must find themselves in one of three states: no communion, partial communion, or full communion.

Contrary to man's experience, there are no grey areas with God. When it comes to truth, God simply cannot be a relativist because He is the Creator of the Universe and *is* Truth, itself. Although we may never know what all of these absolutes are, this side of glory, we can be sure that we *will* know when we get to Heaven. All we can know here is, just as one religion must hold more truth than all the rest, so too must one denomination hold more truth.

Certainly, there is no perfect group of Christians. But a visible group should exist that has all the best answers when it comes to God's revelation. Otherwise, I must believe that God willed the Church to be a scattered, fragmented, invisible entity, only consisting of a small handful of people who miraculously possess the same doctrinal stances. And is that really reasonable? It didn't seem like it. One denomination must stand out from the rest in its ability to steer us in the right direction; to defend a *firm* set of morals and doctrines that, if not capable of eliminating grey areas, certainly highlight apostolic teaching in a modern world. But which one?

I pushed these annoying thoughts to the back of my head. Whatever denomination was lucky enough to get it *most* right, there were Christians who nonetheless existed outside of her. Christ himself pointed this out:

> *And John answered him, saying, "Master, we saw one casting out devils in thy name, and he followeth not us: and we forbad him, because he followeth not us." But Jesus said, "Forbid him not: for there is no man which shall do a miracle in my name, that can lightly speak evil of me. For he that is not against us is on our part. For whosoever shall give you a cup of water to drink in my name, because ye belong to Christ, verily I say unto you, he shall not lose his reward."*
>
> (Mark 9:38-41, KJV)

Sure, it would have been *ideal* for those other Christians (who we might call the "independent disciples") to be part of Christ's troupe (the "organized disciples"). After all, he had hand-picked the leaders of his newly commissioned Church. But although he definitely drew a line by referring to himself and his *organized* Church (the disciples) as "us" (in contrast to the other Christians), Jesus emphasized that the general charity of Christianity was more important.

It seemed to me from this passage that as long as I was honestly seeking the kingdom where I was at, Christ would handle the rest. I had faith that I would somehow make the transition from "independent disciple" to "organized disciple", whatever that meant. God liked this mindset, apparently. Because the kingdom – and the transition – that I had been seeking was revealed to me in a big way.

It happened on my way to visit my fiancé's family in Vegas. I was given a book to read by my good Catholic friend, Patrick Sullivan: *One, Holy, Catholic, and Apostolic* by Kenneth Whitehead. The book retells a summary of Early Church history from a Catholic perspective. The attempt is to convince the reader that through all of its growth in devotions, canon laws, and disciplines, the Roman Catholic Church today is in sacraments, morals, and faith the same One, Holy, Catholic, and Apostolic Church that has continuously existed since its founding by Jesus Christ. Sure, the book was biased (the author was Catholic, after all). But my attempts at critiquing it revealed a startling fact: I was severely uninformed about Early Church history.

There was a gigantic gap from the New Testament to Martin Luther that had quietly existed in my brain, going unnoticed until it was unexpectedly confronted by Pat's book. *Of course,* I thought to myself. *That makes sense, right? All that space is occupied by…by Catholics! Wait, that doesn't sound right…*

At first I was hesitant to look into what the leaders of the Early Church taught. What if they seemed to agree with the book my friend gave me? But I knew I had to do the research. So it was that I dove into Church history. I didn't want to get any more Catholic bias, so I drove to my local (and very Protestant) Christian bookstore to buy a non-Catholic Church history book, *Christianity Through the Centuries; A History of the Christian Church*, by Earle E. Cairns.

> ### *I was severely uninformed about Early Church history.*

As I read, it seemed that certain facts might have been twisted to better fit Protestant ideology. The author's use of vocabulary when describing the Catholic Church was less than flattering. Nevertheless, Cairns couldn't shake the strong resemblance of modern-day Catholicism to the supposedly "pre-Catholic" Early Church. It made me wonder…

When I began to read the Church Fathers themselves – those great Christian Leaders of the first several centuries – I was surprised at what a consensus there really was supporting Catholicism. I was frustrated to find such broad agreement on so many distinctively "Catholic" doctrines. Uncomfortably, I ran into quotes like this one by Ignatius of Antioch in his *Letter to the Philadelphians*, written in A.D. 110:

> "For as many as are of God and of Jesus Christ are also with the bishop. And as many as shall, in the exercise of repentance, return into the unity of the Church, these, too, shall belong to God, that they may live according to Jesus Christ. Do not err, my brethren. If any man follows him

> that makes a schism in the Church, he shall not inherit the kingdom of God."

Then this one, written by Tertullian in his *On the Prescription Against Heretics* in A.D. 200:

> "Was anything withheld from the knowledge of Peter, who is called the rock on which the church should be built, who also obtained the keys of the kingdom of heaven, with the power of loosing and binding in heaven and on earth?...Where was Marcion then, that shipmaster of Pontus, the zealous student of Stoicism? Where was Valentinus then, the disciple of Platonism? For it is evident that those men lived not so long ago,--in the reign of Antoninus for the most part,--and that they at first were believers in the doctrine of the Catholic Church, in the church of Rome under the episcopate of the blessed Eleutherus, until on account of their ever restless curiosity, with which they even infected the brethren, they were more than once expelled."

And this one by Clement of Rome in his first letter to the Corinthians, written in A.D. 96:

> "Our apostles also knew, through our Lord Jesus Christ, and there would be strife on account of the office of the episcopate. For this reason, therefore, inasmuch as they had obtained a perfect fore-knowledge of this, they appointed those presbyters already mentioned, and afterwards gave instructions, that when these should fall asleep, other approved men should succeed them in their ministry."

Also, this one by Irenaeus, written around A.D. 180 in his *Against Heresies*:

> "Since, however, it would be very tedious, in such a volume as this, to reckon up the successions of all the Churches, we do put to confusion all those who, in whatever manner, whether by an evil self-pleasing, by vainglory, or by blindness and perverse opinion, assemble in unauthorized meetings; [we do this, I say,] by

indicating that tradition derived from the apostles, of the very great, the very ancient, and universally known Church founded and organized at Rome by the two most glorious apostles, Peter and Paul; as also [by pointing out] the faith preached to men, which comes down to our time by means of the successions of the bishops. For it is a matter of necessity that every Church should agree with this Church, on account of its pre-eminent authority, that is, the faithful everywhere, inasmuch as the apostolical tradition has been preserved continuously by those [faithful men] who exist everywhere."

Then a quote from Justin "Martyr" in his *First Apology*, written somewhere between A.D. 110 and 165:

"For not as common bread and common drink do we receive these; but in like manner as Jesus Christ our Savior, having been made flesh and blood for our salvation, so likewise have we been taught that the food which is blessed by the prayer of His word, and from which our blood and flesh by transmutation are nourished, is the flesh and blood of that Jesus who was made flesh."

And this one by Origen in his *Homily on Leviticus*, written in A.D. 244:

"Baptism is given for the remission of sins; and according to the usage of the Church, Baptism is given even to infants. And indeed if there were nothing in infants which required a remission of sins and nothing in them pertinent to forgiveness, the grace of baptism would seem superfluous."

Scary, huh? All of that was written *before* the fall of Rome – even before Rome ceased persecuting the Church! And yet there can be seen a firm belief in
- *the organization of Christians,*
  (cf. Acts 15)
- *the authority and hierarchy within the Church,*
  (cf. Matt. 16:18-19; 18:17, John 20:21-23, 1 Tim. 3:15)

- *apostolic succession,*
  (cf. Acts 14:23, 2 Tim. 1:6; 2:2)
- *the primacy of the Church in Rome,*
  (cf. Rom. 1:7; 16:17-20)
- *the doctrine of baptismal regeneration and infant baptism,*
  (cf. John 3:5, Mark 16:16, Acts 2:38-39; 16:15, 33; 22:16, 1 Cor. 7:14, Titus 3:5, 1 Pet. 3:18-21, Col. 2:11-12)
- *the child-like faith that the Eucharist is actually Christ's flesh and blood under the appearances of symbolic bread and wine,*
  (cf. John 6, Mark 14:22-24, 1 Cor. 11:27-29)
- *and even a reference to the Christians who hold to all of the apostolic doctrines as being "Catholic" (meaning "universal")!*
  (cf. Philip. 1:27, Romans 15:6, Matthew 28:19-20)

And that was just the tip of the iceberg! I soon ran into ancient support for other Catholic doctrines, one after another. Not only that, but these early Christians were convinced that Scripture – either explicitly or implicitly – supported these doctrines. At first I attempted to comfort myself with the idea that the Early Church had to fight so many heresies that it was perhaps possible for a "corrupt" Catholic doctrine or two to sneak in.

Using this line of thought, I tried to believe I could write off any teachings of the Early Church that I disagreed with. But I quickly realized how infantile that rational was. After all, as the Body of Christ matured in time, so did the understanding of all the doctrines with which I was having problems. The disagreements I had with Catholic theology didn't dwindle in the course of history – they were underlined and increasingly shoved in my face!

If there was a wide-ranging theological consensus in every period of Church history, where was I to turn? Only to those schools of thought that this consensus labeled as heresy! If I said, *"Show me the evidence of that belief in the Early Church"* it could be pointed out. If I retorted, *"Where and why is this belief in the Church today"* an outline could be given. If I demanded, *"How are these beliefs possibly compatible with Scripture"* countless writings from the saints and today's theologians could walk me through the Bible, touring me through Catholicism.

Slowly, as I counter-referenced the beliefs of the Early Church with Scripture, I was shoved into an uncomfortable corner. I had already been trained as a child in anti-Catholic polemics, but all the arguments that I was taught to mentally rehearse in the event of Catholic inklings seemed weak in the face of historical Christianity. And since my return to Christ, I had come into the possession of books like *The Bible and the Roman Church* by J.C. Macaulay and *Reasoning from the Scriptures with Catholics* by Ron Rhodes (not to mention a host of other material by James White, Norman Geisler, and James McCarthy), so it wasn't as if I was short on the best stuff anti-Catholic scholars had to offer.

Still, merely writing off all recorded Church history as "apostate" between the completion of the New Testament and the revolt of Luther seemed to be a bit of a stretch. Was it really possible that immediately upon the death of the last apostle, the whole Church spontaneously generated all the "Catholic doctrines"? That the first 15 centuries of Christians "got it wrong"? Thinking so, it seemed, would require a great deal of arrogance on my part. All I could do at this point was what I did in the same situation when I was anti-Christian: turn the tables.

Just like before, when I had to do the same thing for Christianity in general, I flipped my view of *Catholic* Christianity from guilty until proven innocent to innocent until proven guilty. If I had been living in a Protestant paradigm, there was only one way to find out. The time came to look at what Catholics had to say in their defense. Having been through the general Christian apologetics run around before, I had a good idea of how to research such things on the internet. Instead, I just typed out "www.catholic.com" in the address bar and hit the enter key.

Maybe I didn't really want *their* answers. Maybe I was afraid their answers would make sense! Or maybe I just wanted to see what would happen. Whatever the case, the site did indeed happen to fit the bill quite nicely. It is the internet home of *Catholic Answers*, one of the United State's largest lay-run apostolates of Catholic apologetics and evangelization. The site hosts a cornucopia of easy to understand information and includes forums for online discussions as well as a library of tracts and quotes from the Early Church Fathers. Pretty good match for what I was after, I think.

As I began my web research and reading of books on Catholic apologetics, I was careful to balance the information out with Protestant counter-point. But just like before, when I was struggling to continue my disbelief in general Christianity, the mounting evidence for this particular group of Christians was quickly becoming overwhelming.

This was especially apparent in a book called *Not by Scripture Alone*, a collection of essays refuting *sola scriptura* (an essential pillar upon which Protestantism stands) by various authors, all edited by Robert Sungenis. Though I still disagree with Sungenis on a few points, that book was remarkable to me in that it not only presented the Catholic stance in an exhaustive and scholarly fashion, but it also answered common Protestant objections. Another book, *Upon This Rock*, by Steve Ray, was helpful as well. I'm no logician, but I think I discovered that the basic case for Catholicism might be broken down into the following three syllogisms:

> *It seemed that disagreeing with the majority vote of Christians throughout history would require a great deal of arrogance on my part.*

1.
   a. **Christ has absolute authority over doctrinal interpretation and Church**

government. (*Matthew 7:29, John 5:19-23*)
- b. **Christ delegated his authority to the united Apostles.** (*Matthew 16:15-19, John 20:19-23*)
- c. **Therefore, the united Apostles (through, with, and in Christ) had absolute authority over doctrinal interpretation and Church government.** (*John 16:12-15, Acts 15*)

2.
- a. **The united Apostles had absolute authority over doctrinal interpretation and Church government.** (*Matthew 10:40, Matthew 18:15-20, Luke 10:16, Acts 5:12-16*)
- b. **The united Apostles authoritatively decided that it was necessary for Church government to individually delegate their authority to successors.** (*Acts 1:15-26; 14:23, 1 Corinthians 3:10, 2 Timothy 1:6; 2:2*)
- c. **Therefore, the united successors of the Apostles have absolute authority over doctrinal interpretation and Church government.** (*Acts 15:6; 16:4, 1 Corinthians 5:3-5, 1 Thessalonians 5:12-13, Titus 2:15, Hebrews 13:7,17*)

3.
- a. **Christ appointed the Apostle Peter as leader of the other Apostles.** (*Matthew 16:15-18, John 21:15-19, 1 Peter 5:1*)
- b. **The Apostles passed down their own authority to other men for the**

               succession of their offices. (*Colossians 1:25, 2 Timothy 1:6; 2:2; 4:1-6, Titus*)
    c.   **Therefore, the successor of Peter's office is the leader of all other successors of the Apostles.** (*Matthew 23:2, John 10:14-16, Romans 16:20*)

Between books like *Not by Scripture Alone* and my other studies, my sense of faith-related authority was shaken. I had never considered that the doctrine of *sola scriptura* (viewing the Bible as the best and only divinely inspired authority) must inevitably lead to chaos and division. Because of its inherent subjectivity and promotion of individualism as opposed to unity, *anyone* could come out of *any passage* with *any interpretation* he or she *feels* that the Holy Spirit is laying on his or her heart.

Two people could argue all they wanted over who the Holy Spirit *truly* spoke to with no way of objectively settling the dispute. Thus, yet another denomination – another split in the Body of Christ – would be born (*http://www.geocities.com/Athens/Troy/6480/solascriptura.html* has more information about the problems with *sola scriptura*). If the united bishops have a perpetual authority, however, then the Holy Spirit protects the Church from doctrinal corruption. When the Church speaks regarding faith-related matters of controversy, the case is closed, the matter is settled. Problem solved.

The more I prayed about it, the more Catholicism began to make sense. I'm not just speaking of the *defenses* Catholics have for various doctrines, dogmas, devotions, or disciplines, dear brother; I'm speaking of their contending *evangelical* points, which speak for themselves. Various aspects of Scripture and Spirit, logic and history, all compellingly point to the necessity – even Divine edict – of *One*, Holy, Universal, and Apostolic Church of Christ. A

> ***Just like before, the mounting evidence was quickly becoming overwhelming.***

visible, organized, and authoritative Church that must persist until the culmination of all things.

If indeed this Church was the Roman Catholic Church, then her apostolic authority alone would require assent to all her other doctrines. Such authority would unite Christians together under the protection of the Holy Spirit and guard them against misinterpretations of Scripture. But could it really be that God prevents the united bishops from binding the Church to errant faith or moral teachings? Could it be that *sola scriptura* was merely an evil tradition of men, inspired by Satan to break apart the Church from the inside out and lead Christians astray? Did the Early Church Fathers – my elders who had lived closer to the time of Christ and the original apostolic teachings – really believe dogmas I thought the Catholics had *invented* in the Middle Ages?

What if...

The idea that only one group of Christians possesses *all* the true doctrines and *none* of the false ones (and consequently, that anyone who wants to fully obey Christ must be in full communion with them) offended me. *But then again,* I thought to myself, *so did the message of the cross, once upon a time.* "I am the Way, the Truth, and the Life; no man comes to the Father but by me" – ring a bell? There is salvation in no other name and there is no other way by which we may have peace with God.

With so many cultures and religions who say differently, it's no wonder we're hated, neglected, or avoided by most of the world. When we talk to our non-Christian friends, we try to approach the subject with gentleness and reverence, but we're often surprised at the negative responses we get. Anyone who is being told he's wrong or at least lacking in essential information can't help but take offense. But does that mean he shouldn't keep an open mind toward what we preach? We pray he does, anyway.

Let me ask you something. If you knew a Christian who seemed to live a pure life, devoted to the Lord, but you knew he had not been baptized, what would you say? Maybe he chooses not to be baptized, even though he knows many other believers who do. Maybe he hasn't had Scripture explained to him about baptism. If you're a true friend to this guy, you'd probably try broaching the subject. If he's never heard about baptism, or at least never understood its importance, you feel a little more comfortable. It was ignorance, not waywardness that kept him from fulfilling Christ's call.

But if after speaking with him you learn that he does understand the concept, yet feels it unimportant and chooses against it, you would be troubled. He would be intentionally disobeying the command of Christ and the Apostles, regardless of his explanation. And what would he tell you if you pressed the issue – if you explained that he *had* to be baptized if he truly wanted to be obedient to Jesus? He would be offended. After all, *he* knows what's right for *him*.

Well, I found out that baptism is just one of many commands and regulations that the Catholic Church believes Jesus Christ gave regarding the Family of God. According to Catholicism's interpretation, he also says Peter is to be the rock upon which the Church bases her leadership (Mark 3:16; Matt. 16:18-19; John 1:42), that she must authoritatively define and defend morals, doctrine, and justice (Matt. 16:19), submit to succeeding authority (Matt. 23:2), identify her infallible protection from corruption of moral or doctrinal teaching (Matt. 10:20; Luke 12:12; John 16:13; John 14:26; Matt. 16:18-19), employ final authority on faith and morals (Matt. 18:17-18), recognize, understand, and – if necessary – bear with the members who are evil, no matter how sinful their actions might be (Matt. 13:24-30; Matt. 13:47-50; Matt. 18:7; Luke 17:1), and maintain a discernable, visible, unity (Matt. 5:14; John 10:16; John 17:11,21,23).

Catholics see other characteristics of Christ's Church throughout Scripture, as well. They feel that the true Church will honor and bless Mary as their own Queen-Mother, the Woman whose soul magnifies the Lord (Luke 1:28, 43, 46, 48; Gen. 3:15; Rev. 12:1-5; John 19:26; Rev. 12:17), forgive and retain sins through confession (John 20:23; 2 Cor. 5:18; 1 John 5:16; 1 John 1:9; James 5:14-16), consume and believe in the real presence of Christ's Body, Blood, Soul, and Divinity in the Eucharist (John 6; 1 Cor. 10:16; 1 Cor. 11:27-29; Mark 14:22, 24; 2 Pet. 1:4) and much, much, more.

I took issue with a few of Catholicism's "interpretations". But the three that seemed most biblical – more biblical, historical, and logical in fact than any alternative Protestant interpretation – were (1) the succession of the Apostles, (2) the Holy Spirit's protection (or, "infallibility") of the faith-related decisions of these successors in ecumenical councils, and (3) the Real Presence of Christ in the Eucharist.

Considering these three topics, it is the Protestant position that seems a bit of a stretch; alternative interpretations of Scripture here are strained and certainly don't take the passages at face value. What's more, if the first two are true, then *every* ecumenical clarification of the Faith that the united bishops have made must also be true. Hence, if I came to believe in the doctrine of apostolic authority and yet disagreed with any doctrines defined by the successors of the Apostles, I would have to conclude that it is I who must be wrong.

I thusly realized that assent to the authority of the Roman Catholic Church meant nothing less than assent to all of her teachings. And what if I found myself conflicted, assenting to that authority, but disagreeing with those teachings? One simple step would suffice. I would need only to humble myself in the face of Christian history. If the living voice of a majority vote from 2,000 years of Christian history disagrees with me, I must be reasonable enough to consider the possibility that perhaps I might be wrong. And for the duration of my limbo between mere assent and genuine conviction regarding any such disagreement, it is my responsibility to study God's Word with the council of the Saints and pray about it.

It became obvious that both *humility* and the willingness to be *reasonable* were essential aids in my explorations of Catholic dogma. But the lingering questions, concerns, and suspicions about

Catholicism were no longer the only objects of my denominational scrutiny. In researching my troubles with the Catholic Church, I had definitely stumbled across some serious problems with Protestantism. What's more, the apparent flaws of Protestantism seemed much more severe.

The first of these problems was with the doctrine of *sola scriptura* – one of the two essential pillars upon which Protestantism stands. *Sola scriptura* states that the Bible is a Christian's only infallible authority. Yet holding the Bible to be the only infallible authority is a self-defeating position since the Bible does not provide its own table of contents. Nowhere within any book of the Bible is there given a complete list of what actually *is* the Bible! And even if there were such a list, how would one know that the book containing it was itself divinely inspired? The Bible did not descend hardbound from the heavens surrounded by angels and beams of light.

Somehow, even though I knew it had taken the Church decades to even *begin* to commit the Gospel to paper and *centuries* to hammer out what was and wasn't divinely inspired, I had failed to make the connection to a simple rule of logic: a fallible cause cannot produce an infallible effect. If a book is infallible, so must be its author. If a collection of books is infallible, so must be the decision of what books belong in that collection. Otherwise, we have infallible books written by fallible authors and a fallible collection of infallible books.

Logically impossible absurdities do not befit the God who is Truth. If I believe the canon of Scripture is infallible, then I must believe that the Church who authored and discerned that canon is also infallible. I must take God at his word (no pun intended) when Christ says that the Holy Spirit will guide us into all truth and teach us all things (cf. John 16:12-18). I must believe that our understanding of God's Word grows, develops, and is clarified in a living way (cf. Matt. 13:31-32). After all, would God let his Word be written and proclaimed infallibly, yet fail to guard against misinterpretation in like manner?

The second problem I had found in Protestantism was with the doctrine of *sola fide*, the idea that we are saved by faith alone (the other "pillar of Protestantism"). If "by faith alone" one means "by grace alone through living faith" then there is no problem. But if *sola fide* means that saving faith occurs *apart* from works, then it is just as self-defeating as *sola scriptura*. At the very least, faith begins with an *act* of repentant submission; a prayer, most likely. Perhaps a tearful fall to the knees. Of course, such an action without faith is empty. But so is a faith without acts. I had never noticed that the only time the phrase "by faith alone" occurs in the Bible is in James 2:24:

> "Ye see then how that by works a man is justified and not by faith [alone]."

I don't know why this came as such a shock to me. I always felt that salvation was the free gift of God – a gift that is never forced on anyone. But a gift must be accepted. Receiving a gift is an action; a work. Holding on to that gift is a work as well. No one can take that gift away from us (cf. John 10:29), but we can surely give it back. If Adam and Eve could throw away the gift of perfect fellowship with God, how much more can we quench the flame of the Spirit within us (cf. 1 Thess. 5:19)? We did nothing to "earn" the gift, and we do nothing to "earn" the right to keep it. Nevertheless, it is a simple fact that we must take it and hold on to it – tightly. A stern warning is given in Hebrews 6:4-6 and James 2: 14-26 for those who do not. Yet somehow this all eluded me.

Down tumbled the two pillars of Protestantism. Without a leg to stand on, the collapse of Protestantism seemed inevitable. But I still had to consider the reasons that these pillars were erected in the first place. Wasn't the Church riddled with poor leaders at the dawn of the Reformation? Well, yes. There were plenty of saints among the lay-people and religious orders (monks), but unfortunately they were few and far between among the priests and bishops. So I could understand how the doctrine of *sola scriptura* – even if unbiblical and illogical – could be welcomed without foresight of disastrous consequences.

And what of *sola fide*? During the course of my studies in Church history, I came to the conclusion that this doctrine was shouted from rooftops not so much to detract from the *works of faith*, but to emphasize the *faith behind works*. Martin Luther was an extremely legalistic and scrupulous person. Unfortunately, while he lived, much of Church leadership placed a bigger priority on the works of faith than they did on the faith of works. It's not difficult to imagine why a person such as Luther, haunted by imperfections and plagued with scrupulosity, would find peace in rearranging the priorities of the time.

I think Luther saw empty works carried out without faith in much of the Church. I think this upset him. And I think he reminded the world (albeit in an equally unbalanced way) that for works to be channels of saving grace, faith must first be present. As ludicrous as it may sound to some, I honestly believe that the faith vs. works argument was in some part a misunderstanding – an issue of semantics – that bred a defensive reaction from both sides. There were other issues that were much more opposed to Catholic doctrine than *sola fide*. If a proper and balanced hearing were given by both Protestants and Catholics then maybe the result would have been a *both / and* stance rather than an *exclusivist* stance.

Are we saved by faith alone? No, we are saved by grace alone. Do we receive that grace through faith alone? Yes. But real faith necessarily begins with and subsists on *works of* faith. We are saved by grace through the prayers, sufferings, and charity of faith; this is *living* faith. If this is the type of faith meant by the doctrine of *sola fide*, then the disagreement between Protestants and Catholics is a simple matter of words and not a real doctrinal difference. Perhaps such a buffoonish tragedy would never have happened if Christians weren't so faithless…if the works of Christians weren't so hollow…who knows what might have been.

My most anti-Protestant conclusions came when I studied the claim that the Catholic Church, which had persisted through all the centuries, had spiritually died. This, supposedly, is the final reason that a new Church had to be formed. Aside from the fact that this is yet another self-defeating position for Protestants (how can a living Church come from a dead Church?), it is blasphemous. The Church is Christ's Body. Christ rose bodily from the dead and lives forever more. Thus, to claim that the Church has died is to claim that his Body has died. It is to claim that he is a liar and all his promises are false. The Church "died"? Blasphemy. Christ – the Head – now sits at the Father's Right Hand, while We – the Body – persist on earth; the bridegroom and the bride are one flesh. And we live on.

When I voiced these findings to my non-Catholic friends and family, more than a few eyebrows were raised. All I wanted was for someone to validate Protestantism in light of what I had been reading. But only a few people even bothered trying. And no one seemed to have the time to read serious Catholic apologetics. *Upon This Rock* by Steve Ray, *One, Holy, Catholic, and Apostolic* by Kenneth Whitehead and *A Biblical Defense of Catholicism* by Dave Armstrong would have done nicely…or maybe Robert Sungenis' *Not by Scripture Alone* or Scott Hahn's *Catholic for a Reason* series…all of these books present, at bare minimum, the logic and psychological brilliance of Catholic Christianity. I was running out of options.

What was I going to do with all of the information I had acquired? I needed to pray about all this…I needed to immerse myself in the Word of God. I knew that if I turned to God in this time of spiritual crisis, I would get his answer. On the one hand, I had become increasingly disenchanted with Protestantism. There were serious and irresolvable errors with the movement on the fundamental level, so far as I could tell. On the other hand, there were still some Catholic doctrines that just didn't seem clear-cut in Scripture. So what was the next step?

Well, after many long Bible studies and prayers, I came to a conclusion. Although I couldn't see all of the Catholic doctrines conclusively *proved* from Scripture alone, I could at least see how the doctrines *complimented* Scripture (I'll write more on that in my third letter to you). And if Catholic teachings were historical and complimented Scripture, wasn't it possible that they were intended for the Christian life? What if…well, what if I was missing out?

I knew from experience that no matter how true something is, you can always find something you don't like about it. You can even argue with it. There is a small group of people that still believe the world is flat, for instance. But there comes a point when you're grasping at hairs, straining gnats, and kicking against the goads. I came to that point with the Catholic Church. To borrow an age old expression: if the Catholic world seemed to be upside down, I decided it might be because I was standing on my head.

Suddenly, I felt a little trapped. I had come to a point where I had to "try on" Catholicism. The thought of nervously poking my toe into the seemingly frigid waters of Catholic culture was intimidating. But a sense of peace washed over me. I remembered that God does not force doctrine on anyone. It's ironic, but I've found that the recognition of freedom in the presence of an awesome God provokes willingness toward submission. We only want to rebel when we believe the lie that our freedom is hampered. Since the Garden of Eden, we've always been free to reject what God offers. Sometimes, as I was beginning to feel might be the case with Protestantism, we take the bits and pieces we're comfortable with and refuse the rest.

What if I was missing out?

"Nevertheless," cautions the Catholic Church, "if we are totally committed to obeying Christ, implementing the fullness of truth into our lives, then we must honestly examine whether or not we are in *full* communion with the One, Holy, Universal, and Apostolic Church that Christ founded – and promised would exist in every generation, the gates of Hell (scandals and sins included) not prevailing."

Once I stuck my toe (or, more literally, my finger) into Catholic waters, it wasn't long before I took a plunge, headfirst! Catholic Culture is so refreshing! It was as if up until this point I had been a child, clinging to the arm of his Father, wishing the heat would go away but afraid to cool off in the pool he built for me.

The world is so wonderful as a Catholic! *Everything* has become a symbol of a higher reality. A common rain shower reminds me of my baptism. Evergreens remind me of eternal life. Candles remind me that Christ is the Light of the World. I could go on and on...

Catholic spirituality utilizes virtually every mundane experience in life and transforms it into a contemplative prayer – an inspiration. All the art, rituals, gestures, and signs that I once thought to be legalistic or meaningless pagan distractions have become for me a means to experiencing the presence of the Holy Spirit. Indeed, they have become a *far* more concrete way to worship God.

A great example of Catholic culture in action is the emphasis Catholics place on the Bible. I am consistently amazed at how Catholic Church services are so saturated with Scripture. In fact, the Church is set up to read through practically the entire Bible every three years! The Church accomplishes this through the Liturgy. The Liturgy is defined as the "people's work" because it is the *communal* celebration and worship of God's Word, not just the work of the pastor.

There is an overwhelming reverence for and devotion to the Bible at Mass. The Scriptures are held high for all to see in procession up to the altar. They are bowed to out of respect for whose words they contain. Catholics trace a small cross over their foreheads, mouths, and chests before they read or hear the Gospels (with the silent prayer: *"May this Gospel be on my mind, that I may meditate on it, on my lips that I may proclaim it, and on my heart that I may believe it."*).

Because of the Liturgy, on any given day, a large part of the Catholic Church may reflect on the same passages from Scripture. This means that if I was visiting another country *tomorrow* and came across a practicing Catholic, I could probably ask him what he thought about our "Bible study" *last weekend*! The idea was always in the back of my head that Catholics hardly ever read the Bible. But the truth is that the very purpose of the Liturgy (the ancient and preferred form of worship at every

Catholic gathering) is the adoration, understanding, and proclamation of God's Word.

As a Protestant, I was accustomed to a pastor picking a passage or two of his choosing and then spending 30 minutes to an hour sharing his thoughts. In Catholic services, you get at least *four* readings; usually one from the Old Testament, one from the Psalms (which is actually sung by everyone), one from the epistles of the New Testament, and one from the Gospels. The greatest thing about this is that the readings are regularly on the same or a similar topic. Thus, you're getting the Bible's message in *context* and witnessing the miraculous *unity* of Scripture. Sometimes I do a double take during the Liturgy, startled at how unified the Bible really is. *No way,* I marvel. *That's really the Old Testament? It sounds so much like the Gospels!*

But perhaps the *most* exciting, refreshing, and thirst-quenching blessing of being Catholic is the centrality of Christ in worship. I don't have to worry so much about my "worship experience" or how "solid" a particular parish (local Catholic community) is, because all parishes of the One, Holy, Catholic, and Apostolic Church celebrate the same Liturgy, the same Sacraments, and the same Catechism, even if they do so by varying means of expression. Enjoying music that lifts my spirit and knowing that the community is one with whom I would enjoy great fellowship is a blessing and conducive to my worship, yes; but the Mass has elevated my worship to a remarkably unconditional (and immeasurably more satisfying) focus.

At any Catholic Church service, because of the Liturgy, the Eucharist, and the universality of doctrine, the focus of worship can be *entirely* on Christ (more on this ahead when I explain the Mass). Unlike my experience with Protestantism, the music, community, and sermon are not conditions for (or impediments to) that focus. The centrality of God's Word – especially in Eucharistic form – trumps every other aspect of worship. It is hard to get distracted from this centrality *precisely because of* the Liturgy and the many symbols and rituals that accompany it.

No longer are there fears of "not being fed", because I know that Christ takes center stage in every Catholic celebration. I will *always* be fed at Mass – mentally, spiritually, *and* physically! It is because of this sense of spiritual security that no longer do I ask what a particular church can do for me, but rather what I, as part of the Church, can offer up before God, who is both spiritually *and* substantially present in every Catholic sanctuary. There is an *object* to which my worship is directed. I no longer worship only in the presence of the Holy Spirit, but also in the real, *substantial* presence of the Son incarnate.

So here I am now, going through the Rite of Catholic Initiation for Adults (RCIA), eagerly awaiting my first communion, and bursting with joy about the Catholic Church. Obviously, a person gets where he or she is spiritually "at" by knowledge, experience, and wisdom. And a person won't remain there unless it seems to be the best option. You are where you are for a reason. So I can't convince you of anything (though I do pray that the Holy Spirit *does* convince you).

Furthermore, if I'm right that the boat I'm in is the least leaky, then it also represents the most truth – and truth doesn't need defending. It is the same yesterday, today, and forever. All I hope for is that by reading these letters, you might better sympathize with and understand me. Consider this an opportunity to reevaluate both your current beliefs and those of the Catholic Church from a clean slate; an unbiased perspective. It is my ultimate desire that you too, will take all the Truth, Beauty, and Love that you have acquired in your spiritual life up to this point and bring it into the Catholic Church, where so much more awaits.

The banquet is prepared. The table is ready. And after nearly two thousand years of development, the menu of choices is diverse; but the heart of the feast remains the same. It was, and is, and always will be; to dine with the Messiah, God with us. That is my humble prayer. For Christ *is* come in the flesh!

His Love,

Brian Forrest Roberts

THE SECOND LETTER

Dear Brother,

I'm sure in your Bible studies you've noticed the overwhelming abundance of the admonishment towards unity. There was only *one* marriage between Adam and Eve, so God's covenant could only apply to the two of them as one cohesive "Body". Likewise only *one* family of Noah, with which God renewed and expanded his covenant. And then only *one* tribe of Abraham in God's next expansion. Then only *one* nation of twelve tribes when God once again renewed, further illuminated, and expanded the covenant with Moses at Sinai. Later, only *one* kingdom of that nation, established in David. And finally only *One* Body of Christ out of that kingdom, a covenant renewal that expands itself to all those on the Earth who would come in through Jesus.

Each of these covenants was visible. The groups were visible and so were the signs under which a person entered them. Why? Because if they weren't, nobody would know where to go to "sign up" for God's Family. The whole of God's plan and people as a Family unit would be undiscernibly confusing in the midst of a disorganized mess!

So God always had a universal front to represent Him and ensure that no one on the outside would be confused about what His people are at least *supposed* to believe. Notice also the familial orientation that each front maintained – others were welcomed to join the expanding Family under a sign, such as circumcision, but only in the context of becoming a full-fledged member.

It is obvious that this Family (in all of its successive covenants and history) has had a tendency to behave in a dysfunctional manner. Adam and Eve defied God and played the blame game in their marriage. Noah got drunk and cursed his kid. Abraham practically sold his wife into prostitution and caused division in his tribe by impregnating his concubine.

God's Family has tended to be a dysfunctional one.

Moses couldn't keep the nation together as a happy Family for the life of him. Rehoboam's lack of prudence as king caused the majority of the Family to schism off of the house of David – the line destined to produce the Messiah – and fall into even greater sin under the good intentions of Jeroboam (see 1 Kings 14:9).

And although a hopeful and submissive remnant has existed in every generation of Christians, massive amputations of Christ's Body have occurred under the scalpels of heretics, rebels, and those in despair throughout the Family's dark history. No wonder those who would dissent against the authoritative unity of the One, Holy, Universal, and Apostolic Church were marked by Paul among those whom believers should avoid (Rom. 16:17-18)!

Why is this important? Well, I want to briefly give you a glimpse of our Family's Christian history by means of the great councils and saints. I've found study of the councils and the heresies they combated to be of immense benefit in gaining a clearer picture of how and why the Church exists.

In this letter you'll find brief summaries of what happened in each council and why it occurred, along with the clear line of successions to St. Peter's office. Following these summaries, you'll learn about a historical Christian who lived between the time of that council and the next. Keep in mind that this letter should not be confused with a complete history of the Church – otherwise, you will quickly notice major names, places, and events not covered. I'm going to focus solely on the developing theology of the Church (see Matt. 13:31-32) and her defense of the Faith.

More explicitly, all that concerns this letter is what each council *publicly and officially* taught regarding *faith and morals*. Remember that only these particular teachings of the councils are what the Church considers "infallible" – that is, protected under the inspiration and guidance of the Holy Spirit. The ways in which these teachings have been *interpreted* by individuals, or the ways in which they have been *applied*, are subject to the same limitations and abuses common in all the ways of men. Likewise, decisions, actions, and speculations regarding social, political, or otherwise *secular* issues also fall under the human (and often sinful) aspect of the Church.

Indeed, the Catholic Church is quick to acknowledge her sins and has even publicly apologized for unchecked corruption in the past. But it is one thing to reform the *organization* – that is to say, the human – aspect of the Church. It is quite another to reform the *idea* – that is to say, the divine – aspect of the Church. The leadership, the culture, and the ways in which we act upon doctrines all change. The doctrines themselves do not.

For example, if you face the problem of a blatantly corrupt bishop, you do everything in your power to get him reformed or out of office. But to condemn the office of bishop itself is to condemn a divine institution; the doctrine of apostolic succession. It would be like pointing the finger at God rather than the sin. We might gain a clearer understanding of a doctrine through careful exploration of God's Word, but we *never* renege on it. That is the very purpose of a high council: to conserve or more clearly define a doctrine in the face of heresy or turmoil.

The first council of the Catholic Church lies within the Sacred Scriptures themselves. Of course, I am speaking of *The Acts of The Apostles*. It's such a fast paced and motion filled book! And it certainly helps us get a glimpse of the key players of the Early Church. But most importantly, it also offers examples of Church government, function, and organization. This is impressive, considering how young the Church was at this time. The book opens with Pentecost and a handful of the faithful and concludes with a flame spreading throughout the known world; a universal (catholic) Church Body!

The council took place at the district of believers that James presided over: Jerusalem. Before we get into it, it is of the utmost importance that we note the following: *it was the first great council of bishops because it was the first great problem to arise.* And no mere conundrum of the minor sense – that is to say an issue that was largely agreed upon even if it remained unheeded. No, this was a great problem in the capital sense – an issue that was great cause for thought and heated debates. In other words, an issue that, if left unchecked, threatened the unity of the Church…

I
The Council of Jerusalem
51 A.D.

Matthew 16:18-19
And I say also unto thee, that thou art Peter, and upon this rock I will build my Church; and the gates of hell shall not prevail against it. And I will give unto thee the keys of the Kingdom of Heaven: and whatsoever thou shalt bind on Earth shall be bound in Heaven: and whatsoever thou shalt loose on Earth shall be loosed in Heaven.

It was no small thing when a council was called. It meant nothing less than a serious challenge to something we thought we had figured out; or at least had largely, up until that point left unquestioned. In the case of the Council of Jerusalem, the problem was Mosaic Law. It seems to make sense that this was the first challenge to Church unity. After all, the first Christians were Jews and had been used to following the Torah, well, religiously. Now were they just supposed to abandon it? The Church was becoming divided. Some said that Christians were obligated to follow every religious and ceremonial law, and others said the Law was done away with. Of particular importance was the question of whether or not an uncircumcised man could be saved. Pay careful attention to the fashion in which this was handled:

> "The apostles and elders met to consider this question. After much discussion, *Peter* got up and addressed them: 'Brothers, you know that some time ago God made a choice among you that the Gentiles might hear from *my* lips the message of the gospel and believe...Now then, why do you try to test God by putting on the necks of the disciples a yoke that neither we nor our fathers have been able to bear? No! *We* believe that it is through the *grace* of our Lord Jesus that we are saved, just as they are.' The whole *assembly* became silent as they listened to Barnabas and Paul...When they had finished, James

spoke up: '...*Simon* has described to us how God at first showed his concern by taking from the Gentiles a people for himself...It is my judgment, therefore, that we should not make it difficult for the Gentiles who are turning to God.'...Then the apostles and elders, with the whole church, decided to choose some of their own men and send them to Antioch with Paul...With them they sent the following letter:

The apostles and elders, your brothers,

To the Gentile believers in Antioch, Syria and Cilicia: Greetings.

We *have heard that some* went out from us *without* our authorization *and disturbed you...It seemed good to the Holy Spirit and to* us *not to burden you with anything beyond the following requirements..."*
(Selections taken from Acts 15, NIV, emphasis added.)

    Notice that Peter was the first one to formally address the leaders gathered. And when he spoke, everyone else shut up and listened. He first declares his divinely appointed preeminence. Then he rebukes them. Finally, he declares a dogma in an almost regal manner: "*We* believe that it is through the *grace* of our Lord Jesus that we are saved..." He doesn't say "*I believe*" but "*We*" – it would be arrogant to say such a thing in a divided crowd who were still debating the matter; unless, that is, you had a recognized, stately authority to pronounce the beliefs of an entire group of people, knowing they would have to comply or ditch the club.

    Also notice that the group is referred to as an *assembly*, indicating an especially governmental organization. James, the bishop of the church the council convened at, only discloses his judgment in the context and preface of Simon Peter's. The apostles (bishops) then draft a letter (these would later be referred to as *apostolic constitutions*) and send it in the hands of one of their own to the breeding grounds of all the trouble, Antioch, Syria, and Cilicia. So a decree was issued through the use of delegates.

Finally, there is something in the constitution itself that is worthy of notice: the acknowledgment that over-seers must be *assigned* their placements, or at least obtain permission. This indicates a hierarchy among the church leadership and indeed a universal or "catholic" Church! The truth is, the Church then and now *requires* organization and a hierarchy within it to function as Christ intended.

- o **The Space Between:** *Heroes of the Faith*
  - ❖ Saint Irenaeus of Lyons (c.130 – 202 A.D.)

Saint Irenaeus did the Church a great favor in his fight against heresy. He was a disciple of Saint Polycarp, who himself was a convert, disciple, and friend of Saint John the Apostle. Irenaeus became bishop of Lyons, where he spent the majority of his Catholic life writing, educating, and preaching. He directed his efforts against Gnosticism in particular, teaching that the Church believed Christ had two natures – fully God and fully man – and also stressed the unity and relationship of the Old and New Testaments. He did a great deal of this relying on John's Gospel because the Gnostics often used that gospel to defend their beliefs.

> "It is possible, then, for everyone in every church, who may wish to know the truth, to contemplate the Tradition of the apostles which has been made known to us throughout the whole world. And we are in a position to enumerate those who were instituted bishops by the apostles and their successors down to our own times, men who neither knew nor taught anything like what these heretics rave about"
>
> - Saint Irenaeus of Lyons; *Against Heresies* 3:3:1, A.D. 189.

II
The First Council of Nicea
325 A.D.

And Linus was ordained successor to Peter, then Anacletus, Clement 1st, Evaristus, Alexander 1st, Sixtus 1st, Telesphorus, Hyginus, Pius 1st, Anicetus, Soter, Eleutherius, Victor 1st, Zephyrinus, Callistus 1st, Urban 1st, Pontain, Anterus, Fabian, Cornelius, Lucius 1st, Stephen 1st, Sixtus 2nd, Dionysius, Felix 1st, Eutychian, Caius, Marcellinus, Marcellus 1st, Eusebius, Miltiades, and Sylvester 1st, who ratified the First Council of Nicea...

    The organization and hierarchal authority that the apostles had set up for their spiritual children had been working very well. The doctrines of the Faith had been guarded carefully against all kinds of heresies and false messiahs in many small councils. These doctrines were held so universally among the Apostles' successors that it became the distinguishing mark between the Church and all those who disagreed with her. Already, Christians who assented to the teaching authority in apostolic succession were called "Catholic", meaning universal. Thanks to the watchful eyes of the bishops, the Body of Christ remained One.

    However, it was only a matter of time. A man named Arius boldly turned his back on Catholic belief by teaching that Christ was not truly God, but rather a pure creature made out of nothing and thus, a son of God by adoption, not by nature. Of course, teachings such as the Trinity and the nature of Christ's relationship with his Father were not fully explored, being mostly dependant on Sacred Tradition. Deeper and more complex doctrines such as those Arius challenged were taught and guarded by the clergy. Since, up to this point, there was a general assent to these particulars of the Faith, there was not yet a need to *figure them out on paper*. So people were left free to speculate.

And here we see the need for the next Ecumenical Council, which was held in the year 325. There were many things the Council confronted. However, it most directly confronted the controversy of Arianism – something new; a tradition of men. Catholics were open to figuring out deeper complexities of what they already believed but would never hold to teachings that contradicted beliefs that were already there. And Arianism did just that and so, was a heresy.

The two most important resolutions of this council were its symbol (what gradually became what we now know as the Nicene Creed) and the decree for which the symbol was drawn up. The bishops, with the aid of the Holy Spirit's preservation from error in public teaching on the Faith, proclaimed on behalf of the undivided Church:

> "We believe in one God the Father Almighty, Maker of all things visible and invisible; and in one Lord Jesus Christ, the only begotten of the Father, that is, of the **substance** of the Father, God of God, light of light, true God of true God, begotten not made, **of the same substance with the Father** [*homoousion to patri*], through whom all things were made both in heaven and on earth; who for us men and our salvation descended, was incarnate, and was made man, suffered and rose again the third day, ascended into heaven and cometh to judge the living and the dead. And in the Holy Ghost. Those who say: There was a time when He was not, and He was not before He was begotten; and that **He was made out of nothing**; or who maintain that He is of another hypostasis or another substance, or that the Son of God is created, or mutable, or subject to change, the Catholic Church anathematizes."

(Catholic Encyclopedia, emphasis added)

And thus, just as with the first council in Jerusalem, the matter was settled. God's authority on His Word had spoken through his vessels, the bishops, just as it had through the Apostles.

Pre-incarnate, the Word was consubstantial with the Father; a separate Person, but of the same substance. Dear Brother, if God had not given a pattern for the authority of the Apostles to us as an organized succession (see Paul's letters to Timothy), how would we know what to do when people argued for new interpretations of the Bible? And when there exist many groups of people contending for that authority, which can we be confident that the Holy Spirit is guarding?

- o **The Space Between:** *Heroes of the Faith*
  - ❖ Saint Cyril of Jerusalem (c.315 – 386 A.D.)

Saint Cyril fought against heresies denying the Real Presence of Christ in the Eucharist. He was a great teacher of the Faith and eventually became bishop of Jerusalem. His instructions are still so clear and poignant that the Church continues to use his writings as a staple for what the Early Church taught and has granted him the honorary title of Church Doctor.

> "The bread and the wine of the Eucharist before the holy invocation of the adorable Trinity were simple bread and wine, but the invocation having been made, the bread becomes the body of Christ and the wine the blood of Christ…
>
> "Then during the Eucharistic prayer we make mention also of those who have already fallen asleep: first, the patriarchs, prophets, apostles, and martyrs; that through their prayers and supplications God would receive our petition."
>
> – Saint Cyril of Jerusalem; *Catechetical Lectures* 19:7, A.D. 350

III
The First Council of Constantinople
381 A.D.

...And Marcus was ordained successor to Peter following Sylvester 1st, then Julius 1st, Liberius, and Damasus 1st, who ratified the First Council of Constantinople...

It was only a few decades later, unfortunately, that what had already been declared in Nicea had to be reinforced. And Apollinaris, another guy in the public eye, became convicted that Christ was not truly a man. Although this reeks of Gnosticism, he had amassed a good following anyway. And if that weren't enough, even more people were siding themselves with the theology of Macedonius, who didn't believe the Holy Spirit was a Divine Person. So this Council had its hands full! It expanded the Nicean Creed to emphasize *homoousion* – the con-substantiality of Christ with the Father – and the divinity of the Holy Spirit. Even if the heretical "denominations" lingered, they were ousted by the authority of the One, Holy, Catholic, and Apostolic Church.

- **The Space Between:** *Heroes of the Faith*
  - ❖ Saint Augustine of Hippo (c.354 – 430 A.D.)

Saint Augustine has been proclaimed by the Church to be the "Doctor of Grace" because of his profound and inspiring defense of salvation by *grace* alone, through works of faith. He was raised by a Christian mother, but was lured by the world into a wild lifestyle, far away from his Christian roots. His mother prayed for his conversion continually and those prayers, eventually, were answered. He became a monk, then a priest, then a bishop, and continues to have a heavy influence on doctrinal reflection.

> "What the universal Church holds, not as instituted by councils but as something always held, is most correctly believed to have been handed down by apostolic

authority. Since others respond for children, so that the celebration of the sacrament may be complete for them, it is certainly availing to them for their consecration, because they themselves are not able to respond."

    – Saint Augustine; *On Baptism, Against the Donatists* 4:24:31, A.D. 400

"I would not believe the Gospel if I were not compelled by the authority of the Catholic Church."

    – Saint Augustine; *Letter to Januarius*, A.D. 400

"By this grace baptized infants too are engrafted into [Christ's] Body, infants who certainly are not yet able to imitate anyone. Christ, in whom all are made alive . . . gives also the most hidden grace of his Spirit to believers, grace which he secretly infuses even into infants. . . . It is an excellent thing that the Punic Christians call baptism salvation and the sacrament of Christ's Body nothing else than life. Whence does this derive, except from an ancient and, as I suppose, apostolic tradition, by which the churches of Christ hold inherently that without baptism and participation at the table of the Lord it is impossible for any man to attain either to the kingdom of God or to salvation and life eternal? This is the witness of Scripture, too. . . . If anyone wonders why children born of the baptized should themselves be baptized, let him attend briefly to this. . . . The sacrament of baptism is most assuredly the sacrament of regeneration"

    – Saint Augustine; *Forgiveness and the Just Deserts of Sin, and the Baptism of Infants* 1:9:10; 1:24:34; 2:27:43, A.D. 412

IV
The Council of Ephesus
431 A.D.

...And Siricius was ordained successor to Peter following Damasus 1st, then Anastasius 1st, Innocent 1st, Zosimus, Boniface 1st, and Celestine 1st, who ratified the Council of Ephesus...

Fifty years later in 431, a man named Nestorius was causing all kinds of problems by his simple assertion that Mary was not the mother of God. But think what this leads to! Not long after he was gaining followers after his tradition, their logical conclusion was that if Mary is not the Mother of God, Christ must have two persons – human and divine – with Mary being mother only of the human. But if that were the case, then the "divine person" would have had to be added to Jesus the human *after* his birth. This could lead to abortion being recognized as an acceptable practice, when you think about it.

If God knits a person together in his or her mother's womb, then the soul is present at conception – in Jesus' case, divinity was present at conception; Mary gave birth to God! This is a great and joyful mystery, that God would set aside a vessel to bear all his fullness into the world. If the ark of the covenant in the Old Testament had to be so meticulously planned and reverently crafted to perfection, how much more so the *human* Ark that would contain the fullness of the actual Deity, Himself!

This council firmly declared, once for all believers to come, the *Theotokos* – that Mary was the Mother of God! Elizabeth knew this long before there arose a need for a council to confirm the dogma, however. In Luke 1:43, Elizabeth cries out "And whence is this to me, that the mother of my Lord should come to me?" Elizabeth recognized Mary as the Mother of God before Christ was born. But somehow, Nestorius' twisted interpretation of Sacred Tradition and Scripture didn't. The Council also confirmed that

Christ was one *Person* with two *natures* – divine and human – joined in that one person.

- o **The Space Between:** *Heroes of the Faith*
  - ❖ Saint Peter Chrysologus (c. 406 – 450 A.D.)

Saint Peter Chrysologus converted as an adult, ultimately becoming the bishop of Ravenna, Italy. His sermons were so eloquent that he became known as "Chrysologus", meaning "golden-words". Quite a few survive to date and largely because of them, he's been given the title of Doctor. He spent his life building churches, fighting heresy (especially Monophysitism, which was beginning to rear its heretical head with increasing frequency), and enforcing internal reform of the Church.

> "We exhort you in every respect, honorable brother, to heed obediently what has been written by the Most Blessed Pope of the City of Rome; for Blessed Peter, who lives and presides in his own see, provides the truth of faith to those who seek it."
>
> – Saint Peter Chrysologus; *Letter to Eutyches*, A.D. 449.

V
The Council of Chalcedon
451 A.D.

...Sixtus 3rd was ordained successor to Peter following Celestine 1st, then Leo 1st, who ratified the Council of Chalcedon...

Despite the Council of Ephesus's declaration that Christ had *two* natures in his Person, by 451 a group of people claiming he had only *one* nature developed under the leadership of Dioscurus, Patriarch of Alexandria, and Eutyches, the president of a monastery outside Constantinople. The polar opposite of Nestorianism, this denomination of Christians believed that the unity of Christ's one Personhood was so strong that whatever human nature he was conceived with was totally engulfed by his divine nature. Since this claim was effectively that Jesus had only one nature, totally God, the heresy came to be known as Monophysitism (*mone physis*, one nature).

The Council condemned monophysitism and declared that Christ had two distinct natures, both true God and true man. It also spread stricter Church discipline in attempt to at least help curb the frequency of wide misinterpretation of the Deposit of the Faith (Sacred Scripture and Sacred Tradition).

- **The Space Between:** *Heroes of the Faith*
  - ❖ Saint Fulgentius of Ruspe (c.465 – 533 A.D.)

A popular preacher, Saint Fulgentius was led to the religious life through Saint Augustine's writings, ultimately becoming bishop of Ruspe. He was exiled on more than one occasion for his opposition to the Arians. Yet he persisted in the work of God; praying, teaching, studying, and helping anyone in need for the rest of his life.

"To Peter, that is, to his church, he gave the power of retaining and forgiving sins on earth."

– Saint Fulgentius of Ruspe; *De Remissione Peccatorum, 2:20,* A.D. 523

VI
The Second Council of Constantinople
553 A.D.

...Hilarius was ordained successor to Peter following Leo 1st, then Simplicius, Felix 3rd, Gelasius 1st, Anastasius 2nd, Symmachus, Hormisdas, John 1st, Felix 4th, Boniface 2nd, John 2nd, Agapetus 1st, Silverius, and Vigilius, who was Peter's successor during the time of the Second Council of Constantinople...

    The discipline promulgated by the Council of Chalcedon did help a bit, as there wasn't a need for this council until nearly one hundred years later. In 553, the Second Council of Constantinople took place because Emperor Justinian I wanted the Church to consider the orthodoxy of three Greek theologians: Theodore, bishop of Mopsuestia, Theodoret of Cyrrhus, and Ebas bishop of Edessa. It was decided that much of the works were greatly influenced by Nestorius and were forthrightly condemned. The Council also underlined the authority of the Council of Chalcedon, since some heretics were pathetically trying to challenge it.

    But who can question the authority of the Holy Spirit in Church leadership that stands in place of the apostles? There was a reason that the apostles set up an organized, hierarchy of leadership, just as there was a reason that they established apostolic succession (1 Cor. 3:10, 1 Tim. 4:14, Eph. 2:20, Tit. 1:5). "May another take his place!"

- **The Space Between:** *Heroes of the Faith*
  - ❖ Saint Isidore of Seville (c.560 – 636 A.D.)

Saint Isidore of Seville was raised in a saintly family but that didn't stop him from being a poor student. Moreover, being a poor student didn't stop him from giving the problem over to God and trying his best, anyway. And that led him to become one of the most brilliant minds of his time. He was a great Bible teacher and apologist, leading many Visigoth Arians into the fold of the One, Holy, Catholic, and Apostolic Church. He became Archbishop of Seville in 601 and used his position to ensure seminaries were in every diocese, while at the same time enforcing reforms in the Church from every angle. He wrote a dictionary, an encyclopedia, a history of the world, and even a liturgy that's still used today in Toledo, Spain. He eventually was pronounced Doctor of Education by the Church.

> "The decrees of the Roman Pontiff, standing upon the supremacy of the Apostolic See, are unquestionable."
>
> - Saint Isidore of Seville, ante A.D. 636

VII
The Third Council of Constantinople
680-681 A.D.

...And Pelagius 1st was ordained successor to Peter following Vigilius, then John 3rd, Benedict 1st, Pelagius 2nd, Gregory 1st, Sabinian, Boniface 3rd, Boniface 4th, Deusdedit, Boniface 5th, Honorius 1st, Severinus, John 4th, Theodore 1st, Martin 1st, Eugene 1st, Vitalian, Adeodatus, Donus, Agatho, and Leo 2nd, who ratified the Third Council of Constantinople...

In 680, the bishops met to discuss Monothelism; a new tradition (denomination) that had sprung up, claiming that Christ did not have a human will. Only his "true God" nature had a will, according to this group. It reminds us of monophysitism, only instead of dealing with the nature of Jesus, it deals with his will. The Church dealt with the problem, as always, through a council, declaring monothelism to be heresy and Christ to have two wills, one for each nature of his one Person. Finally, it anathematized anyone who would knowingly and willingly leave the One, Holy, Catholic, and Apostolic Church for this tradition or any of its leaders.

- **The Space Between:** *Heroes of the Faith*
  - Saint John Damascene (c.676 – 749 A.D.)

A popular saying of Saint John Damascene was, "Show me the icons that you venerate, that I may be able to understand your faith." He loved Christian art – especially the icon, which is a lesson, a story, and a devotional, all in one – and defended it to the Patriarch of Constantinople, Germanus. Since he grew up in Muslim lands, he was well aware of the latest schools of thought and produced volumes of work; commentaries on Scripture, philosophy, and theology. His mission was to curb the growing Muslim influence on the use of images in worship – especially its impact on the Eastern Church.

"The divine Scripture likewise saith that 'the souls of the just are in God's hand'*[Wisdom 3:1]* and death cannot lay hold of them."

    – Saint John Damascene; *Orthodox Faith 4:15*, A.D. 743 (note added)

VIII
The Second Council of Nicea
787 A.D.

...And Benedict 2nd was ordained the successor to Peter following Leo 2nd, then John 5th, Conon, Sergius 1st, John 6th, John 7th, Sisinnius, Constantine, Gregory 2nd, Gregory 3rd, Zachary, Stephen 2nd, Stephen 3rd, Paul 1st, Stephen 4th, and Adrian 1st, who ratified the Second Council of Nicea...

In the year 787, an epic controversy was at a peak – it all centered on the use of images in worship of God or veneration of saints. Some people went too far and felt God was in the images of him, likewise with imagery of saints. Others were on the opposite extreme, influenced by Muslims, believing that all images were evil in and of themselves and that no matter what their use, it amounts to idolatry. They were called the Iconoclasts. The bishops in this council condemned the iconoclasts while at the same time condemning idolatry.

They maintained that images could be honored, cherished, and used in worship without idolatry taking place, much like the cherubim adorning the Ark of the Covenant or the serpent erected on the pole in the Old Testament. Another example of an image being cherished without idolatry taking place might be kneeling at the gravestone of a loved one and placing flowers there in memory of the person whom the engravings or sculptures commemorate. The council also drew up canons of Church discipline to ensure that neither extreme would be reached on such a wide scale again.

- **The Space Between:** *Heroes of the Faith*
  - Saint Theophanes (c.775 – 845 A.D.)

Another staunch defender of icons and sacred images used in worship, Saint Theophanes endured a particularly brutal torture for the stance of the true Church. He grew up in Jerusalem, eventually becoming a priest during the time of the iconoclasts.

After having endured exiles and tortures by those who continued to refuse Church teaching, he was offered the opportunity to recant his position on the use of icons. Of course, he refused. The punishment? Over the course of two grueling days, a 12-line iambic verse was carefully cut into his forehead.

> "These men have appeared at Jerusalem as vessels full of the iniquity of superstitious error, and were driven thence for their crimes. Having fled to Constantinople, they forsook not their impiety. Wherefore they have been banished from thence and thus stigmatized on their faces."
>
> – Saint Theophanes; *The iambic verse cut into the forehead of Saint Theophanes*

IX
The Fourth Council of Constantinople
869 A.D.

...And Leo 3rd was ordained successor to Peter following Adrian 1st, then Stephen 5th, Paschal 1st, Eugene 2nd, Valentine, Gregory 4th, Sergius 2nd, Leo 4th, Benedict 3rd, Nicholas 1st, and Adrian 2nd who ratified the Fourth Council of Constantinople...

In 869, The Fourth Council of Constantinople had to be called because the Church faced the crisis of an irregular council, which had unlawfully appointed a man named Photius as patriarch of Constantinople. The reasons are troubling. Ignatius was the rightful bishop without question and had been so for eleven years! It wasn't until he refused Communion to the regent of Bardas, who was living in open incest, that the Government grew angry. It attempted to unseat Ignatius and impose Photius as a new bishop. Both Ignatius and Photius petitioned the bishop of Rome, Pope Nicholas I, for an authoritative verdict. Nicholas, of course, sided with the bishop who had already been lawfully appointed eleven years prior.

The council condemned Photius in twenty seven canons and recognized Ignatius as the legitimate bishop. Photius in his bitterness formed an anti-Catholic party that spread seeds throughout most of the East, and continued their growth long after his death. Nearly 150 years later, Michael Caerularius took it upon himself to pick up where Photius left off. In 1053, he took unprecedented action; sending a declaration of war, shutting up Latin churches in Constantinople, and venomously slandering the Western Church. On July 16th, 1054, the Roman legates excommunicated Caerularius.

Gradually, however, most of the Eastern churches were swayed by the rhetoric of Caerularius and the habit of turning to Constantinople for religious government. In effect, the Church of the East chose to participate in his excommunication, though some of her bishops vehemently opposed this, such as John III of Antioch. Regardless, as a consequence the Fourth Council of Constantinople in 869 was the last to be held in the East.

- o **The Space Between:** *Heroes of the Faith*
  - ❖ Saint Peter Damian (c.1007 – 1072 A.D.)

The moral state of the Church during the life of Saint Peter Damian reflected the need for one such as him to be sent by God. After enduring a pretty rough childhood, Peter Damian became a priest and founded a hermitage. Disgusted with the increasing prevalence of immorality among clergy, he spent much of his time trying to instill the fear of God into his listeners. Far from abandoning the One, Holy, Catholic, and Apostolic Church he had married himself to, he worked his whole life to further unify her to Christ.

> "What else shall I say? It *[homosexuality – especially pedophilia]* expels all the forces of virtue from the temple of the human heart and, pulling the door from its hinges, introduces into it all the barbarity of vice ... In effect, the one whom ... this atrocious beast has swallowed down its bloody throat is prevented, by the weight of his chains, from practicing all good works and is precipitated into the very abysses of its uttermost wickedness. Thus, as soon as someone has fallen into this chasm of extreme perdition, he is exiled from the heavenly motherland, separated from the Body of Christ, confounded by the authority of the whole Church, condemned by the judgment of all the Holy Fathers, despised by men on earth, and reproved by the society of heavenly citizens. He creates for himself an earth of iron and a sky of bronze ... He cannot be happy while he lives nor have hope when he dies, because in life he is obliged to suffer the ignominy of men's derision and later, the torment of eternal condemnation"
>
> – Saint Peter Damian; *Liber Gomorrhianus*, A.D. 1050

X
The First Lateran Council
1123 A.D.

...And John 8th was ordained successor to Peter following Adrian 2nd, then Marinus 1st, Adrian 3rd, Stephen 6th, Formosus, Boniface 6th, Stephen 7th, Romanus, Theodore 2nd, John 9th, Benedict 4th, Leo 5th, Sergius 3rd, Anastasius 3rd, Lando, John 10th, Leo 6th, Stephen 8th, John 11th, Leo 7th, Stephen 9th, Marinus 2nd, Agapetus 2nd, John 12th, Leo 8th, Benedict 5th, John 13th, Benedict 6th, Benedict 7th, John 14th, John 15th, Gregory 5th, Sylvester 2nd, John 17th, John 18th, Sergius 4th, Benedict 8th, John 19th, Benedict 9th, Sylvester 3rd, Benedict 9$^{th\ ll}$, Gregory 6th, Clement 2nd, Benedict 9th, Damasus 2nd, Leo 9th, Victor 2nd, Stephen 10th, Nicholas 2nd, Alexander 2nd, Gregory 7th, Victor 3rd, Urban 2nd, Paschal 2nd, Gelasius 2nd, and Calistus 2nd, who ratified the First Lateran Council...

It wasn't until more than two centuries later, in 1123, that a council had to be called. This time the crisis wasn't heresy or schism, but a need for social and religious reform. What would haunt the Church in later years, the State was getting too mixed up in Her affairs. The bishops recognized a need to deal with this and so, once again gathered together to figure out how to deal with the situation. As a result of the Great Schism of the Eastern Church (which was still a gradual process the West was getting used to), this was the first time a council was held in Rome, home of Peter's successor, the Pope.

Since the topics were so diverse, the canons promulgated by this council are as well. It ended the random grants of Church benefices by laymen, reestablished freedom of episcopal and abbatial elections, took strong steps toward the separation of Church from State, and confirmed that only the Church emanates spiritual authority. Most importantly, however, it ensured emperors knew it was not their place to interfere in papal elections.

- **The Space Between:** *Heroes of the Faith*
  - ❖ Saint Bernard of Clairvaux (c.1090 – 1153 A.D.)

After his mother died, Saint Bernard convinced several friends and family to join the Cistercian Order with him. He thrived there and after awhile, he was sent with twelve other monks to found a new monastery, destined to be called the Abbey of Clairvaux. The life he lived was of such holiness and love that his name became renowned throughout the Christian world – even the Pope came to him for advice. His life was also marked with the gift of miracles, if even a handful of the many well-documented stories are true. He was offered a bishopric on many occasions, humbly turning down the offer every time. His work makes him stand out to such an extent that he has been given the title, Doctor of Devotions.

> "Since then you see that Christ in one person has two natures, one by which he always was, the other by which he began to be, and always knew everything in his eternal essence but temporally experienced many things in his temporal essence; why do you hesitate to grant that, as he began in time to be in the flesh, so also he began to know the ills of the flesh by that kind of knowledge which the weakness of the flesh teaches? Our first parents would have been wiser and happier to have remained ignorant of that kind of knowledge, since they could only attain it by folly and misery."
>
> - Saint Bernard of Clairvaux; *On the Steps of Humilty and Pride*, A.D. 1125.

XI
The Second Lateran Council
1139 A.D.

...And Honorius 2nd was ordained successor to Peter following Callistus 2nd, then Innocent 2nd, who ratified the Second Lateran Council...

Only sixteen years later, the Second Lateran Council was held. The short years between the two councils were filled with turmoil, all because of a double-papal election! There were two camps within the upper hierarchy of apostolic succession, each wanting to elect a different pope. The majority camp was swayed toward Cardinal Pietro Pierleone, who was eagerly attempting to buy and force his way into the Chair of St. Peter. The minority recognized Pierleone for what he was; grossly immoral and tied to the State by both family and desire.

What the minority had going for them, however, was that though they were few in number, four of them were cardinal bishops – meaning they had a leading role in the election – and five of those left to elect the next pope were also against Pierleone. They used their weighty influence to move the currently dying Pope Honorius II from the Lateran to St. Gregory's, near the Frangipani towers.

Since they were then the first to know of his passing, they wasted no time in burying him the morning of. Immediately thereafter, they elected Gregory Papareschi, Cardinal of San Giorgio, to be the new pope, taking the name of Innocent II. Later that day, Pierleone and his corrupt party assembled in the Church of St. Mark. That group of bishops elected *him* as pope under the name of Anacletus II. But too late, of course. God had already allowed a successor to be appointed and until his passing, there could be no other pope.

Yet what is appealing to God does not always seem so to people. The city of Rome sided with Anacletus. With his copious disbursement of wealth from family or plundered from the Church, who wouldn't? He was a popular guy. And Innocent, whose virtues met up to the name he took, fled to France. However, if he was rejected by Rome, he was welcomed by the world as the legitimate bishop. In a few short years, the stubborn Anacletus died and although he had a successor, the ruse was over. Even the pretend-successor was convicted by the sin and came to the feet of the true Pope Innocent II.

So, to wipe out the last traces of Rome's schism, Innocent held the tenth council since that of Jerusalem. In it, many errors and reform abuses, both by the clergy and the people, were condemned. The pope deposed all those who had obtained any kind of position in the Church from the anti-pope, Anacletus, or anyone partisan to him. Some heresies that were left unchecked were officially condemned (two active denominations had arisen, following the errors of Peter of Bruys and Arnold of Brescia). The council also promulgated ecclesiastical morals and discipline to help ensure such scandal would not soon again so easily happen.

- o **The Space Between:** *Heroes of the Faith*
  - ❖ Saint Malachy (c.1094 – 1148 A.D.)

After becoming Archbishop of Armagh in 1132, Saint Malachy worked to restore a great deal of Church discipline and in his diocese, was largely successful. He became a close friend of Saint Bernard of Clairvaux, who writes of his triumph in reforming Church morality during his time on earth. His life is marked with other great accomplishments, including the founding of the great Abbey of Mellifont in 1142. Perhaps the most interesting aspect of his life, however, is that like St. Bernard, the Lord worked miracles through Malachy. And not only that, it is said he had the gift of prophecy, though he didn't publish or circulate the idea. However, this gift seems to have been confirmed when, in 1597, a set of prophecies he wrote in secret was discovered in Rome. Among other things, they predicted the line of the next 112 popes from his day. So far, one could argue they have all come true.

"In the final persecution of the Holy Roman Church there will reign Peter the Roman, who will feed his flock amid many tribulations, after which the seven-hilled city will be destroyed and the dreadful Judge will judge the people. The End."

– Saint Malachy; *From the Prophecies of Saint Malachy*

XII
The Third Lateran Council
1179 A.D.

...And Celestine 2nd was ordained successor to Peter following Innocent 2nd, then Lucius 2nd, Eugene 3rd, Anastasius 4th, Adrian 4th, and Alexander 3rd, who ratified the Third Lateran Council...

In 1179, the Third Lateran Council was called. There had always been false claimants to be the pope. These anti-popes usually never caused serious schism; but Anacletus gave new temptations toward the effort and the bishop of Rome wanted to put an end to it. Not only that, but the separation between Church and State was definitively vague and as a result, more and more immorality was creeping into the Church. The purpose of this council was to address each of these issues; not a small matter for a world-wide institution. Only the Holy Spirit Himself may restrain abuses within such a large group, and he seemed more interested in adding pressure towards reform and reorganization.

However, as always He would go about this within the bounds of His covenant; within the boundaries of the One, Holy, Catholic, and Apostolic Church who had remained the faithful, visible, guardian of the Faith since Christ handed it down to her. Thus did the council work to restore the Church discipline that had been waning and, as always, deal with any heresies or denominations that had been springing up (most notably in this time period, that of Peter Waldes' denomination: the Waldensians, who believed in extreme poverty, literal and independent interpretations of the Bible, the abandonment of spouses in order to pursue celibacy, and the refutation of an authoritative Church – sometimes to the point of murder, as was the case with Blessed Peter Cambiano, who was stabbed to death by three Waldensians for preaching the importance of Catholic unity and teaching).

Preventing schisms by better regulating and monitoring papal elections, keeping a close eye on the moral life of the clergy, and maintaining a tight track-record for where money is going were among the many issues dealt with through the promulgation of this council's canons.

- The Space Between: *Heroes of the Faith*
  - ❖ Saint Anthony of Padua (c.1195 – 1231 A.D.)

Another saint – and probably the most popular – known for miracles, Saint Anthony of Padua was a Franciscan monk and evangelist. He was acclaimed for his simple teaching of Christ and immovable stance against heretics and secular philosophies. So many wonders and miracles are recorded of his short life that they could fill a book by themselves. Many are very hard to refute because of the number and variety of witnesses and accounts. When his body was exhumed 336 years later, his tongue was found to be completely incorrupt. He has been given the title, Doctor of Evangelism.

> "You cannot see your face if you look into troubled and moving water. If you want to see Christ's face appear in you when you look, sit down and be quiet."
>
> – Saint Anthony of Padua; *The Sermons of Saint Anthony: Festival Sermons; the Ascension of the Lord*

XIII
The Fourth Lateran Council
1215 A.D.

...And Lucius 3rd was ordained successor to Peter following Alexander 3rd, then Urban 3rd, Gregory 8th, Clement 3rd, Celestine 3rd, and Innocent 3rd, who ratified the Fourth Lateran Council...

Early in the next century, 1215, Pope Innocent III achieved his great desire for another council. There were heresies to be combated, problems to solve, matters to discuss. Among these was the need for a dogmatic definition of what occurs in the Eucharist; though the Real Presence of Christ in the most Blessed Sacrament was an apostolic belief handed down through the ages, clarification of it was needed. Also, a decision had to be made on how to put a handle on immoral clergy; was there any way to stop it? These were among the tasks that this council set before itself.

The heresies at the time may have contributed to the desire for figuring out the Real Presence on paper. Albigensianism was becoming popular among the people. In this belief, the principle of evil and the principle of good are both equal and ultimate forces. The evil created all material things, the body included. The good was responsible for all things spiritual. Thus, Christ only *appeared* to have a physical body. His birth and death were illusory, not actual, since his apparent body was actually celestial. However, he pretended to endure suffering and death as an instruction for the people. Thus, the only way to Heaven was through becoming a member of Christ's Church, the Albigenses.

But the Church had faith in the incarnation since the beginning. And more than that, that the incarnated God was among us; that God really had come in the flesh through the Eucharist. Explaining the metaphysics of it through "transubstantiation" helped to stamp out Gnosticism and any of its spawn in the true Church. The council condemned the Albigenses. As far as the other issues went, the Church thought it good to hold annual provincial councils towards moral reform and reinforce the importance of the sacrament of confession by requiring it once a year for all people.

- o **The Space Between:** *Heroes of the Faith*
  - ❖ Saint Bonaventure (c.1221 – 1274 A.D.)

As a child, Bonaventure contracted a serious illness. When Saint Francis of Assisi prayed for him, he was cured. After he got older, he studied liberal arts and became a Franciscan teacher at a university. There, he drew many to a deeper understanding of St. Francis's way towards Christ. His writings continue to inspire today. He was named the Seraphic Doctor by the Church.

> "I shall speak to you of grace; and more necessary is grace for us than the Law; to receive which grace fruitfully Mother Church and the Apostle Paul urge us. And in the beginning we shall beg the Lord that our words may zealously serve grace, and the intention of our mind, if it has grace, be strengthened in words to be able to say something, which is for the praise of God and the salvation of our souls."
>
> – Saint Bonaventure; *Conferences on the Seven Gifts of the Holy Spirit: Conference I; Preliminary Tract on Grace*

XIV
The First Council of Lyons
1245 A.D.

...And Honorius 3rd was ordained successor to Peter following Innocent 3rd, then Gregory 9th, Celestine 4th, and Innocent 4th, who ratified the First Council of Lyons...

In 1245, a council was prompted mainly for two reasons; a troublesome and heretical emperor and persecution at the hands of Islam. Emperor Frederick II, highly interested in Islam, seemed determined to gain control of God's Church. He pressured the cardinals to do as he pleased and attempted to bribe the pope toward his side. In turn, Pope Innocent the IV swiftly held a council to excommunicate him. To help stop persecution of Christians, the sixth crusade was launched, which ultimately led to the restoration of Jerusalem to the Church.

- o **The Space Between:** *Heroes of the Faith*
  - ❖ Saint Thomas Aquinas (c.1225 – 1274 A.D.)

Thomas Aquinas is perhaps the most widely known saint in Christianity. Besides Mary, probably no other saint has as many honorary titles. At five years old, he was given by his parents to a Benedictine monastery, where he surprised his teachers again and again by the fervor of his study and the devotion he paid to God; about Whom, he only asked one thing: *What is He?* Eventually he was sent to the University of Naples, where his teachers thought such a mind could be best served. It was there that he became so interested in Aristotle. Although he was born nobility, he chose the habit of a poor, Dominican friar. He traveled to Rome, then Paris, and finally Cologne, where he would finish his studies under his greatest teacher, Saint Albert the Great.

His writings mark the Catholic Church's unity. The doctrinal explanations he presents continue to be some of the best we have. The *Summa Theologiae* (Sum of Theology) is hands down the work he is best known for. In it, he attempts to present the whole of Catholic theology. However, it remains unfinished. After celebrating mass one day in 1273, he stopped writing. When asked why, all he said was, "I cannot go on.... All that I have written seems to me like so much straw compared to what I have seen and what has been revealed to me." He passed away only a few months later. The Church has called him the Angelic Doctor.

> "Hence we must say that for the knowledge of any truth whatsoever man needs divine help, that the intellect may be moved by God to its act. But he does not need a new light added to his natural light, in order to know the truth in all things, but only in some that surpasses his natural knowledge"
>
> – Saint Thomas Aquinas; *Summa Theologiae*, I-II, 109:1

XV
The Second Council of Lyons
1274 A.D.

...And Alexander 4th was ordained successor to Peter following Innocent 4th, then Urban 4th, Clement 4th, and Gregory 10th, who ratified the Second Council of Lyons...

Pope Gregory X called the Second Council of Lyons in 1274 with sincere hopes that the schismatic Eastern Church would merge back with the One, Holy, Catholic, and Apostolic Church. The council produced the dogmatic constitution of the *filioque* – that the Holy Spirit proceeds from *both* the Father and the Son – and the reconciliation attempts failed miserably. Also, the rules for papal elections were better laid down in this council.

- **The Space Between:** *Heroes of the Faith*
  - Saint Clare of Montefalco (c.1268 – 1308 A.D.)

Clare joined a Franciscan convent as a young woman and with them set up Holy Cross Convent at Montefalco in 1290, under the rule of St. Augustine. There, she spent her life, quietly adoring God and living righteously, with a special devotion to the Passion of Christ and His cross. She was perfectly content with a simple life, revolving around prayer and worship. Clare's passion for Christ consumed her with such a fire that people wondered how such a kind a cheerful girl's health could keep up with her vigils and fasting. Her example displayed the virtues of a humble relationship with God, right up to the day of her death, in 1308.

She had always spoken with Christ about His cross and the "coincidence" seemed miraculously appropriate that when her body was prepared for burial, an unexplainable emblazoned cross was discovered on her chest, directly over her heart. What's more, the corpse showed no signs of deterioration and to this day, remains incorrupt. Her peaceful body continues to lie at

Montefalco, Italy, in the Church of the Holy Cross, where Augustinian nuns continue to honor her name.

> "If you seek the cross of Christ, take my heart; there you will find the suffering Lord."
>
> – Saint Clare of Montefalco, shortly before her death.

XVI
The Council of Vienne
1311-1313 A.D.

...And Innocent 5th was ordained successor to Peter following Gregory 10th, then Adrian 5th, John 21st, Nicholas 3rd, Martin 4th, Honorius 4th, Nicholas 3rd, Martin 4th, Honorius 4th, Nicholas 4th, Celestine 5th, Boniface 8th, Benedict 11th, and Clement 5th, who ratified the Council of Vienne...

The Council of Vienne became *ecumenical* (meaning bishops were convoked from the whole world) in 1312 and was called due to controversy and heresy. New denominations had sprung up around their leaders - the Fraticelli, the Beghards, the Beguines, and the Quietists. The heresies among these groups were diverse, but the general idea was one common to the New Age movement; that we have an inner union with God which enables us spirituality perfect enough to indulge in fleshly desires (Luther would later remind us of this with his infamous statement "be a sinner, and let your sins be strong, but let your trust in Christ be stronger"). All of them were deposed or suppressed. Another interesting aspect of this council was that it initiated education in the languages of the Orient.

- o **The Space Between:** *Heroes of the Faith*
  - ❖ Saint Catherine of Siena (c.1347 – 1379 A.D.)

Even at the age of six, little Catherine experienced visions from God. In her large family, these were disregarded in preference toward secular responsibilities, which according to her parents' clear wishes, included a good marriage. Catherine did indeed have a good marriage – the best possible – though it wasn't the one her parents had in mind. When she was sixteen, she was admitted to the Third Order of St. Dominic for a religious life. Out of her intense love for God, she busied herself with all sorts of charities and service work, not neglecting her own house chores in the process! It was readily apparent to all those whom she served that she burned with the Holy Spirit and people streamed out to learn from her. The Church experienced serious tumult during her life, and she was an earnest peace activist in the face of this. Her efforts toward reformation and a call to continuing conversion in the Church won the hearts of many, including many changed clergy – even the pope! It was for this and her great teachings that the Church awarded her the title of Doctor in 1970.

> "Eternal Trinity, Godhead, mystery deep as the sea, you could give me no greater gift than the gift of yourself. For you are a fire ever burning and never consumed, which itself consumes all the selfish love that fills my being. Yes, you are a fire that takes away the coldness, illuminates the mind with its light, and causes me to know your truth. And I know that you are beauty and wisdom itself. The food of angels, you gave yourself to man in the fire of your love."
>
> – Saint Catherine of Siena; *A Treatise On Divine Providence*

XVII
The Council of Constance
1414-1418 A.D.

...And John 22nd was ordained successor to Peter following Clement 5th, then Benedict 12th, Clement 6th, Innocent 6th, Urban 5th, Gregory 11th, Urban 6th, Boniface 9th, Innocent 7th, Gregory 12th, and Martin 5th, who ratified the Council of Constance...

Over half a century later, Satan decided to launch his next major attack; and it was big. The aftereffects of this great tremor were to play a key role in the Devil's hope to destroy Christ's Bride – or at the very least confuse her and all those who look upon her. The Enemy made sure to keep the Church's hands full. There was major heresy to be dealt with, anti-popes grasping for authority, and worldwide ("catholic") social and structural problems springing up among both clergy and laity.

It may be argued that the storm began its ominous thunder in the late 1370's. An anonymous Teutonic mystic, part of the Dominican "Friends of God" society, set quill to parchment and authored *Theologia Germanica* – a little volume that would be of profound influence to Martin Luther. With this, the clouds grew and became grey.

John Wycliffe was an influential teacher at Oxford who, though beginning with honest and internal reform rhetoric, was gradually more embittered toward papal problems. Humanism was taking hold of the world and he was influenced by a growing, nationalistic, malice toward ecclesial authority. With this, those clouds darkened and churned.

The world had developed a strong middleclass, who, now knowing the pleasures of their own extra money, resented the economic drain of Church expenses. Can you hear the wind, rising?

And worst of all, after the cardinals had rightfully elected Urban VI as successor to Peter, they reacted negatively to his leadership and presumed the power to elect another in his place, beginning a schism that recalls the second Lateran council. We may envision the first blazes of lightning, crackling across the black heavens.

    Over the next several years, things became more and more muddled. The cardinals continued to muck things up. The laity continued to exhibit increasing dissatisfaction with the Church leadership. By 1414, not only had the schism not been resolved but with the passing of both Pope Urban VI and the antipope Clement VII, each of the two competing lines had subsequently elected successors to Peter!

    Pope Gregory XII, the third after Urban VI, saw an even greater indignity at the hands of the cardinals when they tried to "depose" both him and Benedict XIII (from the line of Clement VII) in favor of Alexander V. It was as if the corrupt bunch of cardinals realized what a mess they had gotten themselves in and threw up their hands in frustration. "Well, there's no ironing this out – might as well start over!" After the death of Alexander V, John XXIII was elected as another anti-pope. Thus, by the close of 1410 there were two lines of anti-popes refusing to acknowledge the fact that those in Urban VI's were the true successors to Peter since he was rightfully elected first.

    Enter the Council of Constance in 1414. Though the council lasted four years, it proved the Holy Spirit's protection over the Sovereign God's One, Holy, Catholic, and Apostolic Church. Benedict XIII and John XXIII were finally and totally deposed, ending the lines of antipopes and securing Gregory's position. However, to aid in clearing up the confusion this scandalous schism caused, the pope resigned so that a fresh successor to Peter might be chosen and the Church could return to some sense of security. Martin V was elected in his stead, the line was preserved, a successor to Peter occupied the chair of Rome, and Christ's promise remained sure: the powers of Hell had not prevailed against His Church.

    The next thing to do within this council was to deal with the wildfire that Wycliffe had started. Its sparks had fanned into flame with the ensuing ecclesiastical chaos of the anti-popes. If Wycliffe had been frustrated with the Church before, the shameless irresponsibility of the papal office during his last years drove him to emotionally volatile and irrational conclusions.

Since it was obvious to him that the Church was not serving her role as an authority, Wycliffe concluded that Catholics could only rely on Scripture for their authority. Thus, this man gave birth to the novel tradition of *sola scriptura*, a slightly more liberal version of an earlier Waldensian tradition. Unfortunately, this overreaction (even if understandable) set a wheel in motion that allowed Satan to better enter the minds of the believers; twisting their interpretations of Scripture as far away from the One, Holy, Catholic, and Apostolic Church as possible without fear of the bishop's correction.

This is exactly what happened to Wycliffe before he died. Without reading the Bible in the context of consistent church teaching, the commentaries of the early fathers, and Sacred Apostolic Tradition together, he arrived at all sorts of new doctrines and oppositions to the historical Church.

After his death, Wycliffe's teachings spread quickly and fell on the eager ears of those who no longer wanted to put their money in the Church, whose leadership had been displaying such negligence. Among these followers was a priest named John Hus. Even after Wycliffe's innovative doctrines were condemned, Hus continued to not only believe them, but publicly support and spread them. To turn on the Church is tantamount to turning on Christ, since the two are covenanted together in a mystical marriage, and so Hus in a way, excommunicated himself before the Church could. But he went much farther than that. He launched an all out verbal attack against the Church, trying to pull members out of her. At the Council of Constance, both Wycliffe's and Hus's teachings were condemned.

The council took great strides in reformative efforts; it worked out a massive schism, encouraged the laity with new discipline, ensured more frequent minor councils, and dealt with particularly destructive heresies the best way it knew how.

Although the council had served the present well, it did not safeguard the future. In his wisdom and for His own purposes, God did not will for such protection just yet. Then again, the Lord does bring more glory to His name by making his people weak first.

- o **The Space Between:** *Heroes of the Faith*
  - ❖ Saint Joan of Arc (c.1412 – 1431 A.D.)

Pretty much everyone has at least heard of this saint. It surprises some that the Catholic Church canonized her since it was an ecclesial court that had her executed. But the Church doesn't claim perfection – only *protection* when it comes to official, public, teaching on faith or morals; and even then, only in very specific circumstances. Joan was a commoner; a shepherdess. But even at the age of 13, she was graced by the Holy Spirit with visions. In 1428, she received one she could not ignore – to find the "true king" of France and help him reclaim his throne. And that is just what she did.

With a banner reading *"Jesus, Mary"* in hand, she inspired and amassed many followers, leading them to one victory after another. Those miraculous victories brought Charles VII to the throne. She was captured, however, and sold to the English, where she was tried and executed as a heretic. 23 years later, her case was retried and she was acquitted – only too late to keep her from earning the crown of martyrdom. Through all of this, she never rejected or abandoned the One, Holy, Catholic, and Apostolic Church she believed in.

> "About Jesus Christ and the Church, I simply know they're just one thing, and we shouldn't complicate the matter."
>
> - Saint Joan of Arc, at her trial

XVIII
The Council of Florence
1431-1439 A.D.

...And Eugene 4th was ordained successor to Peter following Martin 5th, ratifying the Council of Florence...

In 1431, a series of councils was launched, culminating in the 17th Ecumenical Council: Florence. At the top of this council's agenda was a reunion of the Eastern and Western Churches, after years of negotiation. Various circumstances of the time pressed the issue, including the persistence of Islam, the weakness of Constantinople, and a floating idea that a council held more power than the Pope. The Council of Florence confirmed that the Pope, as successor to St. Peter, who was the leader of all the apostles, is in turn leader of all the apostles' successors. No longer could people attack the headship of the Roman Pontiff without directly violating the decision of a great council.

Although the reasons for the Eastern schism were primarily territorial and politically driven, there were some doctrinal differences to be settled if there was to be any kind of union. Among these was the procession of the Holy Spirit from the Father and the Son, Purgatory, and papal supremacy over the patriarchs of the East. Miraculously, the majority of the Greeks conceded on all these points and more. Although the union was short-lived for a large portion of the Eastern Church, it was nonetheless a great step in the right direction, and evidence for hope that a total and final union could one day be achieved.

[Note: Since the "P" word was introduced here for the first time, I only think it considerate to help clear up some common misunderstandings regarding Purgatory. Like Catholics, Protestants believe in "Purgatory" – the transition from earthly sinfulness to heavenly perfection when our bodies die – Protestants just don't give the experience a name and usually don't think

there's any prolonged suffering involved. The word "purgatory" doesn't occur in the Bible, but neither does the word "trinity". In both instances, however, the doctrine is clearly inferred by what is revealed in Scripture. I would point to the following passages for a basic biblical understanding of purgatory: Matthew 18:23-35, Psalm 51:7-10, 1 Corinthians 3:12-15, and Matthew 5:21-26. It is unfortunate that, as we've seen happen so many times already in our journey through Church history, this doctrine could be taken advantage of by certain people for profitable gains. This is the sin of simony. And like all other sins, it is simultaneously condemned and prone to be committed by a Church full of sinners saved by grace. As we will see soon, this particular sin was a primary cause in the even greater misfortune of the Protestant Exodus from Catholicism.]

- **The Space Between:** *Heroes of the Faith*
  - Saint Catherine of Genoa (c.1447 – 1510 A.D.)

Saint Catherine of Genoa wanted to enter a convent when she was 13, but was refused due to her youth. She let the idea go willingly, trusting in God's call for her vocation. Three years later, that call came in a marriage to Giuliano Adorno, a Genoese nobleman, by the request of her parents. The marriage was initially a cross for Catherine to bear. Her husband blew his money on everything but her, was heart-wrenchingly unfaithful, and had a violent temper. Her response was a gentle submission to her husband and commitment to prayer and devotion. Slowly but surely, God honored those efforts. She led her husband to conversion and the two worked with the sick and the poor for the rest of their lives. The experiences and doctrinal teachings her writings relate have gained high praise within the Church. Her story is one of hope and encouragement to many others who endure troubled marriages.

> "I see that as far as God is concerned, paradise has no gates, but he who will may enter. For God is all mercy, and his open arms are ever extended to receive us into his

glory. But I see that the divine essence is so pure - purer than the imagination can conceive--that the soul, finding in itself the slightest imperfection, would rather cast itself into a thousand hells than appear, so stained, in the presence of the divine majesty. Knowing, then, that purgatory was intended for her cleaning, she throws herself therein, and finds there that great mercy, the removal of her stains… I see that the souls in purgatory behold a double operation.

"The first is that of the mercy of God; for while they suffer their torments willingly, they perceive that God has been very good to them, considering what they have deserved and how great are their offences in his eyes. For if his goodness did not temper justice with mercy (satisfying it with the precious blood of Jesus Christ), one sin alone would deserve a thousand hells. They suffer their pains so willingly that they would not lighten them in the least, knowing how justly they have been deserved. They resist the will of God no more than if they had already entered upon eternal life.

"The other operation is that satisfaction they experience in beholding how loving and merciful have been the divine decrees in all that regards them. In one instant God impresses these two things upon their minds, and as they are in grace they comprehend them as they are, yet each according to her capacity. They experience thence a great and never-failing satisfaction which constantly increases as they approach to God. They see all things, not in themselves nor by themselves, but as they are in God, on whom they are more intent than on their sufferings."

– Saint Catherine of Genoa; *Treatise on Purgatory*

XIX
The Fifth Lateran Council
1512-1517 A.D.

...And Nicholas 5th was ordained successor to Peter following Eugene 4th, then Callistus 3rd, Pius 2nd, Paul 2nd, Sixtus 4th, Innocent 8th, Alexander 6th, Pius 3rd, Julius 2nd, and Leo 10th, who ratified the Fifth Lateran Council...

Again, almost a full century passes before the Church finds itself in enough of a mess to call a great council in 1512. Atheism was a growing trend in the minds of the people and the Church had the foresight to address and condemn it, along with the Averroes philosophy, which claimed the soul to be mortal. As always, general reform decrees were promulgated. However, censorship was also brought onto the tables in this council as a way to control the spread of dissent against Church teaching. Finally, the idea that a council held more power than the pope who convened / ratified it was unequivocally condemned. The council closed in the year 1517. Only a few short months later, one, troubled, self-loathing man would reinvent the Church in a way that none of his long line of heretical predecessors had dreamed.

- o **The Space Between:** *Heroes of the Faith*
  - ❖ Saint John Houghton (c.1487 – 1535 A.D.)

John Houghton lived through a most horrific period in Christianity. The chaos of Protestantism, as soon as the idea was sparked, spread like wildfire through the Universal Church, multiplying its own doctrinal differences and scriptural interpretations incessantly. The new churches lured or pulled members from the One, Holy, Catholic, and Apostolic Church from every angle. Every issue of the Catholic Faith was up for grabs and as Protestant numbers grew, so naturally did her denominations. The Church was in desperate need of immediate defense of dogmas to ensure the stability of Christian beliefs.

In the midst of this nightmare, Houghton was earning degrees from Cambridge in civil and canon law. By the time he became a parish priest, King Henry VIII had set up his new church, proclaiming himself the supreme head of the Church in England (among his chief reasons for doing so was to change moral laws regarding divorce, remarriage, and sexual immorality.) Saint John Houghton was the first person to oppose this. His stance for Truth and Christ's Church was rewarded by imprisonment.

Still refusing to sign the King's "Oath of Supremacy", he was slowly dragged through the streets both as a form of torture and public ridicule. Then he, along with friends he had inspired, was hanged. However, the form of hanging used was not like what we're accustomed to today. He stood in a cart, which was gradually rolled away, and the noose was designed more to choke a person to death, rather than break his neck. But Houghton was being killed for treason, so hanging was too good for him. Instead, they removed the noose so he could gasp for air and regain his senses. Then he was disemboweled, gently, so as to prolong his suffering and entertain the onlookers.

The executioner was able to lift John's pulsating heart out a little bit while he was still conscious. John dazedly looked at his own beating heart and said, "Sweet Jesus, what will you do with my heart?" As his life sped away, the executioner hurriedly sliced off his head. The corpse was then quartered. Finally, the pieces were hung on display in different spots around London. He died with four other companions following him, who also took a stand for Christ, the first among many martyrs in the Tudor persecutions.

> "Our Holy Mother the Church has decreed otherwise than the king and parliament have decreed, and therefore, rather than disobey the Church, we are ready to suffer."
>
> – Saint John Houghton, at his executioner's scaffold

XX
The Council of Trent
1545-1563 A.D.

...And Adrian 6th was ordained successor to Peter following Leo 10th, then Clement 7th, Paul 3rd, Julius 3rd, Marcellus 2nd, Paul 4th, and Pius 4th, who ratified the Council of Trent...

It was on October 31, 1517 that the harsh tapping of a hammer echoed off of nearby windows and buildings. Martin Luther had posted his 95 theses, immediately recognized as heretical in nature, onto the door of a church. Although on the face, it seemed that much of the work was aimed toward the prevalent abuses of indulgences by some clergy at the time, the heart of it was an attack on the very system of penance, as well as the authority of the Church. As the tremors and challenges increased and the arguments came to a boil, in 1545 the Council of Trent met to thoroughly defend the same deposit of Faith that had been guarded against so many others before Luther.

Ultimately, it condemned the views of Luther, Calvin, and others like them in the instantly fragmenting Protestant Church. It also further emphasized and defined the Sacraments, teachings on marriage, purgatory, indulgences, the use of images in devotional life, and much, much, more. The reason so many teachings had to be explored and defined in *complex* ways was because so many teachings were being challenged and attacked in *competing* ways. No other council has had to stand up to such viscous, nebulous, and wide-spread heresy – and no other council has come out with such insightful clarification on so many issues.

The resulting attitude of those who remained loyal and faithful to the One, Holy, Catholic, and Apostolic Church Christ inaugurated was of great conviction and evangelistic zeal. Thus did Trent launch the conservative backlash against Luther and other dissenters that counter-reformed morals and life within the Church.

- The Space Between: *Heroes of the Faith*
  - ❖ Saint Francis De Sales (c.1567 – 1622 A.D.)

Saint Francis De Sales was born to one of those families that place a great deal of stress on carrying on the family name. His parents were wealthy, powerful, and respected and wanted as much for their son. Their hope was for him to become a lawyer. He obeyed their wishes, studying at Clermont College in Paris and the University of Padua, where he earned a doctorate in law. He returned home and found a rewarding position as Senate advocate.

One day, he perceived a voice that compelled him, *"Leave all and follow Me."* Francis recognized the Holy Spirit's work in him and understood the message to be a call to priesthood. Of course, his parents disagreed. So he prayed earnestly about it and eventually, his devotion won over his family. He became a missionary priest in the diocese of Geneva, Switzerland – the very hotbed of Calvinism. People thought he was crazy when he said he intended on bringing 60,000 sheep back to the fold.

For three years, he must have felt they seemed right. Doors were slammed in his face, rocks were thrown at him, and he almost froze to death on many occasions. At the close of those first three years, his cousin – the only companion to come with him to Geneva – left him all alone and Francis didn't have a single convert to show for it. But true to his nature, he patiently waited for God and kept up his work and prayer in the meantime. Finally, God inspired Francis with a new method of preaching; if people wouldn't listen to him face to face, they might *read* what he had to say when he left.

So Francis De Sales busied himself by writing tracts and stuffing them under doors. That's right. Saint Francis De Sales was the first tract-writer! Between those messages and his constant kindness and generosity, the people of Geneva slowly warmed up to him and listened to what he had to say. By the time he left, tens of thousands of Calvinists had left the church that Calvin invented and returned to the One, Holy, Catholic, and Apostolic Church that Christ founded.

Francis eventually became a bishop and was turned to time and again by many in the Church, clergy and layperson alike. His writings on Christian living and the apologetics collected in his tracts are still used today. It is for them that the Church has declared him Doctor of the Counter Reformation.

"Our Lord and Master sends us to the Church in our difficulties and variances (Matt. 18:16-17). St. Paul teaches how we ought to *behave in* it (1Tim. 3:15); *he called* together *the ancients of the Church* militant (Acts 20:17); he showed them that they are *placed* by *the Holy Ghost* (ibid. 28); he is *sent* by *the Church*, with St. Barnabas (ibid. 13:1,3); he is *received by the Church* (ibid. 15:4); *he confirmed the Churches* (ibid. 41); *he ordained for them priests in every Church* (ibid. 14:22); *he assembled the Church* (ibid. 26); *he saluted the Church* at Caesarea (ibid. 18:22); *he persecuted the Church* (Gal. 1:13). How can all this be understood of an invisible Church? Where should one seek it to lay complaints before it, to converse in it, to rule it? When it sent St. Paul, and received him, when he confirmed it, ordained priests in it, assembled it, saluted it, persecuted it – was this in figure or in faith only, and in spirit? I am sure that everybody must see that these were visible and perceptible acts on both sides. And when he wrote to it, did he address himself to some invisible chimera?"

"...Shall I say further this word? Your fine church has not contented itself with cutting off from the Scripture entire books, chapters, sentences, and words, but what it has not dared to cut off altogether it has corrupted and violated by its translations. In order that the sectaries of this age may altogether pervert this first and most holy rule of our faith, they have not been satisfied with shortening it or with getting rid of so many beautiful parts, but they have turned and turned it about, each one as he chose, and instead of adjusting their ideas by this rule they have adopted it to the square of their own greater or less sufficiency."

"Now will you remain asleep during this shock which your masters have given to the Church? Consider with yourselves, I pray you. Luther in the books which he has composed on the Councils is not content with tearing down the stones that are visible, but goes so far as to sap the very foundations of the Church. Who would credit this of Luther, that great and glorious reformer, as Beza calls him? How does he treat the great Council of Nice? Because the Council forbids those who have mutilated themselves to be received into clerical ministry, and presently again forbids ecclesiastics to keep in their houses other women besides their mothers or their sisters: - 'Pressed on this point,' says Luther, 'I do not allow [the presence of] the Holy Spirit in this Council…'"

"We are not hesitating as to whether we should receive a doctrine at haphazard, or should test it by the application of God's Word. But what we say is that when a Council has applied this test, our brains have not now to revise but believe. Once let the canons of Councils be submitted to the test of private individuals, - as many persons, so many tastes, so many opinions."

"The article of the real presence of Our Lord in the most Holy Sacrament had been received under the test of many Councils. Luther wished to make another trial, Zwingle another trial on that of Luther, Brentius another on these, Calvin another, - as many tests so many opinions. But, I beseech you, if the test as applied by a General Council be not enough to settle the minds of men, how shall the authority of some nobody be able to do it? That is too great an ambition."

- St. Francis De Sales; *The Catholic Controversy, Saint Francis De Sales' Defense of the Faith*

XXI
The First Vatican Council
1869-1870 A.D.

...And Pius 5th was ordained successor to Peter following Pius 4th, then Gregory 13th, Sixtus 5th, Urban 7th, Gregory 14th, Innocent 9th, Clement 8th, Leo 11th, Paul 5th, Gregory 15th, Urban 8th, Innocent 10th, Alexander 7th, Clement 9th, Clement 10th, Innocent 11th, Alexander 8th, Innocent 12th, Clement 11th, Innocent 13th, Benedict 13th, Clement 12th, Benedict 14th, Clement 13th, Clement 14th, Pius 6th, Pius 7th, Leo 12th, Pius 8th, Gregory 16th, and Pius 9th, who ratified the First Vatican Council...

The Council of Trent had done such an exhaustively good job that it wasn't until 1869 – more than three centuries later – that Vatican I met, and only over general issues. The assembly touched bases on matters of faith and morals, emphasizing a need for a revival in religious life, as well as a restatement of the Faith, as defined up to that point. In doing so, the bishops recognized the need to infallibly clarify that the bishop of Rome, by himself, had the God-given protection of the Holy Spirit over what he officially proclaimed as the Church's teachings on matters of faith or morals. In other words, the pope's teachings are infallible only under certain, very strict circumstances. As always, there were new philosophies, interpretations of Scripture, and traditions of men to deal with. And of these, Vatican I particularly condemned the Rationalists, who placed human reason above the Church as the test of all truth and rejected any belief based on faith alone.

- o **The Space Between:** *Heroes of the Faith*
  - ❖ Saint Maxamilian Kolbe (c.1894 – 1941 A.D.)

Maxamilian Kolbe was born to a fiscally poor but spiritually rich Catholic family in Poland, during the time Russia occupied it. His father was a Polish freedom fighter and was eventually executed as a traitor. Around the age of 12, after his first Communion, the Virgin Mary appeared to him in a vision. "I asked the Mother of God what was to become of me," he says of it, "Then she came to me holding two crowns, one white, the other red. She asked if I was willing to accept either of these crowns. The white one meant that I should persevere in purity and the red that I should become a martyr. I said that I would accept them both." Four years later, he entered the Franciscan Order and began studies in Rome. There, he started the *Immaculata Movement*, which was devoted to conversions, opposition to Freemasonry, devotion to Mary, and the adoration of Christ. At 24, he was ordained a priest in Rome. It was around that time that he was hit with tuberculosis, which would cause him suffering for the rest of his life.

His missionary travels took him back to Poland and from there to Japan and India. When he arrived back in Poland, he started a radio station to aid in news and evangelization. In 1939, the Nazis invaded. Kolbe, who had been housing 3,000 Polish refugees (most of whom were Jewish) and continuing in anti-Nazi publications was arrested and transferred to Auschwitz. There, he ministered to other prisoners, preached the Gospel, heard confessions, and with smuggled bread and wine, celebrated mass. He was severely abused by the guards for these efforts. After an escape from the camp in 1941, the order was given that ten men be executed for each one that had escaped.

One of those chosen to die was Francis Gajowniczek, a young married man with children. Saint Maximilian Kolbe requested to be taken in the man's place for the sake of his wife and children and the request was granted. They placed him and the others selected in a starvation chamber. Kolbe encouraged them with song and the Good News. After two weeks of *not dying*, the Nazis decided to end it with a lethal injection. Thus did Saint Maximilian get the crown of martyrdom he had been promised in the vision so many years before.

"No one in the world can change Truth. What we can do and should do is to seek truth and to serve it when we have found it. The real conflict is the inner conflict. Beyond armies of occupation and the hecatombs of extermination camps, there are two irreconcilable enemies in the depth of every soul: good and evil, sin and love. And what use are the victories on the battlefield if we ourselves are defeated in our innermost personal selves?"

– St. Maximilian Kolbe in the last issue of his publication, *The Knight*

XXII
The Second Vatican Council
1962-1965 A.D.

...And Leo 13th was ordained successor to Peter following Pius 9th, then Pius 10th, Benedict 15th, Pius 11th, Pius 12th, John 23rd, and Paul 6th, who ratified the Second Vatican Council...

In 1962, Pope John XXIII called the second Vatican council. Vatican II took place in the context of tumultuous times, politically, spiritually, and philosophically. There was a definite need to render the Faith in such a way that it could better be communicated to the modern era. The Council also underscored the fact that, since the Church is composed of sinners, a constant need for reform and revival is and always will be needed. The call to continuing conversion in the Christian life could be understood in light of this. Over 2,500 bishops were in attendance (the number rose to over 3,000 before it was over), making it the largest assembly in the history of the Church.

The bishops wrestled over how to live and teach the Faith in a way discernable to the changing world, while maintaining orthodoxy to Church teaching. Some were horrified at the alteration of any detail, while others wanted to abandon large chunks of what they felt were outdated customs. In a way, the two sides balanced each other out, ensuring a relative norm was kept in the decision making process. A picture of a cross was used as a poetic way of describing this dichotomy; the vertical beam aimed at God and the horizontal beam outstretched toward men are both needed to make the whole.

Although there were no particular dogmas proclaimed, nor heresies condemned at this council, the impact was immense. Developments in the liturgy and Church practice were usually very gradual, taking place slowly over a long period of time. The changes made by Vatican II were major and put into effect as soon as the council closed. For instance, although Latin was to remain the universal tongue of the Church; masses, prayers, and documents were to be written in the vernacular (so as to become more accessible for curious seekers, lazy Catholics, and interested press). In addition, the altar was to be positioned so that the priest faced the people. The importance of a good homily was also stressed.

In general, a much greater emphasis was put on the role lay-people play in the function and life of the Church. It could be argued that, along with ecumenism, all the changes have this for their intent. A "new evangelization" continues to result from this council, producing dedicated apologists, missionaries, theologians, and – most importantly – converts.

- **The Space Between:** *Heroes of the Faith*
  - Blessed Mother Teresa of Calcutta (c.1910 – 1997 A.D.)

Few people in our generation are unaware of Mother Teresa. You'd think she had the fortune and fame, glamour and glitz of Hollywood. But what this deeply wrinkled old woman had was of far greater value than the wealth measured by the world's standards. What attracted so many to her was not *her* at all, but Christ radiating from within her. She became a missionary nun and teacher in India in 1928, unceasingly serving anyone in need. Teresa became known for her ability to feel God's love for the most unlovable people and to offer her humble little body for God's use, wherever needed. When she hugged a deathly ill person, to her that person lay in God's place and to the person, it was a hug from God.

She founded the *Congregation of the Missionaries of Charity* in 1950 and in 1957, that group began the work it became most known for: loving and serving lepers in disastrous areas. Mother Teresa lived in the slums of Calcutta for many years, learning the needs of the individuals in her community. When possible, she traveled the world, requesting support and love for those in need.

She received many awards for her compassion and charity during her earthly life, including the Nobel Peace Prize. Her missionaries now continue her legacy, working in 30 different countries.

> "In each of our lives Jesus comes as the Bread of Life– to be eaten, to be consumed by us. That is how he loves us. He also comes as the Hungry One, hoping to be fed with the bread of our life, with our hearts that love and our hands that serve. In so doing, we prove that we have been created in the image and likeness of God, for God is love. When we love we are like God. This is what Jesus meant when he said: 'Be perfect as your heavenly Father is perfect.'"
>
> – Blessed Mother Teresa of Calcutta, *Total Surrender*

***

And there were wolves and sheep, saints and sinners, weeds and wheat; yet the Family of God persisted as a city of light, a beacon set on a hill for all to know and see. The One, Holy, Catholic, and Apostolic Church continued to grow and the Gates of Hell have not prevailed.

***

    I've tried to demonstrate the "theological thread" of the Church, which may be traced back to Christ through the saints, the councils, and apostolic succession. I've highlighted the lives of Christians who held on to that thread; whose examples have proven that in even the worst of generations, there were those who lived according to the Gospel. Remember God's own decision regarding the wicked cities of Sodom and Gomorrah: if there were only *ten* righteous people there, he would have spared the whole population (cf. Genesis 18:20-33). If such were God's standards for the namesakes of depravity, how much more so can we count on his protection over the Mystical Body of Christ (cf. Matthew 16:18; 28:20)?

    Even during the Church's darkest days, I don't think anyone honestly believes that *all* the good Catholics had vanished. Wherever in history there were bad priests, there were good bishops. Wherever there were bad bishops, there were good popes. Wherever there were bad popes, there were good monks. Wherever there were bad monks, there were good lay-people. And wherever else the Church was weak, well, Christ was made all the stronger (see 2 Corinthians 12:9). We simply cannot throw the baby out with the bath water – especially since in this case, the baby would be the Body of Christ, Himself!

    I recently heard someone say that he thought the Catholic Church was mostly "dead" – devoid of a relationship with the Holy Spirit – and had been so for at least the past thousand years. What an atrocious and foolishly ignorant absurdity! Can it really be said that the Church who produced Saints Thomas a' Becket, Francis of Assisi, Patrick, Gregory, Basil, Augustine, Thomas Aquinas, Francis de Sales, Jean de Chantal, Catherine, Theresa of Avilla, Thomas a' Kempis, Kolbe, Mother Theresa, Padre Pio, Peregrine, Anthony of Padua, John of the Cross, and *thousands* more like them – the greatest heroes and heroines, poets and thinkers, martyrs and mystics of all Christian history – in every generation of even the darkest ages of the Church, is now or ever was spiritually dead?

The Church who produced the High Mass and Gregorian Chant? The Church who constructed stained glass to preach even to the non-practicing illiterate and the great cathedrals to make even kings feel small? The Church who is singularly responsible for the greatest charity efforts of all time? The largest body of Christians to remain one in faith, morals, and Sacraments? The Roman Catholic Church? She's dead? Absurd.

Is the Church sinful, in need of constant internal reformation, and continuing conversion? Always. But unsalvageable, devoid of the Holy Spirit, and worthy of abandon? Never! For to abandon Christ's Church, his Body, is to abandon Christ. And to abandon Christ is to abandon our salvation. It would be at worst mortally sinful and at least gravely hypocritical to point the finger at your brothers and sisters in Christ – no matter how unfaithful they may be – and judge their sin to be a problem too great to bear.

Furthermore, let us suppose you are right. Let's suppose that you really are the brilliant Light of Christ in a Church full of disgusting sinners. Isn't it entirely illogical to say that your absence is the only solution to a corrupt Church? If you, so righteous and full of the Holy Spirit, really are the Church's last hope, how can your absence do anything but harm Christ's Body? Perhaps my words sound sarcastic. But they are true.

Without even going into in-depth historical studies, I've shown that the Catholic Church that exists today can be traced back to Christ. All of its competitors are traced back to mere men who either left her or never committed to her. You have to admit, the Early Church sure sounds Catholic! When everything's said and done, the Catholic Church

Starting a new Church is impossible because Christ is not divided.

does at least *seem* to be the oldest of the bunch. After all, the splits came *out of* the Catholic Church, not the other way around. And taken into the larger context of history, Martin Luther might at first glance be mistaken as just another heretic in a long line behind him. Sure, he meant well. The especially poor Catholic leadership of the time compels us to sympathize with his anti-Catholic conclusions. He sincerely believed he was right.

But so did all the other heretics. They all (sincerely) felt that *their* way was the best way to know God. All heretics have the good intention of reforming or "salvaging" the Church that disagrees with them. However, for reformation to take place, it must be internal. A Body is organic, growing from within. It can't be violently operated on from without, as if it were a machine. For all the high motives, we know a heretic from a reformer when he or she chooses to leave the Church, rather than work for reformation from within; for this is *rebellion*, not *reformation*.

For all his high hopes and motivations, Luther didn't reform the Church. He – perhaps unconsciously – abandoned her and attempted a new one; one he *felt* was in line with *his* thinking, just like all of his heretical predecessors. But starting a new Church is impossible. The Church is Christ's Body, therefore the Church is Christ (cf. Acts 9:4-5). And Christ is not divided. It's interesting that, when referring to Christianity's struggle against heresy before the time of Luther, Protestants say "*the* Church taught" such-and-such, but the terminology becomes much vaguer when referring to that same struggle *after* Luther.

Why? Because no longer (for Protestants) does a universal Church speak with one voice, proclaiming dogma or condemning heresy. Now when considering the truth of a doctrine or moral teaching, Protestants must say something like, "Well, Methodism used to teach *this* but now is considering something *else*, while Baptists for the most part disagree *here*, thus making the Presbyterian stance a majority opinion, *if* you don't take into account the Church of England…" and so on and so on.

Protestantism has one central point around which all "protest" revolves: the all sufficiency of Christ *alone*. It is this "mere Christianity" that the original Protestants felt must be the solution to the problem of largely corrupt Church leadership (notice I don't say "entirely"). The idea was that Church leadership was so bad, it was necessary to strip away any doctrine, discipline, or devotion that didn't explicitly refer to Christ. But there were three problems with this idea. First, it ignored any *Christ-centered interpretation* of a doctrine proposed for rejection. Second, it assumed that doctrines rejected were not part of Christ's revealed deposit of the Faith. Third, it skipped a step. Instead of blaming the real culprit – man's sinfulness – it blamed the doctrines of the Church.

As I studied these three problems with stripping away doctrines, I came to three respective conclusions. In relation to the first problem, I discovered that Catholicism *does* in fact believe in the all sufficiency of Christ alone, just as fervently as Protestantism. Every doctrine that a Protestant might take issue with is entirely centered on Christ (as I'll somewhat explain in my next letter to you), existing through him, with him, and in him – efficacious only because of the Incarnation.

In relation to the second problem, I quickly discerned a majority vote amongst the Early Church Fathers in *favor* of Catholic doctrines; the "democracy of the dead" has declared Catholic teaching to be the original Tradition of Christ and the Apostles.

In relation to the third problem, I noticed the prevalence throughout all of history to point the finger at God rather than at *ourselves* – a desire to say, *"Ok God, seems your way isn't working. But don't worry! I'll take it from here..."* Unfortunately, though the original Protestants obviously had good intentions, the fruit of their attitude (*sola scriptura*) reflects this desire. Because Luther popularized Wycliffe's modified version of an innovative Waldensian tradition (that the Bible is humanity's only infallible authority), Satan succeeded in confusing and fragmenting the Body of Christ on a scale grander than anything prior or since.

Luther himself seems to have lamented this, observing the chaos unleashed by Protestantism. Patrick F. O'Hare, in his *The Facts About Luther,* quotes a very distressed Martin Luther as saying, *"This one will not hear of Baptism, and that one denies the sacrament, another puts a world between this and the last day: some teach that Christ is not God, some say this, some say that: there are as many sects and creeds as there are heads. No yokel is so rude but when he has dreams and fancies, he thinks himself inspired by the Holy Ghost and must be a prophet."*

Perhaps God gave Luther a prophetic glimpse of what would be caused by rebellion against the authoritative leadership Christ vested in the Church. In 1600, there were around 100 new "churches" of Christians. Three hundred years later that number had grown to about 1,000. By 1981 there were over 20,000. In 2001, according to *World Christian Encyclopedia* – a Protestant publication – the groups following individual interpretations of Scripture outside of the One, Holy, Catholic, and Apostolic Church had splintered into nearly 34,000 (See 2 Peter 1:20, 3:15-16).

We know that God is not the author of confusion. But how can anyone looking at general Christianity from the outside *not* see confusion? If God didn't author thousands of splits – and rebellions – against the One Body, who did? Does the spirit of this nebulous, indefinable, young, and invisible "church" of Protestantism really sound like something of God? What if there was one *universal in creed, faith, sacraments, and morals* – with councils occurring every so often to maintain that unity – that can be traced back to Christ himself?

Would *One* (Eph. 4:4-5, 1 Cor. 10:17, John 10:16), *Holy* (1 Tim. 1:15, Eph. 5:25-27), *Catholic* (Acts 2:5, Col. 1:5-6, 1 Pet. 3:8, Rom. 15:6), and *Apostolic Church* (John 6:70, Heb. 5:4, Titus 1:5-9) founded by *Christ* (Matt. 16:18, Luke 10:16) fit the bill more nicely? And what if the Early Church Fathers – the elders, leaders, and bishops who lived so close to the Apostles – agreed that these characteristics marked the true Church? Dear Brother, have you ever even *read* the biblical and historical commentary provided for you by these great heroes of the Faith?

Today there is a great stress on "discovering" the Early Church; the idea being that the original Church, because it was so close to the Apostles guardianship, must have been a model for continuing generations. What better way to do so than to read what the Early Church has to *say*? Shouldn't we want to be sure that we're behaving, believing, and celebrating as they did?

    Pax Christi,

    Brian Forrest Roberts

THE THIRD LETTER

Dear Brother,

In my previous letter I tried to help you grasp a thread to the Church's history. I wanted you to see that, as heresies and schisms occurred, One Church remained Holy, Catholic, and Apostolic to defend the faith with authority only apostolic succession can provide. I also provided you with some examples of great Christians through every period of the Church.

This time, I want to focus on five points in Catholicism that make most Protestants feel uncomfortable, yet are of the utmost importance to the Family of God. In order, they are the Catholic view of the Church, God's Word, Mary, the Communion of the Saints, and the Mass. Why these five? Because together they do an amazing job of representing God's Family and demonstrating how it works.

Think about it. The Church is God's Covenant Family. God's Word reveals important aspects of how that Family functions. Mary, as Mother of the Family, is an amazing symbol and fulfillment of that Covenant. The Communion of the Saints realizes the transcendent Oneness in Body that the Covenant Family shares through the work of Christ and the Holy Spirit. And the Mass is the Family meal; the celebration where it all comes together and the Family truly becomes bone of His bones and flesh of His flesh – blood relatives!

> *Everything about the Church is aimed at a deeper understanding and appreciation of your Family in Christ.*

Everything about the Church is aimed at a deeper understanding and appreciation of your Family in Christ. The five I've just mentioned, though they best illuminate that Family, are among the most hotly contested by Protestants.

You might wonder why I've limited my presentation of Catholicism to just five topics; but as I said before, apologetics are only a secondary intention of these letters. There are scores of other books that explain and defend Catholic doctrines exhaustively (see Appendix 1 for a suggested reading list). Besides, if you come to believe the first of my five explanations (that the Roman Catholic Church has the infallible authority, protection, and perpetuity of Christ on earth in doctrinal and moral judgment), then all other Catholic stances, no matter how uncomfortable they make you, must also be true.

Though I will handle some frequent questions or challenges regarding the five issues I've selected, I'm more interested in letting the Catholic Faith defend itself. I'm convinced by faith and reason that the Catholic Church holds the *fullness* of truth – and truth compels us all, once we are even subtly aware of it. That's because regardless of what we want to believe, truth is truth; it will never change.

So much time is spent trying to "defend the Faith" – and defending the Faith is a good thing, don't get me wrong. But if what we believe is really true, then it should somehow resonate in our beings – even if we don't like it – and nag at us to come closer, even if instead we run away. That's why I'm trying to write these letters from an evangelical stand-point, letting the rhyme and reason of the Church – the good sense and facts – speak for themselves. And I think the five topics I've selected for this letter work well together for this purpose.

Each of the five sections will present the Church's clear teachings on the subject, how it can be seen to be complementary with the Bible, and what the first several hundred years of Church leaders had to say about it. As you read, try to discern your attitude. Have you automatically written off the subject as untrue? If so, no amount of biblical evidence or the teaching of the Early Church will convince you. But if you truly want to seek God's kingdom, you'll begin by writing off *yourself*, so to speak. Why don't you begin by asking the Holy Spirit to protect you from error and keep you in line with the Gospel Truth? And while you're at it, pray the same for me!

I hope you'll find this information useful…

What is the Church?

What is the mission of the Church and what are its marks? Is it easy to distinguish? Doesn't it simply consist of those who repentantly follow Christ?

Just the Facts, Please! *Dispelling Ignorance*

CATECHISM OF THE CATHOLIC CHURCH

778 The Church is both the means and the goal of God's plan: prefigured in creation, prepared for in the Old Covenant, founded by the words and actions of Jesus Christ, fulfilled by his redeeming cross and his Resurrection, the Church has been manifested as the mystery of salvation by the outpouring of the Holy Spirit. She will be perfected in the glory of heaven as the assembly of all the redeemed of the earth (cf. Rev 14:4).

779 The Church is both visible and spiritual, a hierarchical society and the Mystical Body of Christ. She is one, yet formed of two components, human and divine. That is her mystery, which only faith can accept.

866 The Church is one: she acknowledges one Lord, confesses one faith, is born of one Baptism, forms only one Body, is given life by the one Spirit, for the sake of one hope (cf. Eph 4:3-5), at whose fulfillment all divisions will be overcome.

867 The Church is holy: the Most Holy God is her author; Christ, her bridegroom, gave himself up to make her holy; the Spirit of holiness gives her life. Since she still includes sinners, she is "the sinless one made up of sinners." Her holiness shines in the saints; in Mary she is already all-holy.

868 The Church is catholic: she proclaims the fullness of the faith. She bears in herself and administers the totality of the means of salvation. She is sent out to all peoples. She speaks to all men. She encompasses all times. She is "missionary of her very nature" (AG 2).

869 The Church is apostolic. She is built on a lasting foundation: "the twelve apostles of the Lamb" (Rev 21:14). She is indestructible (cf. Mt 16:18). She is upheld infallibly in the

> truth: Christ governs her through Peter and the other apostles, who are present in their successors, the Pope and the college of bishops.

The Church is not and can never be an obstacle toward your relationship with Christ. That is because the Church is Christ's Body and therefore, in a mystical way, Christ himself. It can never be tainted or destroyed. Protestants will sometimes admit this inescapable reality and retreat to a comparison of the Church to Noah's ark. The idea is that Noah's ark (the Catholic Church) accrued so many barnacles (pagan traditions of men) that it began to sink (poor leadership and morality). People like Luther, Calvin, and Knox saw this and decided to scrape the barnacles off to restore the Church to its original New Testament simplicity.

Of course this assumes the "barnacles" scraped off really were false doctrines, the cause of problems, and progressively added long after the Apostles' passing. If this is true, a Protestant should (religiously speaking) feel more "at home" when reading the Early Church Fathers than a Catholic. Well. Here's a link to the Fathers of the Early Church online:

http://www.newadvent.org/fathers/

I invite you to read about the Early Church in her own words. I don't think you'll find something that looks at all like the average Protestant conception of barnacle-free New Testament simplicity. Throughout this and other sections of the letter I'm currently writing, I will provide you with quotes from the Early Church that prove Catholic Christianity wasn't an invention of the Dark Age, but rather from the very beginning a *"kingdom…like a grain of mustard seed, which a man took, and sowed in his field: which indeed is the least of all seeds: but when it is grown, it is the greatest among herbs, and becometh a tree, so that the birds of the air come and lodge in the branches thereof"* (Matt. 13:31-32).

The Church *is* like an ark. It is a house that God builds for his people, who are saved by entering inside through the waters of baptism (1 Pet. 3:18-21). But the Church is also like an *acorn* (or, as the parable above demonstrates, a mustard seed). In the Bible we find many Catholic doctrines in "acorn" form, not yet fully explored or developed, such as the Trinity, purgatory, the two natures of Christ, and the seven Sacraments. As the acorn grows into a tree, the Church explores and clarifies her Faith, better understanding God's revelation with every passing generation. It is this voice of history that the Church listens to when taking firm stances on tough moral or faith issues. G.K. Chesterton called it "the democracy of the dead".

The Catholic Church believes God graced her with the fullness of the Way, the Truth, and the Life intended by Christ for *all* peoples – not just Christians. The *normative* means of entry is the new circumcision, the water Baptism. Just as the Old Covenant required an outsider to be circumcised in order to become a Family member, so the New Covenant fulfills this requirement with Baptism (see Col. 2:11-12).

The old circumcision affected the flesh, a shadow foretelling the new circumcision that would affect the spirit. This is not a work of man, nor is it something man deserves. Someone *else* baptizes a person out of *obedience* to God. From beginning to end, no matter the way you slice it, baptism is about *grace*, not merit. Catholics believe that in a very real way, this grace brings a person into Jesus Christ himself. As members of Christ, each of us are members of his Body, and therefore members of one another – *the Church*.

But that's not to say that the Church excludes the possibility of salvation for the un-baptized. Rather, each person is subject to the degree of Truth God has helped him or her to perceive. In the progressive understanding of God's Word, the person becomes accountable for what he disregards the moment he's aware of its Truth. It is in the free and knowing rejection of Truth that the person chooses separation from God, who is Truth, Himself. So if an un-baptized person doesn't know any better, it's one thing. If he does, it's flat out disobedience and sinful. Once a person is baptized properly (that is, the way Jesus commanded: *in the Name of the Father, and of the Son, and of the Holy Spirit*), he's entered into the Church and is in at least partial communion with Her. But he's called to so much more...

There is so much to what God has revealed to us! And the Church believes we are each called to continuing conversion; to incessantly seek the Kingdom of God, learning and experiencing more and more of the Christian life. For instance, a person might know of God; but he's called to know God as *Trinity*. The same person might learn of God as Trinity; but he'd still be called to know the Trinity as *Family*. Or another example: a person might know of the Passover; but he's called to know the *Eucharist*. The same person might learn of the Eucharist; but he's called to know the Eucharist as the *Real Presence*. So we see that there is a constant growth in our understanding of all Truth.

It's a seemingly impossible task – but the Church points the way. It brings the consensus of all theology and philosophy together under the sovereignty of Father, Son, and Holy Spirit. The Church never presumes to know *everything* about God's Word. Instead, She leaves much room for debate. Yet as issues threaten unity, God has promised to protect Her exploration of revelation. Under the authority of Peter's successor, the universal decisions on faith, morals, or sacraments that She publicly teaches and proclaims are binding on all those who come to understand them and hear the ring of Truth. Such clarifications are called *dogmas*.

The Church teaches that Peter was the leader of the disciples, and that Christ commissioned him with special tasks. Wherever Peter was, there was the primacy of the Church. Peter went from Jerusalem to Antioch to Rome and it was there that he and Paul were martyred. Since this was his final resting place, his successors have dwelt there ever since.

As heresies and spin-off "churches" grew, the Catholic Church has come to be specified as the "Roman" Catholic Church for this reason. She is the only one to trace her authority back to *Peter* and from him to Christ. The whole of Church authority is based on Christ's promises to the apostles and their succession, Peter's successor still being leader.

Think of it. Every bishop in the Catholic Church today had hands laid on him by an older bishop; had breath breathed on him; and the same that did so experienced the same from his predecessor, and his before him, and his before him…all the way back to Christ, who breathed on the original apostles and said, "receive the Holy Spirit." To me, that's powerful. That's unity, continuity, and authority. That's what we *need*.

If we are called to obey Christ and to live fully according to his Word, how are we to discern truth from error? Who's to say what biblical interpretation has greater weight? Where is the final authority? If we believe it is the Bible and not the Church, then the Bible must be a fallible collection of infallible books, since it was the Church who determined what books were Sacred Scripture. That means we trust we're right, but could be wrong, since God never gave us a set canon.

If we, however, have the *faith* that Christ invests in the Church His own infallibility, then we have no problem. Our line of faith and reason trace back to Christ. Moreover, the Scriptures themselves testify that the Church is the "pillar and foundation of Truth" (1 Tim. 3:15). If that is so – and we must at the very least respect the authority of our priests and bishops (Heb. 13:17) – then how could a split from the visible Church be justified? When did these verses cease to be applicable?

As a Protestant, I remember many times in my home groups when troubling issues would come up – issues that were not and could not be clearly defined by mainline Protestantism – such as masturbation, remarriage, almsgiving, and the death penalty. We would each take turns mumbling our opinion, eye each other nervously, and eventually move on to the next subject. There just weren't enough obvious verses referring to these things. Each of us could hold our own opinion…but it didn't feel like enough.

How could we discern biblical responses to modern-day issues like cloning or artificial womb technology? We would be grasping at hairs at best, and we *knew it*. Enter the Catholic Church. How nice it is to *know* where we should stand in regards to these and so many other issues…all thanks to the authority of the One, Holy, Catholic, and Apostolic Church by the power vested in Christ.

Everyone can enjoy these benefits. Full communion with God, His Family, and His Life. Not only can they enjoy it, but they are *called to it*. And as each person discerns that call in his heart, he makes a choice to accept or reject it. Salvation is found only in God's Covenant with humankind; His *Church* through Christ. Yet there are many who don't know about Baptism, but nevertheless participate in God's Love through what they *do* know. And there are many baptized who don't understand the necessity of the other Sacraments, but nevertheless have a strong relationship with Christ through what they *do* understand. The point is that the Church is commanded to *eradicate ignorance* through evangelism so each person *can* achieve the fullness of his calling. What a shame it would be for us to let someone live out their mortal life with only a partial sharing in the Divine Life.

Ah, and just because Catholicism holds the deepest and most clear understandings of God's Word, that doesn't mean that all Catholics have a better relationship with God than everyone else. Get this – it doesn't even have to mean your *average* Catholic has a better relationship with God. In fact, it could very well mean that *more* Catholics are choosing *separation* from God! How is this possible? Well, as I said before, you are only held accountable for what you have come to understand and recognize is true (assuming you are not choosing to remain willfully ignorant). Let's look at the following verses:

> John 9:41
> Jesus said unto them, *If ye were blind, ye should have no sin: but now ye say, We see; therefore your sin remaineth.*

> Romans 2:13-15
> For not the hearers of the law are just before God, but the doers of the law shall be justified. For when the Gentiles, which have not the law, do by nature the things contained in the law, these, having not the law, are a law unto themselves: Which shew the work of the law written

> in their hearts, their conscience also bearing witness, and their thoughts the mean while accusing or else excusing one another...

> James 3:1
> My brethren, be not many masters, knowing that we shall receive the greater condemnation.

So stop and think about it. Each of these verses reveals a striking truth – the more you know, the more you're held accountable. If Catholicism provides an atmosphere where you have the greatest opportunity for the most of what God wants for you, then it is simultaneously the atmosphere prone to the greatest failings. Many Catholics would make good Protestants, but not many Protestants would make good Catholics. That is because there is a higher understanding of Truth involved and consequently a higher obligation to pursue and assent to it. It's easier to let go of moral and doctrinal stances than it is to confess them. Every denomination of Christianity that has broken off from full communion with the Catholic Church has surrendered portions of the Faith handed down by the Apostles.

If a Catholic became Protestant, he could find a group of *other* Christians whose interpretations of Scripture were compatible with his lifestyle. The ex-Catholic could then feel free to focus only on *his* one-on-one relationship with God; able to ignore his Mother, his brothers and sisters in Heaven, and the taxing burdens of what his Father considers "healthy living". The Protestant, however, would suddenly upon becoming *Catholic* find himself surrounded by an enormous Family of Heaven and Earth, cheering him on to the finish line in a race full of obstacle courses of temptation and liberalism, which were previously thought not to have mattered.

There's a lot for a Catholic to live up to! And realistically, it's probably impossible. That is where the Sacraments come in. Many people, including some Catholics, confuse the Sacraments for magic, but the difference is profound. Magic is an attempt to *control* God for selfish purposes. A Sacrament is an attempt to *obey* God with faith in his promises. Each of the Church's seven Sacraments is commanded in God's Word – and they each serve a vital purpose. The Church is a Family, built on God's covenant, driven towards an ever deepening understanding of His Word. We enter that covenant under the sign of Baptism and then, hopefully, choose to grow in the Faith that has taken us in. When we're ready to make a committed choice, we receive the Sacrament of Confirmation to open ourselves more fully to the life of the Spirit and make a firm profession of faith.

Still, since there's so much to fully enjoying the life God intended, we relive the act and method of our covenant by receiving the Body, Blood, Soul, and Divinity of our Lord in the Eucharist, under the appearance of bread and wine. This not only consummates the paschal sacrifice of God's own Lamb, it also empowers us with extra grace to continue living well. Eventually, we either discern a call to marry a spouse or consecrate ourselves to the Church. Why? Well, certainly to be a sign of Christ but also to have full-time partners in the race to heaven! Whether a spouse or the clergy, we get added encouragement to stand fast and stay strong.

Yet even after all this, we are prone to fall. And when we do, Christ saw to it that the story of the Prodigal Son would come true – there's always a spiritual father to turn to in confession and repentance; and he'll *always* welcome you home. Refreshed, unburdened, and empowered, we are once again fully equipped to live as God wants us to. It's psychological genius, really. Then again, it *is* the Church of God we're talking about.

And when our time on this earth is finally up and God is about to call us home, He still wants *someone* to be with us physically, to better remind us of His presence, spiritually. When we are very ill or on our deathbeds, we receive the Anointing of the Sick. The Sacrament has been known to miraculously heal on occasion, but more often than not it is a time of quiet compassion between God and his suffering child. The Family draws near and prepares our hearts for the God we will soon be wonderfully embracing.

So even though the call to the fullness of Truth is a high one, God more than amply provides the grace needed for *anyone* to live it. And what a life it is! It is nothing short of the Heavenly Liturgy; the Lamb's Supper; the Divine Life. God wants nothing but the best for all his children. And the prayer and goal of the Church is to bring as many back to the utmost of what God intended as is possible.

Everything true, everything honorable, everything just, everything pure, everything lovely, everything of good report – anything of virtue or praise in your philosophy or theology – all of it can be brought with you into the One, Holy, Catholic, and Apostolic Church where so much more awaits you! That is the purpose of evangelism. The incarnation of the Word inaugurated a New Covenant with the *entire world*.

In effect, Christ didn't draw a circle around himself and say *everyone's out*; he drew a circle around the planet and said *everyone's in.* Every person on this world has the opportunity to draw near to God, solely because of what Christ has done for him. We are the Family of God. And the more deeply we understand and experience that, the more deeply we understand and experience the Trinity.

How does one recognize the Family, then? Surely it isn't some nebulous, invisible, entity. It's not simply a philosophical ideal. That's not how real families exist. As the history of the Church shows, it is a very visible kingdom. Usually, we need only become formal citizens. We discern the true kingdom from the imposters by finding out which one can be traced back to the *true King*.

Many follow the King's advice and commands – and that's very good. But how many are traced back to the King, Himself? The Catholic Church is the only historical entity to whom the keys of the kingdom were given. The Catholic Church *is* that kingdom. And suddenly all the parables about the King handing over his trust and authority to a steward while He's away make perfect sense. Christ says His Church is "the light of the world", comparing it to "a city set on a mountain" that *can't* be hidden

(Matt. 5:14). It *must* be visible and have certain marks that set it apart from all the rest, or else it becomes very hard for someone to find and enter it.

The first obvious question is: how many denominations were around at the time of Christ? Well, just one. How many can claim to be that one? To have existed in all generations (Matt. 16:18, 28:20)? How many have, in practice, pronounced Mary "blessed" *throughout* all those generations (Luke 1:48)? How many, throughout all those generations, have taught not as the Pharisees did, but as one having authority (Mark 1:22)? Come on. I know you know the answer...

> *We discern the true kingdom from the imposters by finding out which one can be traced back to the true King.*

For 2,000 years the Church has existed despite bitter opposition. As a Protestant, one of the evidences I relied on most frequently for the Divine origins of the Bible was its survival and preserved organization against all odds. As a Catholic, I can say the same thing of my Church. The Church is composed of sinful, fallible, human beings. How on earth could it be possible for it to preserve its organization and unity for so long? Most great nations only last for several hundred years, but *two thousand*? Not only that, but the Church is the most vigorous and fruitful in the world, with over a billion members! I attribute it to nothing and no one less than the Holy Spirit.

Over and over again, I have referred to the Church by Her grandest title: *One, Holy, Catholic, and Apostolic*. And these are in fact the four marks that set her apart from the rest. The Church is One (Rom.12:5, 1; Cor.10:17, 12:13) in that She has one set of doctrines (Phil. 1:27, 2:2; Jude 3) and is the only Bride of Christ (Eph. 5:23–32). She may grow in her understanding of those doctrines (John 16:12–13) and come up with new customs, disciplines, devotions, or habits to emphasize them, but She'll never contradict them. The Church is Holy, not in that her members are perfect (Matt 7:15; Acts 20:29; Luke 17:1; John 6:70; Matt. 7:21–23) but in that she is redeemed by Christ and is the source and guardian of the Sacraments, which produce holiness and grace (Eph. 5:25–27; Rev. 19:7–8; Eph. 5:26). The Church is Catholic (meaning, Universal) because God conceived Her for all peoples (Matt. 28:19–20) and bonds Her together as a common Family; as early as 107 A.D. the Church was referred to as "Catholic". The Church is Apostolic (Eph. 2:19–20) in that She traces her leadership back to the apostles through direct succession (Acts 1:24-25, 6:6, 14:23; 2 Tim. 2:2), guarding and passing down their teaching (both oral and written) through the generations (2 Thes. 2:15). What other Church bears these marks?

Scripture Speaks! *What the Bible Says*

What if the Church was Founded and Protected by Christ?

> Matthew 16:18
> And I say also unto thee, that **thou art Peter, and upon this rock I will build my church; and the gates of hell shall not prevail against it.** And I will give unto **thee** the **keys of the kingdom** of heaven: and whatsoever **thou** shalt bind on earth **shall be bound in heaven**: and whatsoever **thou** shalt loose on earth shall be loosed in heaven.

Here, Jesus reveals a few key aspects of the One, Holy, Catholic, and Apostolic Church. First, the real one is the one founded by Christ. Second, Peter has a prime role to play in it (God never changes a name lightly). Third, by inference, the Church is somehow oriented around and traced back to him. In fact, Christ calls the Church a kingdom – the keys of which belong to Peter. And fourth, it will last…

> Matthew 28:20
> Teaching them to observe all things whatsoever I have commanded you: and, lo, **I am with you alway, even unto the end of the world.** Amen.

…in fact, Christ said that Church would exist for him to be with right up to the point when he returns.

> Ephes. 5:23
> For the husband is the head of the wife, even as Christ is the head of the church: **and he is the saviour of the body.**

Many scholars think the word used for "savior" here might better be translated as "preserver". Regardless, the meaning is the same. After Jesus set up the Church, he began to protect it – to save it – and continues to do so today.

> 1 Cor. 11:26
> For as often as ye eat this bread, and drink this cup, ye do shew the Lord's death **till he come.**

This passage indicates that the Church of the Apostles will be celebrating communion until Christ comes back.

> Eccles. 3:14
> I know that, **whatsoever God doeth, it shall be for ever: nothing can be put to it, nor any thing taken from it**: and God doeth it, that men should fear before him.

God the Son began the New Covenant Church. According to this verse, when could there be a time when that action is thwarted or undone? Could the whole Church ever become apostate? When would it be okay to leave and start a new one?

> Hebrews 13:5
> Let your conversation be without covetousness; and be content with such things as ye have: for **he hath said, I will never leave thee, nor forsake thee**.

Another example of the Church's Divine protection.

> Luke 1:33
> And he shall reign over the house of Jacob for ever; and **of his kingdom there shall be no end.**

We already saw that the Church is Christ's kingdom. This verse tells us that the kingdom will exist perpetually. If someone didn't like the first one, and so set up a competing kingdom – based on the same principles and the same King – would it be the same as the original? Of course not! Only the one founded by the King is the legitimate kingdom.

> Luke 1:48
> …for, behold, **from henceforth all generations** shall call me blessed.

The Blessed Mother certainly understood what this meant! Christ's kingdom would exist throughout all generations; consequently, those members of the true kingdom would in practice bless the one by whom the King entered into the world.

> John 17:11
> And now I am no more in the world, but these are in the world, and I come to thee. Holy Father, **keep through thine own name those whom thou hast given me, that they may be one, as we are.**

Here, Christ invokes the Name of God in his determination for the Divine protection of his Church. Which Church was founded by Christ and has exhibited a decisive unity in Sacraments and doctrines throughout all generations? Only the One, Holy, Catholic, and Apostolic Church.

What if the Church is the Final Authority on the Faith?

> Matthew 18:15-17
> Moreover if thy brother shall trespass against thee, go and tell him his fault between thee and him alone: if he shall hear thee, thou hast gained thy brother. [16] But if he will not hear thee, then take with thee one or two more, that in the mouth of two or three witnesses every word may be established. [17] And if he shall neglect to hear them, tell it unto the church: but **if he neglect to hear the Church, let him be unto thee as an heathen man and a publican.**

Where in this passage does Jesus say to consult the Bible? What does he say is the final authority before judgment is made?

> 1 Tim. 3:15
> But if I tarry long, that thou mayest know how thou oughtest to behave thyself in the house of God, **which is the church of the living God, the pillar and ground of the truth.**

What is the pillar and foundation of Truth? According to this passage, how may we discern truth from falsehood? How may we judge between differing interpretations of Scripture?

> 2 Tim. 3:16-17
> All scripture is **given by inspiration of God**, and is **profitable** for doctrine, for reproof, for correction, for instruction in righteousness: [17] That the man of God may be perfect, thoroughly furnished unto all good works.

Where does this verse declare Scripture to be the final authority? Certainly it confirms Scripture's Divine origins and profitability – but does it say that the Bible *alone* is our infallible authority? Read verse 17 in context; a man may be perfect *if* he has sound doctrine, correction, and instruction. The problem is that the previous verse only says that Scripture is *profitable* for such gains.

Certainly a person could come to know God and get by with the Scriptures alone; but is that what God intended?

> John 14:26
> But the Comforter, which is the Holy Ghost, whom the Father will send in my name, he **shall teach you all things**, and **bring all things to your remembrance, whatsoever I have said** unto you.

This passage reveals two aspects of the Church's authority and special protection. Firstly, the Catholic Church has all of God's revelation in Sacred Scripture and Sacred Tradition. The Holy Spirit reminded the apostles of what Christ handed down to them so they could hand it down to their successors. Secondly, when the Church asks questions about God's revelation, she will be able to give an authoritative answer. The Holy Spirit will guide the Catholic Church into deeper understandings of what she already believes.

> Titus 2:15
> These things speak, and exhort, and rebuke **with all authority**. Let no man despise thee.

No wonder Paul could tell Titus that his oral teaching, which represented the living voice of the Church, had "all authority"!

What if the Church Must be One?

John 17:21-23
That they all may be one; as thou, Father, art in me, and I in thee, that they also may be one in us: **that the world may believe that thou hast sent me.** [22] And the glory which thou gavest me I have given them; **that they may be one, even as we are one:** [23] I in them, and thou in me, **that they may be made perfect in one; and that the world may know that thou hast sent me, and hast loved them, as thou hast loved me.**

Here, Jesus prays for a unity so intense, so complete, that it compares to the familial relationship between the Persons of the Trinity. He also says that the Church has as much glory as He does. And why? So that the world isn't confused about which Church is the true one and what it means to be in the Family of God. In what denomination has that prayer been answered?

Romans 16:17
Now I beseech you, brethren, **mark them which cause divisions and offences contrary to the doctrine which ye have learned; and avoid them.**

Did your church's founder cause division in the Body of Christ? Does it teach the whole Word of God, as handed down to the Apostles? (see 2 Thes. 2:15) Or does it teach things contrary to what were held true by its predecessors?

1 Cor. 1:10-13
Now I beseech you, brethren, by the name of our Lord Jesus Christ, **that ye all speak the same thing, and that there be no divisions among you; but that ye be perfectly joined together in the same mind and in the same judgment.** [11] For it hath been declared unto me of you, my brethren, by them which are of the house of Chloe, that there are contentions among you. [12] Now this I say, that every one of you saith, I am of Paul; and I of Apollos; and I of Cephas; and I of Christ. [13] **Is**

> **Christ divided?** Was Paul crucified for you? Or were ye baptized in the name of Paul?

In what Christian group do all the members universally speak the same things in worship? Which group has an authoritative teaching body and government that agrees upon, clearly states, and exhaustively explains doctrine and the Christian life?

> Galatians 1:8-9
> But **though we**, or **an angel from heaven**, preach any **other gospel** unto you than that which **we** have preached unto you, let him be **accursed**. [9] As we **said** before, so **say** I now again, **If any man preach any other gospel** unto you than that ye have **received**, let him be **accursed**.

Here Paul asserts that there is only one gospel and even bishops can fail it. But does that mean that the whole Church to which the bishop claims to be committed is straying as well? Or is it only the heretic and his followers? Obviously the One, Holy, Catholic, and Apostolic Church remains! The dissenters are the ones who leave, are expelled, or are eventually condemned – precisely because they preach another gospel. If there is only one Deposit of apostolic teaching, what denominations have existed throughout all generations to guard it? Which ones have even a *claim* to the kind of authentic authority required to do so?

What if the Church Must be Holy?

> Matthew 18:7
> **Woe unto the world because of offences!** for it must needs be that offences come; but woe to that man by whom the offence cometh!

Christ knew the world would feel the suffering inflicted by corrupt or failing periods of Church leadership…

> Luke 17:1
> Then said he unto the disciples, **It is impossible but that offences will come**: but woe unto him, through whom they come!

…he was being realistic. He had set up a Divine Institution; a New Covenant Family of God that would be under the Holy Spirit's protection and guidance. Nevertheless, the stewards of the Kingdom and stand-ins for the King would still be human, with all the fallibility and frailty that come with it. So sins and scandals were not only to be expected, but Christ even went so far as to say that it would be *impossible* for them not to come! The *fallible Church* (all members of the Family, individually) would stray from the *infallible Church* (the Teaching Voice and Spirit of the Magisterium on Sacred Scripture and Sacred Tradition) and whenever that happened, so would sin and scandal.

> John 6:70
> Jesus answered them, Have not **I chosen you** twelve, and one of you is a **devil**?

Even one of the original apostles whom Jesus chose rejected Christ and committed the most atrocious sin and scandal the Church has ever known. So do we abandon Peter and the rest of them and of our own accord start something new? No. We pray God's will be done, look forward to a day when things change, offer our sufferings up with the Lord (see Col. 1:24), and submit to the authority He has placed over us. Why? Because regardless of the hypocrisy and sins of mere men, we know that the Holy Spirit protects Church teaching – in a mysterious and paradoxical way, we can trust the Church, even if we can't trust her members!

> Matthew 7:21-23
> **Not every one that saith unto me, Lord, Lord, shall enter into the kingdom of heaven; but he that doeth the will of my Father which is in heaven.** [22] Many will say to me in that day, Lord, Lord, have we not prophesied in thy name? and in thy name have cast out devils? and in thy name done many wonderful works? [23] And then will I profess unto them, I never knew you: depart from me, **ye that work iniquity.**

Here again Christ asserts that his Church is not devoid of corrupt, hell-bound, sinners who refuse the holiness God offers them through the fullness of His Family.

> Mark 2:17
> When Jesus heard it, he saith unto them, They that are whole have no need of the physician, but they that are sick: **I came not to call the righteous, but sinners** to repentance.

All of this was a natural consequence of God's love for all peoples. Of course there would be sin and scandal in His Church – it is a hospital for sinners, full of sinners, run by sinners, and intended for sinners! Yet in Christ, we have a wonderful faith…

> Ephes. 5:25-27
> Husbands, love your wives, even as Christ also loved the church, and gave himself for it; [26] That **he might sanctify and cleanse it with the washing of water** by the word, [27] That he might present it to himself a **glorious church**, not having spot, or wrinkle, or any such thing; but that it should be **holy and without blemish.**

Jesus' own righteousness and His redemptive Incarnation gives anyone who enters the Church (through the new "circumcision" sign of the New Covenant: water baptism [see Col.

2:11-13]) a new and eternal life, clothed and empowered by the holiness of Christ. The grace of God through Christ can keep us perfect from then on, according to our cooperation.

> Rev. 19:7-8
> Let us be glad and rejoice, and give honour to him: for the marriage of the Lamb is come, and his wife hath **made herself** ready. [8] And to her was granted that she should be arrayed in fine linen, clean and white: for the fine linen is **the righteousness of saints**.

Again we see that though our efforts don't deserve the label of "holiness", God's free grace in the Sacraments – if we obediently receive them – does give us the righteousness and holiness necessary for Heaven.

> 2 Cor. 5:21
> For he hath made him to be sin for us, who knew no sin; that **we might be made the righteousness of God in him.**

Through Christ, with Christ, and in Christ, the grace of God truly obliterates our sins, regenerates us, and empowers us to keep free from sin. Since it is the Church who is given, protects, presents, and dispenses the Sacraments that accomplish this (through Christ and not of herself) she is holy.

What if the Church Must be Catholic?

Matthew 28:19-20
Go ye therefore, and **teach all nations**, baptizing them in the name of the Father, and of the Son, and of the Holy Ghost: [20] **Teaching them to observe all things whatsoever I have commanded you**: and, lo, I am with you alway, even unto the end of the world. Amen.

Rev. 5:9-10
And they sung a new song, saying, Thou art worthy to take the book, and to open the seals thereof: for thou wast slain, and hast redeemed us to God by thy blood **out of every kindred, and tongue, and people, and nation;** [10] And hast made us unto our God kings and priests: and we shall reign on the earth.

We see in these passages that Christ's Church is global, and consists of exotic cultures and peoples from all over the world. Yet they are members by one baptism. And they have one body of teachings: the Sacred Tradition of Christ, as explored, clarified, defended, and handed on by the Magisterium and pointed to in Sacred Scripture.

Galatians 3:28
There is **neither Jew nor Greek**, there is neither bond nor free, there is neither male nor female: for **ye are all one in Christ Jesus**.

Though this Church is present on every populated continent, it celebrates the same Person, the same faith, the same hope, the same love.

Romans 15:6
That ye may with **one mind and one mouth** glorify God, even the Father of our Lord Jesus Christ.

All over the planet, from sunrise to sunset, one Church worships the same God *together* with one, resounding, voice. Though the local customs or traditions may vary, every Mass has the Liturgy of the Word and the Liturgy of the Eucharist – the basic structure and prayers are universal. With one mind, all the peoples of the earth call on the Lord for mercy and pray as he taught them.

> Philip. 1:27
> Only let your conversation be as it becometh the gospel of Christ: that whether I come and see you, or else be absent, I may hear of your affairs, that ye stand **fast in one spirit, with one mind striving together for the faith** of the gospel;

What other group has this kind of unity? Can they literally fulfill this passage?

What if the Church Must be Apostolic?

> Ephes. 2:20
> And are **built upon the foundation of the apostles** and prophets, Jesus Christ himself being the chief corner stone;

The Church must be Apostolic. Which Church traces its authority in an unbroken line back to the Apostles as Her foundation?

> 1 Cor. 12:12-27
> For **as the body is one**, and hath many members, and **all the members of that one body, being many, are one body**: so also is Christ. [13] For **by one Spirit are we all baptized into one body**, whether we be Jews or Gentiles, whether we be bond or free; and have been all made to drink into one Spirit. [14] For the body is not one member, but many. [15] If the foot shall say, Because I am not the hand, I am not of the body; is it therefore not of the body? [16] And if the ear shall say, Because I am not the eye, I am not of the body; is it therefore not of the body? [17] If the whole body were an eye, where were the hearing? If the whole were hearing, where were the smelling? [18] But now hath God set the members every one of them in the body, as it hath pleased him. [19] And if they were all one member, where were the body? [20] But now are they many members, yet but one body. [21] And the eye cannot say unto the hand, I have no need of thee: nor again the head to the feet, I have no need of you. [22] Nay, much more those members of the body, which seem to be more feeble, are necessary: [23] And those members of the body, which we think to be less honourable, upon these we bestow more abundant honour; and our uncomely parts have more abundant comeliness. [24] For our comely parts have no need: but God hath tempered the body together, having given more abundant honour to that part which lacked: [25] That **there should be no schism in the body;** but that the members should have the same care one for another. [26] And whether one member suffer, all the members suffer with it; or one

> member be honoured, all the members rejoice with it. [27] Now ye are the body of Christ, and members in particular.

Here, we are told to respect each other's individual gifts and places in the Body of Christ, and that members of the Church have different positions of leadership and authority to prevent schism.

> 1 Tim. 3:1-4
> This is a true saying, If a man desire **the office of a bishop**, he desireth a good work. [2] A bishop then must be blameless, the husband of one wife, vigilant, sober, of good behaviour, given to hospitality, apt to teach; [3] Not given to wine, no striker, not greedy of filthy lucre; but patient, not a brawler, not covetous; [4] One that ruleth well his own house, having his children in subjection with all gravity;

Here, the bishop is referred to having an "office". What's significant about this is that an office requires succession in order to be maintained.

> 1 Cor. 3:10
> According to the grace of God which is given unto me, as a wise masterbuilder, I have laid the foundation, and **another buildeth thereon.** But let every man take heed how he buildeth thereupon.

Paul refers to his future successors, who will build on what God revealed through him, and warns them of teaching falsely.

> Acts 1:20
> For it is written in the book of Psalms, Let his habitation be desolate, and let no man dwell therein: and **his bishoprick let another take.**

Here is an example of apostolic succession. The Apostles ordained bishops as they spread the gospel. When they had all passed away, the bishops they had granted their authority were the leaders of the Church. We can trace all of the Church's bishops back to the original Apostles.

> 2 Tim. 4:1-5
> **I charge thee** therefore before God, and the Lord Jesus Christ, who shall judge the quick and the dead at his appearing and his kingdom; [2] Preach the word; be instant in season, out of season; reprove, rebuke, exhort with all longsuffering and doctrine. [3] **For the time will come when they will not endure sound doctrine; but after their own lusts shall they heap to themselves teachers, having itching ears; [4] And they shall turn away their ears from the truth, and shall be turned unto fables.** [5] But watch thou in all things, endure afflictions, do the work of an evangelist, make full proof of thy ministry.

Paul ordained Timothy as his successor and warned him of coming heresies and schismatic groups who would reject the God-given authority of the Church. Does this passage remind you of King Henry VIII and the anti-church he set up?

> Acts 8:14-24
> Now when the apostles which were at Jerusalem heard that Samaria had received the word of God, **they sent unto them Peter** and John: [15] Who, when they were come down, prayed for them, that they might receive the Holy Ghost: [16] (For **as yet he was fallen upon none of them**: only they were baptized in the name of the Lord Jesus.) [17] **Then laid they their hands on them, and they received the Holy Ghost.** [18] And when Simon saw that **through laying on of the apostles' hands the Holy Ghost was given,** he offered them money, [19] Saying, Give me also this power, that on whomsoever I lay hands, he may receive the Holy Ghost. [20] But **Peter said** unto him, Thy money perish with thee, because thou hast thought that the gift of God may be purchased with money. [21] Thou hast neither part nor lot in this matter: for thy heart is not right in the sight of God. [22] Repent therefore of this thy wickedness, and pray God, if perhaps the thought of thine heart may be forgiven thee. [23] For I perceive that thou art in the gall of bitterness, and in the

> bond of iniquity. [24] Then answered Simon, and said, Pray **ye** to the Lord for me, that none of these things which ye have spoken come upon me.

Notice here that it required the God-given authority of ordained clergy (in this case, two of the original bishops – authority that Christ breathed on them) to allow these Christians to be fully open to the Holy Spirit's indwelling presence. This is an example of Confirmation.

> Acts 20:28-31
> Take heed therefore unto yourselves, and **to all the flock, over the which the Holy Ghost hath made you overseers,** to feed the church of God, which he hath purchased with his own blood. [29] For I know this, that **after my departing shall grievous wolves enter in among you, not sparing the flock. [30] Also of your own selves shall men arise, speaking perverse things, to draw away disciples after them.** [31] Therefore watch, and remember, that by the space of three years I ceased not to warn every one night and day with tears.

Paul addresses the bishops that would start where he left off, his successors. He is also very clear that the Church will have evil men that enter in and come out of Her. Verse 30 seems almost prophetic of Luther, who went from "reformer" to "rebel" by condemning the Church's authority and doctrines, rather than just her sins. This is yet further evidence of the need for God's protection in matters of the Faith. How can a fallible, sinful, human organization survive with universal doctrine preserved, except by the hand of God?

What if Peter is Eminent in Scripture Because of His Appointed Leadership?

> Matthew 16:17-19
> And Jesus answered and said unto him, Blessed **art thou, Simon Barjona**: for flesh and blood hath not revealed it unto thee, but my Father which is in heaven. [18] And I say also **unto thee,** That **thou** art **Peter,** and **upon this rock I will build my church**; and the gates of hell shall not prevail against it. [19] And I will give **unto thee** the **keys of the kingdom of heaven**: and **whatsoever thou shalt bind on earth shall be bound in heaven: and whatsoever thou shalt loose on earth shall be loosed in heaven.**

This passage is ridiculously clear. Simon is blessed, his name is changed (something which indicates a massive positional change throughout the Bible and implies an enormous role to play in God's plan), he's told that the Church will be built on him, the keys to heaven are given to him, and he has ultimate teaching authority. This reminds us of a prophecy...

> Isaiah 22:22
> And the **key of the house of David** will I lay upon his shoulder; so **he shall open, and none shall shut; and he shall shut, and none shall open.**

Sound familiar? To be given the keys to the kingdom meant you were the prime-minister. You represented the King while he was away and had all of his authority.

> 1 Peter 5:1
> **The elders** which are among you **I exhort, who am also an elder**, and a witness of the sufferings of Christ, and also a partaker of the glory that shall be revealed:

Peter has authority above all other bishops (translated "elders" in the KJV), even though he is a bishop himself.

Matthew 17:24-27
    And when they were come to Capernaum, they that received tribute money **came to Peter**, and said, Doth not your master pay tribute? [25] He saith, Yes. And when he was come into the house, Jesus prevented him, saying, What thinkest thou, Simon? of whom do the kings of the earth take custom or tribute? of their own children, or of strangers? [26] Peter saith unto him, Of strangers. Jesus saith unto him, Then are the children free. [27] Notwithstanding, lest we should offend them, **go thou to the sea**, and cast an hook, and take up the fish that first cometh up; and when thou hast opened his mouth, thou shalt find a piece of money: that take, **and give unto them for me and thee**.

The tax collectors weren't fooling around. They went straight to the leader of the disciples to get to Jesus. And Jesus sends Peter back to them to represent Himself and the rest of the disciples.

Mark 16:7
    But go your way, tell his disciples and **Peter** that he goeth before you into Galilee: there shall ye see him, as he said unto you.

The angel marks Peter apart from the rest of the disciples because of his special position of leadership.

Luke 22:32
    But I have prayed for **thee**, that thy faith fail not: and when thou art converted, **strengthen thy brethren**.

Christ was deeply concerned about Peter because it was Peter's task to lead his brethren.

John 21:15-17
    So when they had dined, **Jesus saith to Simon Peter**, Simon, son of Jonas, lovest thou me more than these? He saith unto him, Yea, Lord; thou knowest that I love thee. **He saith unto him, Feed my lambs.** [16] He saith to him again the second time, Simon, son of Jonas, lovest thou

me? He saith unto him, Yea, Lord; thou knowest that I love thee. **He saith unto him, Feed my sheep.** [17] He saith unto him the third time, Simon, son of Jonas, lovest thou me? Peter was grieved because he said unto him the third time, Lovest thou me? And he said unto him, Lord, thou knowest all things; thou knowest that I love thee. **Jesus saith unto him, Feed my sheep.**

Peter was appointed leader over all the Church in Christ's absence...

John 10:16
And other sheep I have, which are not of this fold: them also I must bring, and they shall hear my voice; and **there shall be one fold, and one shepherd.**

...so that when Christ ascended, Peter could be the one shepherd over the one fold.

Acts 5:2-11
And kept back part of the price, his wife also being privy to it, and brought a certain part, and laid it at the apostles' feet. [3] But **Peter said,** Ananias, why hath Satan filled thine heart to lie to the Holy Ghost, and to keep back part of the price of the land? [4] Whiles it remained, was it not thine own? and after it was sold, was it not in thine own power? why hast thou conceived this thing in thine heart? **thou hast not lied unto men, but unto God.** [5] And Ananias hearing these words fell down, and gave up the ghost: and great fear came on all them that heard these things. [6] And the young men arose, wound him up, and carried him out, and buried him. [7] And it was about the space of three hours after, when his wife, not knowing what was done, came in. [8] And Peter answered unto her, Tell me whether ye sold the land for so much? And she said, Yea, for so much. [9] **Then Peter said unto her, How is it that ye have agreed together to tempt the Spirit of the Lord? behold, the feet of them which have buried thy husband are at the door, and shall carry thee out.** [10] **Then fell she down straightway at his feet, and yielded up the ghost: and the young men came in, and found**

her dead, and, carrying her forth, buried her by her husband. [11] And great fear came upon all the church, and upon as many as heard these things.

Peter stands in place of Christ, on earth. Thus, Peter's judgment carried with it the judgment of God.

What if Paul Rebukes Peter For Hypocrisy Because Peter's Leadership Has so Much Influence?

> Galatians 2:11-14
> But when Peter was come to Antioch, I withstood him to the face, because **he was to be blamed.** [12] For before that certain came from James, he did eat with the Gentiles: but when they were come, he withdrew and separated himself, fearing them which were of the circumcision. [13] And the other Jews dissembled likewise with him; insomuch that Barnabas also was carried away with their dissimulation. [14] But when I saw that they walked not uprightly according to the truth of the gospel, I said unto Peter before them all, If thou, being a Jew, livest after the manner of Gentiles, and not as do the Jews, **why compellest thou** the Gentiles to live as do the Jews?

It was precisely because of Peter's influence over the entire Christian world as Church leader that Paul was so upset over his hypocrisy. The same kind of hypocrisy could be seen in another man after God's own heart...

> 2 Samuel 12:1-14
> And the Lord sent Nathan unto David. And he came unto him, and said unto him, There were two men in one city; the one rich, and the other poor. [2] The rich man had exceeding many flocks and herds: [3] But the poor man had nothing, save one little ewe lamb, which he had bought and nourished up: and it grew up together with him, and with his children; it did eat of his own meat, and drank of his own cup, and lay in his bosom, and was unto him as a daughter. [4] And there came a traveller unto the rich man, and he spared to take of his own flock and of his own herd, to dress for the wayfaring man that was come unto him; but took the poor man's lamb, and dressed it for the man that was come to him. [5] And David's anger was greatly kindled against the man; and he said to Nathan, As the Lord liveth, the man that hath done this thing shall surely die: [6] And he shall restore the lamb fourfold, because he did this thing, and because he had no pity.

[7] And Nathan said to David, Thou art the man. Thus saith the Lord God of Israel, **I anointed thee king over Israel,** and I delivered thee out of the hand of Saul; [8] And I gave thee thy master's house, and thy master's wives into thy bosom, and gave thee the house of Israel and of Judah; and if that had been too little, I would moreover have given unto thee such and such things. [9] Wherefore hast thou despised the commandment of the Lord, to do evil in his sight? **Thou hast killed Uriah the Hittite with the sword, and hast taken his wife to be thy wife, and hast slain him with the sword of the children of Ammon.** [10] Now therefore the sword shall never depart from thine house; because thou hast despised me, and hast taken the wife of Uriah the Hittite to be thy wife. [11] Thus saith the Lord, Behold, I will raise up evil against thee out of thine own house, and I will take thy wives before thine eyes, and give them unto thy neighbour, and he shall lie with thy wives in the sight of this sun. [12] For thou didst it secretly: but I will do this thing before all Israel, and before the sun. [13] And David said unto Nathan, I have sinned against the Lord. And Nathan said unto David, The Lord also hath put away thy sin; thou shalt not die. [14] Howbeit, **because by this deed thou hast given great occasion to the enemies of the Lord to blaspheme,** the child also that is born unto thee shall surely die.

...Yet his position as king remained. So did Peter's position as leader of the Church. Nowhere does Christ guarantee that the leaders of the Church will be perfect or even average – only that the Faith itself would be protected. There have certainly been plenty of "great occasions" when popes or bishops made a poor spectacle of the Church.

What if Some Have a Specific Calling to the Priesthood?

> 1 Peter 2:9
> But ye are a chosen generation, **a royal priesthood, an holy nation**, a peculiar people; that ye should shew forth the praises of him who hath called you out of darkness into his marvellous light:

> Exodus 19:6
> And ye shall be unto me **a kingdom of priests, and an holy nation.** These are the words which thou shalt speak unto the children of Israel.

Both in the Old and New Covenants, we are all called "priests". Yet in the New, as with the Old, there is a group of those specifically called to the priesthood. More and more we see the Catholic Church most perfectly fulfills the Old Covenant in the New.

> Hebrews 13:17
> **Obey** them that have the **rule over you**, and **submit yourselves**: for **they watch for your souls, as they that must give account**, that they may do it with joy, and not with grief: for that is unprofitable for you.

We see in this verse a command from God to obey our spiritual superiors. This command indicates both hierarchy within the organized Church and a new priesthood. Milk has an expiration date. We eventually decide to toss eggs out, too. What about this verse? Is it still in affect? Certainly. And it was in affect when every heretic throughout the ages left the Church. So did they forget about this passage?

What if Priests Are Our Spiritual Fathers in The Family of God?

>Matthew 23:9
>And **call no man your father** upon the earth: for one is your Father, which is in heaven.

Some people cite this verse, complaining that it's a sin to regard anyone as a spiritual father-figure. But is that really what Jesus meant? Or is it another case where Jesus is using hyperbole to emphasize a point? Let's see what some other passages have to say…

>Mark 11:9-10
>And they that went before, and they that followed, cried, saying, Hosanna; Blessed is he that cometh in the name of the Lord: [10] Blessed be the kingdom **of our father David,** that cometh in the name of the Lord: Hosanna in the highest.

>Luke 16:24
>And **he cried and said, Father Abraham, have mercy on me,** and send Lazarus, that he may dip the tip of his finger in water, and cool my tongue; for I am tormented in this flame.

>Acts 7:2
>**And he said, Men, brethren, and fathers, hearken;** The God of glory appeared unto our father Abraham, when he was in Mesopotamia, before he dwelt in Charran,

>1 Thes. 2:11
>As ye know how **we exhorted and comforted and charged every one of you, as a father doth his children,**

>1 John 2:1
>**My little children,** these things write I unto you, that ye sin not. And if any man sin, we have an advocate with the Father, Jesus Christ the righteous:

>1 John 2:12-14

> **I write unto you, little children,** because your sins are forgiven you for his name's sake. [13] **I write unto you, fathers,** because ye have known him that is from the beginning. I write unto you, young men, because ye have overcome the wicked one. **I write unto you, little children,** because ye have known the Father. [14] **I have written unto you, fathers,** because ye have known him that is from the beginning. I have written unto you, young men, because ye are strong, and the word of God abideth in you, and ye have overcome the wicked one.

…Obviously then, Christ is not to be taken literally when he says "call no man father". He's simply emphasizing the infinitely greater position of the *Heavenly* Father. Otherwise He would be in sin Himself, along with the Apostles and Stephen.

What if Christ Appointed the Apostles as his Stand-ins until his Return from the Father's Right Hand?

> Matthew 9:6-8
> But that ye may know that the Son of Man hath **power on earth to forgive sins,** (then saith he to the sick of the palsy,) arise, take up thy bed, and go unto thine house. [7] And he arose, and departed to his house. [8] But when the multitudes saw it, **they marveled, and glorified God, which had given such power unto men.**

What's interesting here is that while Matthew is speaking of *Christ's* authority to forgive sins (much to the chagrin of the Pharisees) he finds it important to note the people's joy over how God gave such power to *men* (plural). This at least gives us a sneaking suspicion that there is more to this passage than meets the eye…

> Matthew 18:18
> **Verily** I say unto you, whatsoever ye shall **bind** on earth **shall be bound in heaven**: and whatsoever ye shall **loose** on earth **shall be loosed in heaven.**

…and in fact, later in Matthew's Gospel, we come to understand the glorious truth. Only two chapters after Christ grants the keys of the kingdom to Peter, he grants the same binding and loosing authority to the rest of the Apostles (and thus, to their successors).

> John 20:21-23
> Then said Jesus to them again, "Peace be unto you: **as my Father hath sent me, even so send I you.** [22] And when he had said this, **he breathed on them**, and saith unto them, "Receive ye the Holy Ghost: [23] **Whosoever sins ye remit, they are remitted unto them; and whosoever sins ye retain, they are retained.**

John's Gospel clarifies. What does this passage say about the authority and grace given to the Apostles? How were the

Apostles sent? What does this mean for the Church? Did the Apostles have the authority to forgive sins?

> 2 Corinthians 2:10
> To whom ye forgive anything, I forgive also: **for if I forgave anything, to whom I forgave it, for your sakes I it in the person of Christ**…

> 2 Corinthians 5:18
> And all things are of God, who hath reconciled us to himself by Jesus Christ, **and hath given to us the ministry of reconciliation**…

The Apostles had a ministry of reconciliation – they forgave sins "in the person of Christ". Whenever believers had mortally sinned (that is, of their own free will, jumped out of their Heavenly Father's saving hand), they could step back into the Light by confessing their sins out loud and in the open.

> 1 John 1:9
> **If we confess our sins**, he is faithful and just to forgive us our sins, and to cleanse us from all unrighteousness.

> Acts 19:18
> And many that believed came, and **confessed, and shewed their deeds.**

Believers understood that if they wished for reconciliation with God, they should go to God's representatives: the bishops and priests. But this would not be possible in a Church without structure, government, and the priestly authority of Christ. This would require Christ to have appointed stand-ins, while he was physically absent, so that he could rest heavy hearts and guilty consciences with spoken words of sure forgiveness. Where in the Bible is the command to keep sins bottled up in the privacy of one's own mind? Where does the Bible say that Jesus Christ doesn't forgive sins through human vessels? Does it seem like the Catholic position of bishops and priests as Christ's stand-ins is more Scriptural?

What if the Church is Christ's Body?

> 1 Cor. 12:12
> For as **the body is one**, and hath many members, and all the members of that one body, being many, are one body: **so also is Christ**.

> 1 Cor. 12:27
> Now **ye are the body of Christ**, and members in particular.

> Ephes. 1:22-23
> And hath put all things under his feet, and gave him to be the head over all things to **the church, which is his body, the fullness of him** that filleth all in all.

Your body is not your house. It is you – a part of you, anyway. You also are a mind (or, "head") and a soul (or, "spirit"). Gnostic Christianity would say that the body (along with all matter) is evil and an obstacle to God. But Catholic Christianity has historically fought this idea because God *created* matter, "knits" the body together in a mother's womb, and consistently uses matter as a means to convey grace throughout scripture.

Your body is not the whole you, but it *is you*. Well, if the Church is Christ's Body then that means the Church is also Christ! Because the Bride of Christ is one flesh with Christ, the Bride is, in a mystical way, Christ himself. And if the Church *is* Christ than the Church could never be an obstacle *to* Christ. Far from it! If the Church is Christ's Body, then she must in some way bear the characteristics and attributes of Christ himself…but how?

> Romans 7:4
> Wherefore, my brethren, ye also are become dead to the law **by the body of Christ**; that ye should be married to another, even to him who is raised from the dead, that we should bring forth fruit unto God.

> Romans 12:4-5
> For as we have **many members in one body**, and all members have not the same **office**: So **we, being many,**

are one body in Christ, and every one members one of another.

Ephes. 3:4-6
   Whereby, when ye read, ye may understand my knowledge in the **mystery of Christ** which in other ages was not made known unto the sons of men, as it is now revealed unto his holy apostles and prophets by the Spirit; That the Gentiles should be fellow heirs, and **of the same body**, and partakers of his promise in Christ by the gospel:

Ephes. 4:11-12
   And he gave some, apostles; and some, prophets; and some, evangelists; and some, pastors and teachers; For the perfecting of the saints, for the work of the ministry, for the edifying of **the body of Christ**:

1 Cor. 1:12-13
   Now this I say, that every one of you saith, I am of Paul; and I of Apollos; and I of Cephas; and I of Christ. **Is Christ divided?** was Paul crucified for you? or were ye baptized in the name of Paul?

Ephes. 4:15-16
   But speaking the truth in love, may grow up into him in all things, which is **the head, even Christ: From whom the whole body fitly joined together** and compacted by that which every joint supplieth, according to the effectual working in the measure of every part, maketh increase of the body unto the edifying of itself in love.

These passages further illustrate the mystery of the Church's identity. If the Church is Christ's mystical Body, then we can know she possesses the same attributes of Christ. Christ is both human and divine, a Person of the Trinity. The Church is both human (but unlike Christ, usually sinful) and divine (in that she shares in and is sanctified by Christ's Body, Blood, Soul, and Divinity, just as God planned from all eternity) and is "triune" in the sense that She is a separate Person (the Bride) from her Head (Christ) and her Soul (the Holy Spirit). Christ is organized, as is the Church. Christ is perpetual, as is the Church. Christ is not confused in doctrine, neither is the Church. In all things: as is Christ, so is the Church.

It is because of this mysterious union that denominational Christianity outside of the original Church – the One, Holy, Catholic, and Apostolic Body of Christ – is absolutely and literally impossible. You may go to a non-Catholic "church", but if you have a relationship with Jesus (and especially if you're baptized) you have a partial communion with Catholicism anyway. Though not in name, in fact, you are a member of the real Church. The true Church. The *only* Church. The Roman Catholic Church.

> Ephes. 5:25-28
> **Husbands, love your wives, even as Christ also loved the church,** and gave himself for it; [26] That he might sanctify and cleanse it with the washing of water by the word, [27] That he might present it to himself a glorious church, not having spot, or wrinkle, or any such thing; but that it should be holy and without blemish. [28] So ought men to love their wives **as their own bodies. He that loveth his wife loveth himself.**

This passage helps us understand how the Bride of Christ can also be identified as his One Body. The husband is one flesh with his bride – they are no longer two, but one! The Husband (the Christ) is the head of his Body; the Bride (the Church) is the body of her Head.

> Acts 9:4-5
> And he fell to the earth, and heard a voice saying unto him, Saul, Saul, **why persecutest thou me?** [5] And he said, Who art thou, Lord? And the Lord said, **I am Jesus whom thou persecutest**: it is hard for thee to kick against the pricks.

It doesn't get any clearer than this. Jesus clearly identifies himself with the Church Saul had been persecuting. The Church is truly Christ's Body. The Church is Christ!

Honor your Fathers! *The Elders Cry Out*

*"Through countryside and city [the apostles] preached, and **they appointed their earliest converts, testing them by the Spirit, to be the bishops and deacons of future believers.** Nor was this a novelty, for bishops and deacons had been written about a long time earlier...Our apostles knew through our Lord Jesus Christ that there would be strife for the office of bishop. For this reason, therefore, having received perfect foreknowledge, **they appointed those who have already been mentioned and afterwards added the further provision that, if they should die, other approved men should succeed to their ministry.**"*

- Pope Clement I, *Letter to the Corinthians* 42:4–5, 44:1–3 (A.D. 80).

*"Ignatius . . . **to the church also which holds the presidency**, in the location of the country of the Romans, worthy of God, worthy of honor, worthy of blessing, worthy of praise, worthy of success, worthy of sanctification, and, **because you hold the presidency** in love, named after Christ and named after the Father."*

- Ignatius of Antioch, *Letter to the Romans* 1:1 (A.D. 110)

*"When I had come to Rome, I [visited] Anicetus, whose deacon was Eleutherus. And after Anicetus [died], Soter succeeded, and after him Eleutherus. **In each succession and in each city there is a continuance of that which is proclaimed by the law, the prophets, and the Lord.**"*

- Hegesippus, *Memoirs*, cited in Eusebius, *Ecclesiastical History* 4:22 (A.D. 180)

*"But since **it would be too long to enumerate in such a volume as this the successions of all the churches**, we shall confound all*

those who, in whatever manner, whether through self-satisfaction or vainglory, or through blindness and wicked opinion, assemble other than where it is proper, by **pointing out here the successions of the bishops of the greatest and most ancient church known to all, founded and organized at Rome by the two most glorious apostles, Peter and Paul—that church which has the tradition and the faith with which comes down to us after having been announced to men by the apostles. For with this Church, because of its superior origin, all churches must agree, that is, all the faithful in the whole world. And it is in her that the faithful everywhere have maintained the apostolic tradition.***"*

- Irenaeus, Against Heresies 3:3:2 (A.D. 189)

"I shall at once go on, then, to exhibit the peculiarities of the Christian society that, as I have refuted the evil charged against it, I may point out its positive good. **We are a body knit together as such by a common religious profession, by unity of discipline, and by the bond of a common hope.** *We meet together as an* **assembly** *and* **congregation***, that, offering up prayer to God as with* **united force***, we may wrestle with Him in our supplications. This violence God delights in. We pray, too, for the emperors, for their ministers and for all in authority, for the welfare of the world, for the prevalence of peace, for the delay of the final consummation.* **We assemble to read our sacred writings***, if any peculiarity of the times makes either forewarning or reminiscence needful. However it be in that respect, with the sacred words we nourish our faith, we animate our hope, we make our confidence more steadfast; and no less by inculcations of God's precepts we confirm good habits."*

- Tertullian, *Apology* 39:1 (A.D. 197)

"*[The apostles] founded churches in every city, from which all the other churches, one after another, derived the tradition of the faith, and the seeds of doctrine, and are every day deriving them, that* *they may become churches. Indeed, **it is on this account only that they will be able to deem themselves apostolic, as being the offspring of apostolic churches. Every sort of thing must necessarily revert to its original for its classification.** Therefore the churches, although they are so many and so great, comprise but the one primitive Church, [founded] by the apostles, from which they all [spring]. In this way, all are primitive, and all are apostolic, while they are all proved to be one in unity...*

*"...**Then let all the heresies, when challenged to these two tests by our apostolic Church, offer their proof of how they deem themselves to be apostolic.** But in truth they neither are so, nor are they able to prove themselves to be what they are not. Nor are they admitted to peaceful relations and communion by such churches as are in any way connected with apostles, inasmuch as **they are in no sense themselves apostolic because of their diversity as to the mysteries of the faith."***

- Tertullian, *Demurrer Against the Heretics* (A.D. 200)

*"But we who hope for the Son of God are persecuted and trodden down by those unbelievers. For the wings of the vessels are the churches; and **the sea is the world, in which the Church is set, like a ship tossed in the deep, but not destroyed**; for she has with her the skilled Pilot, Christ. And she bears in her midst also the trophy (which is erected) over death; for she carries with her the cross of the Lord. For her prow is the east, and her stern is the west, and her hold is the south, and her tillers are the two Testaments; and the ropes that stretch around her are the love of Christ, which binds the Church; and **the net which she bears with her is the layer of the regeneration which renews the believing, whence too are these glories. As the wind the Spirit from heaven is present, by whom those who believe are sealed**: she has also anchors of iron accompanying her, viz., the holy commandments of Christ Himself, which are strong as iron. **She has also mariners on the right and on the left, assessors like the holy angels, by whom the Church is always governed and defended.** The ladder*

in her leading up to the sailyard is an emblem of the passion of Christ, which brings the faithful to the ascent of heaven. **And the top-sails aloft upon the yard are the company of prophets, martyrs, and apostles, who have entered into their rest in the kingdom of Christ.*"*

- Hippolytus, *Christ and AntiChrist* 59 (A.D. 200)

"Since, according to my opinion, ***the grades here in the Church, of bishops, presbyters, deacons,*** *are imitations of the angelic glory, and of that economy which, the Scriptures say, awaits those who, following the footsteps of the apostles, have lived in perfection of righteousness according to the Gospel."*

- Clement of Alexandria, *Stromata* 6:13 (A.D. 202)

"We are not to credit these men, nor go out from ***the first and the ecclesiastical tradition****; nor to believe otherwise than as* ***the churches of God have by succession transmitted to us****."*

- Origen, *Commentary on Matthew* (~A.D. 244)

"The Lord says to Peter: 'I say to you,' he says, 'that you are Peter, and upon this rock I will build my Church.' . . . On him [Peter] he builds the Church, and to him he gives the command to feed the sheep [John 21:17], and **although he assigns a like power to all the apostles, yet he founded a single chair [cathedra], and he established by his own authority a source and an intrinsic reason for that unity.** *Indeed, the others were that also which Peter was [i.e., apostles],* **but a primacy is given to Peter, whereby it is made clear that there is but one Church and one chair.** *So too, all [the apostles] are shepherds, and the flock is shown to be one, fed by all the apostles in single-minded accord.* **If someone does not hold fast to this unity of Peter, can he imagine that he still holds the faith? If he [should] desert the chair of Peter upon**

whom the Church was built, can he still be confident that he is in the Church?"

- Cyprian of Carthage, *The Unity of the Catholic Church* 4; 1st edition (A.D. 251)

*"Therefore **the power of remitting sins was given to the apostles**, and to the churches which they, sent by Christ, established, and to **the bishops who succeeded to them by vicarious ordination**."*

- Firmilian, *To Cyprian*, Epistle 75:16 (A.D. 256)

*"From which things it is evident that all the prophets declared concerning Christ, that it should come to pass at some time, that being born with a body of the race of David, **He should build an eternal temple in honor of God, which is called the Church, and assemble all nations to the true worship of God. This is the faithful house, this is the everlasting temple; and if any one hath not sacrificed in this, he will not have the reward of immortality.** And since **Christ was the builder of this great and eternal temple**, He must also have an everlasting priesthood in it; and there can be no approach to the shrine of the temple, and to the sight of God, except through Him who built the temple. David in the sixth Psalm teaches the same, saying: 'Before the morning-star I begat Thee. The Lord hath sworn, and will not repent; Thou art a priest for ever, after the order of Melchizidec.'"*

- Lactantius, *Divine Institutes* 4:14 (A.D. 310)

*"This gave occasion for an **Ecumenical Council** [i.e. Nicea], that the feast might be everywhere celebrated on one day, and that the heresy which was springing up **might be anathematized**. It took place then; and the Syrians submitted, and the Fathers pronounced the Arian heresy to be the forerunner of Antichrist, and drew up a suitable formula against it. And yet in this, many as they are, they ventured on nothing like the proceedings of these three or four*

men. *Without pre-fixing Consulate, month, and day, they wrote concerning Easter, 'It seemed good as follows,' for it did then seem good that there should be a general compliance;* **but about the faith they wrote not, 'It seemed good,' but, 'Thus believes the Catholic Church'; and thereupon they confessed how they believed, in order to shew that their own sentiments were not novel, but Apostolical; and what they wrote down was no discovery of theirs, but is the same as was taught by the Apostles.***"*

- Athanasius, *Councils of Ariminum & Seleucia,* 5 (A.D. 362)

"Far be it from me to speak adversely of **any of these clergy who, in succession from the apostles, confect by their sacred word the Body of Christ** *and through whose efforts also it is that we are Christians."*

- Jerome, *Letters* 14:8 (A.D. 396)

"The unanimity of peoples and nations keeps me here. [The Catholic Church's] authority, inaugurated in miracles, nourished by hope, augmented by love, and confirmed by her age, keeps me here. **The succession of priests, from the very see of the apostle Peter, to whom the Lord, after his resurrection, gave the charge of feeding his sheep** *[John 21:15–17], up* **to the present episcopate, keeps me here. And last, the very name Catholic, which, not without reason, belongs to this Church alone, in the face of so many heretics, so much so that, although all heretics want to be called 'Catholic,' when a stranger inquires where the Catholic Church meets, none of the heretics would dare to point out his own basilica or house.***"*

- Augustine, *Against the Letter of Mani Called "The Foundation"* 4:5 (A.D. 397)

What is the Word of God?

In what ways was revelation given to us? How do we know the Word of God from everything else?

Just the Facts, Please! *Dispelling Ignorance*

CATECHISM OF THE CATHOLIC CHURCH

68 **By love, God has revealed himself and given himself to man.** He has thus provided the definitive, superabundant answer to the questions that man asks himself about the meaning and purpose of his life.

73 **God has revealed himself fully by sending his own Son**, in whom he has established his covenant for ever. The Son is his Father's definitive Word; so there will be no further Revelation after him.

96 **What Christ entrusted to the apostles, they in turn handed on by their preaching and writing**, under the inspiration of the Holy Spirit, to all generations, until Christ returns in glory.

97 **"Sacred Tradition and Sacred Scripture make up a single sacred deposit of the Word of God"** (DV 10) in which, as in a mirror, the pilgrim Church contemplates God, the source of all her riches.

100 **The task of interpreting the Word of God authentically** has been entrusted solely to the Magisterium of the Church, that is, to the Pope and to the bishops in communion with him.

141 **"The Church has always venerated the divine Scriptures as she venerated the Body of the Lord"** (DV 21): both nourish and govern the whole Christian life. "Your word is a lamp to my feet and a light to my path" (Ps 119:105; cf. Is 50:4).

The Word of God is of the utmost importance to all Christians, whether they make use of that knowledge or not. It is in God's revealed Word that we get essential grace, knowledge, wisdom, and inspiration necessary to live the way God intended. No group realizes or emphasizes that more than the Catholic Church. Unfortunately, many myths and outright lies have been spread about Christ's Church, feeding off the fear and doubt bred into Protestants. Hopefully, I can with God's help attempt to dismantle some of these mistruths and give a good explanation of Catholic beliefs.

First, keep in mind that Christianity didn't start with the written Word. It began with the incarnated Word, God's Eternal Son made flesh. It was the Holy Spirit, sent into the world by means of Christ's redemptive work, Who fueled the Church's movement and growth. Early Jewish converts "received the word with all eagerness, examining the scriptures daily to see if these things were so" (Acts 17:11). It took the Apostles *interpreting* those same scriptures they had been reading or hearing all their lives for them to understand them in enlightening new ways. They were giving these people the same gift Jesus had given them on the Emmaus Road (see Luke 24:44-49). Christ revealed how the Old Testament points to him and his kingdom and further, that those scriptures could not be understood apart from their *fulfillment*.

The Apostles, not the Bible, with the incarnated Christ as the cornerstone, are the foundation of the Church (see Eph. 2:19-22). Yet the Bible remains indispensable to Christians because in its pages, God comes lovingly to meet his children through his written revelation. It is a single book about Jesus Christ and yet it is a collection of 73 books that took 1,600 years to write. In the same way, it is about many things and yet only about one thing: Christ. That's only possible because the Holy Spirit is its true Author, though He used humans to write it. So what's the logical conclusion? As the Catechism explains, "the books of Scripture firmly, faithfully, and without error teach that truth which God, for the sake of our salvation, wished to see confided to the Sacred Scriptures" (see 2Tim 3:16, CCC 105-107). It is no more "just" a book than Christ was "just" a man or the Eucharist is "just" a piece of bread.

So where did we get the Bible? It didn't just fall out of the sky...it was gradually revealed and acknowledged as divinely inspired. We know this much: by 100 B.C. the Old Testament was the same as we know it now. When Jews started to inhabit areas outside of Palestine, they slowly lost the Hebrew language in preference of the increasingly universal Greek of the times. When they eventually needed a retranslation of the Old Testament into Greek, they produced what we know today as the Septuagint. The Septuagint is the complete Old Testament found in the Catholic Bible and was the version quoted and read by Jesus and his disciples.

The disciples didn't even *begin* to write the New Testament until at the very earliest 10 years after Christ's Ascension. For over three centuries, the writings of the New Testament were read aloud in congregations of Christians and for the most part, there was a general consensus on the collection. By the end of the fourth century, several minor councils and papal decrees supported that collection. Since nobody really questioned the books that were accepted, there was really no need for a council to dogmatically state the obvious. Remember, general councils were called only when there was a pressing issue or controversy at hand. For 12 centuries, there wasn't.

However, in the 16th century, a few men who had abandoned and rebelled against the Church took away seven books and accepted only the Hebrew versions of Daniel and Esther. They taught that these books contained ideas contrary to the rest of the Bible, which basically meant they contradicted their own novel theories. Some had the false impression that the contemporary Jewish canon of the Old Testament was the same used at the time of Christ. The Scriptures they removed had been almost unanimously accepted by all of Christianity up to that point. Although some of the original Protestant Bibles contained these books (the King James Version being one), they were ultimately dropped altogether.

In the meantime, the Universal Church retained the same books they had been acknowledging as Scripture and reading on

Sundays for the past sixteen hundred years! Again, this was and is the same Septuagint canon of the Old Testament that *Christ* used and cited. We know this because there are slight variations in syntax and vocabulary between the Hebrew and Septuagint versions of the Old Testament. Usually, when the New Testament quotes the Old Testament, the vocabulary and syntax of the Septuagint is used (for evidence of this, I suggest comparing verses found on the following website:
http://www.scripturecatholic.com/septuagint.html).

Because the Bible had been attacked and there was now a controversy surrounding it, the Church finally found Herself in a place where the subject had to be closed. The true canon of Scripture was thus made dogma (a decision protected by God from error) and the issue was settled.

So that's how we *got* the Bible. But where do we go from there? The Bible is 73 books long and written from all sorts of perspectives for all sorts of audiences. So it is understandable that there are many things scattered throughout Scripture that seem contradictory. A person could isolate three passages and find another three passages that say something completely different. There's a good analogy that's been floating around for awhile – I first ran into it when I read Pat Madrid's book, *Where is That in the Bible?*

Read the following sentence out loud: "I never said you stole that." That's easy enough to understand, right? But place the emphasis on any given word. "*I* never said you stole that." Everyone else did. Or, "I *never* said you stole that." But I would do anything to prove it. "I never *said* you stole that." I only thought it. "I never said *you* stole that." Your mother did. "I never said you *stole* that." You lied and you cheated to get it, but you didn't outright steal it. Finally, "I never said you stole *that*." You stole everything else.

You begin to see the problem. Even when you take a passage in context, it doesn't guarantee you're reading it in the way the author intended. In order to do that, the author's background, current situation, audience, culture of the time, contemporary literary techniques, and much, much, more must be taken into account. This can be quite a challenge for serious scholars, let alone the average reader. However, this is also where Sacred Tradition comes in.

When I say Tradition, I don't mean the collected customs, disciplines, or devotions that the Church has developed over time. Those would fall under "tradition" in the lower-case "t" sense. It's one of those cases where the same word can have multiple meanings. So when we refer to Tradition in the capital "T" sense, we aren't referring to traditions of men; we're referring to the handing down of the Word of God.

> *Even when you take a passage in context, it doesn't guarantee you're reading it in the way the author intended.*

Sacred Tradition broadcasts the Word of God in its entirety – both oral and written – through the living voice of the Church. The guidance of the Holy Spirit entrusted it to the Apostles and it has been faithfully guarded, expounded, and handed down ever since through apostolic succession. Tradition acts as a lens, focusing the light of Scripture through the wisdom and experience of the Church, which has been collected from the time of the apostles right on down to today. It is not separate from the Scriptures; it is another facet of the same thing: the Word of God. Both Scripture and Tradition are necessary to best understand God's Word. We need each of them when we study. In 2 Thessalonians 2:15, St. Paul sums it up:

> "Therefore, brethren, stand fast, and hold the **Traditions** which ye have been taught, whether **by word, or** our epistle."
> (emphasis added)

The Apostles did not communicate the Gospel by writing alone. In fact, it was transmitted mostly in unwritten form, just like today! Stop and think about it.

When you were led to the Lord, how did it happen? Was it a sermon? Did someone explain God's plan of salvation to you? Were you prompted to pick up a Bible by someone? Chances are, you received the Gospel person-to-person, just like it was preached almost 2,000 years ago. And that's a fairly good example of Sacred Tradition in action. The only difference is the Catholic Church has the united bishops, led by the pope, to guard it from error (see Luke 10:16). This teaching authority of the Church is called the "Magisterium".

Here are some good analogies people have used. Think of Scripture as a gold fish. Apostolic Tradition is the water in which the goldfish swims. And the Magisterium is the bowl that keeps the water – and with it, the fish – from splashing all over the floor. Or, returning to the "light and lens" analogy, if Scripture could be compared to light and Tradition could be compared to a lens, then the Magisterium is the boy who focuses the light through the lens to burn away any heresy!

In this way we can see how all three legs must be present for the stool to stand. God's Word is not entirely bound to Scripture. Nor does Scripture tell us to base God's Word – or our Faith – entirely on a book. Rather, we are to examine Tradition and Scripture together under the authority of the Church, which God gave us as the pillar and foundation of Truth.

Scripture Speaks! *What the Bible Says*

What if the Necessity of Tradition is Evident in Scripture?

> Isaiah 59:21
> As for me, this is my covenant with them, saith the Lord; My spirit that is upon thee, and **my words which I have put in thy mouth, shall not depart out of thy mouth, nor out of the mouth of thy seed, nor out of the mouth of thy seed's seed,** saith the Lord, **from henceforth and for ever.**

This prophecy refers to the oral Tradition of God's Word. Can you think of a place that has preserved that oral Tradition, even as it grew with the New Covenant, all these past thousands of years?

> Joel 1:3
> **Tell** ye your children of it, and let your children **tell their children**, and their children another generation.

Yet again, we find precedence for Sacred Tradition that hasn't been committed to writing.

> Deut. 31:9-12
> And Moses wrote this law, and delivered it unto the priests the sons of Levi, which bare the Ark of the Covenant of the Lord, and unto all the elders of Israel. [10] And Moses commanded them, saying, **At the end of every seven years, in the solemnity of the year of release, in the feast of tabernacles, [11] When all Israel is come to appear before the Lord thy God in the place which he shall choose, thou shalt read this law** before all Israel in their hearing. [12] Gather the people together, men, and women, and children, and thy stranger that is within thy gates, **that they may hear, and that they may learn, and fear the Lord your God, and observe to do all the words of this law:**

Most Israelites only *heard* the Law once every seven years. How many Israelites do you think had a study Bible? And where were the Scriptures in the midst of those seven years? They had to get God's Word from the lips of the priests.

> Malachi 2:7
> For **the priest's lips should keep knowledge,** and they should seek the law **at his mouth**: for he is the messenger of the Lord of hosts.

Why from the lips of the priest? Because he is the messenger of the Lord; the guardian of God's Word.

> Mark 13:31
> Heaven and earth shall pass away: but **my words shall not pass away.**

It took almost 400 years for the New Testament to be written and collected, and another 1,000 for the printing press to be invented. Where was God's Word then? Had it passed away? Or was it communicated orally and guarded by the Church?

> Mark 3:14
> And he ordained twelve, that they should be with him, and that he might send them forth **to preach**

> Mark 16:15
> And he said unto them, Go ye into all the world, **and preach the gospel** to every creature.

How come Jesus didn't ever command his disciples to write things down or hand out Scriptures? Why to preach? And he never said he wanted the preaching to stop; so what did Christians do after the last apostle died and the New Testament still wasn't finalized? How did they receive the Word?

> Acts 15:27
> We have sent therefore Judas and Silas, **who shall also tell you the same things by mouth.**

Why not by letter?

> Romans 10:17
> So then faith cometh by **hearing**, and hearing by the word of God.

Why not reading?

> 2 Tim. 1:13
> **Hold fast the form of sound words, which thou hast heard of me**, in faith and love which is in Christ Jesus.

So Paul's oral teachings (what Timothy heard) didn't pass away with him? They lived on through Timothy? Sounds a lot like Sacred Tradition, to me.

> 2 Tim. 4:2
> **Preach the Word**; be instant in season, out of season; reprove, rebuke, exhort with all longsuffering and doctrine.

> 2 Tim. 4:6-7
> For I am now ready to be offered, and the time of my departure is at hand. [7] I have fought a good fight, I have finished my course, I have kept the faith:

After God takes him home, Paul instructs Timothy to preach the Word, not write it.

> 1 Peter 1:25
> But the word of the Lord endureth for ever. And **this is the word which by the gospel is preached** unto you.

The spoken Word that is preached – oral Tradition – endures forever? That would only be possible if the apostles had successors to preserve and continue to preach it.

> 2 Peter 1:12

> Wherefore **I will not be negligent to put you always in remembrance of these things,** though ye know them, and be established in the present truth.
>
> 2 Peter 1:15
> Moreover **I will endeavour that ye may be able after my decease to have these things always in remembrance.**

How would that be possible for him to do "after [his] decease"? Since this was his last letter, he can only be referring to the authority and Sacred Tradition that his office would leave behind with his successors.

> 2 John 1:12
> Having **many things** to write unto you, **I would not write with paper and ink: but I trust to come unto you, and speak face to face, that our joy may be full.**
>
> 3 John 1:13
> **I had many things to write,** but I will not with ink and pen write unto thee:

John prefers to transmit God's Word orally, through Sacred Tradition, rather than committing the Word to paper. And how do we know what those "many things" are? Only through Apostolic Tradition, which guards and preserves everything he taught.

> 1 Cor. 11:2
> Now I praise you, brethren, that ye remember me in all things, and **keep the ordinances, as I delivered them to you.**

Paul praises these Christians for holding to the Tradition he preached.

> Ephes. 4:20
> But ye have not so **learned Christ**…

What's important about this rebuke? He writes to them (Scripture) about what he preached to them (Tradition) and refers them *back* to what he preached! They learned Christ from Tradition, not the Scriptures.

> Philip. 4:9
> Those things, which ye have both **learned**, and **received**, and **heard**, and **seen** in me, **do**: and the God of peace shall be with you.

Here, Paul is clearly referring to Tradition, not Scripture.

> Col. 1:5-6
> For the hope which is laid up for you in heaven, whereof **ye heard before** in **the Word of the truth of the gospel**; [6] Which is come unto you, as it is in all the world; and bringeth forth fruit, as it doth also in you, since the day ye heard of it, and knew the grace of God in truth:

This refers to the Tradition the received before he wrote the letter. It also refers to the Catholicity of the Church ("as it is in all the world").

> 1 Thes. 1:5
> For our gospel **came not unto you in word only, but also in power, and in the Holy Ghost,** and in much assurance; as ye know what manner of men we were among you for your sake.

Paul calls the Tradition the Thessalonians had previously received to mind.

> 1 Thes. 4:2
> For **ye know what commandments we gave you** by the Lord Jesus.

He does so again, here.

> 2 Thes. 2:5

> Remember ye not, that, when I was yet with you, **I told you these things?**

Once again, here.

> 2 Thes. 2:15
> Therefore, brethren, stand fast, and **hold the Traditions which ye have been taught, whether by word, or our epistle.**

Finally, he leaves no room for question. Sacred Tradition is just as binding as Sacred Scripture!

> 2 Thes. 3:6
> Now we command you, brethren, in the name of our Lord Jesus Christ, that ye **withdraw yourselves from every brother that walketh disorderly, and not after the Tradition which he received of us.**

But he reminds them of it, just to be sure.

> Matthew 2:23
> And he came and dwelt in a city called Nazareth: **that it might be fulfilled which was spoken by the prophets, He shall be called a Nazarene.**

The problem? This prophecy is no where to be found in Scripture. It is an oral Tradition. Some people mistakenly think it refers to Judges 13:5. But Judges 13:5 refers to a *Nazirite*, not a Nazarene. Nazirite means "set apart as sacred", coming from the word "nazir", meaning "vowed". Check out Numbers chapter six to find out more about the conditions of the Nazirite vow, which Samson (the person referred to in the context of Judges 13:5) took.

> Matthew 15:3
> But he answered and said unto them, Why do ye also transgress the commandment of God by **your** tradition?

> Mark 7:9

> And he said unto them, Full well ye reject the commandment of God, that ye may keep **your own** tradition.

Galatians 1:14
> And profited in the Jews' religion above many my equals in mine own nation, being more exceedingly zealous of the traditions of **my fathers**.

Col. 2:22
> Which all are to perish with the using; after the commandments and doctrines **of men**

What's the connection between all these verses? They all refer to personal traditions of men, not the Sacred Tradition passed down as God's Word. Jesus referred to the Pharisees custom of giving things to the temple so that they wouldn't feel spiritually obligated to care for their parents. Paul was referring to Old Covenant commands that were better fulfilled by New Covenant commands. The far greater context of Scripture speaks of Sacred Tradition as being the Word of God.

Matthew 23:2-3
> Saying, **The scribes and the Pharisees sit in Moses' seat:** [3] **All therefore whatsoever they bid you observe, that observe and do;** but do not ye after their works: for they say, and do not.

Here, Jesus reinforces the oral Tradition of Moses' seat (cathedra), which is fulfilled in the oral Tradition of Peter's seat (cathedra). Even if the successor is a hypocrite, he still sits in the authority God gave him.

Acts 20:35
> I have shewed you all things, how that so labouring ye ought to support the weak, and to **remember the words of the Lord Jesus, how he said, It is more blessed to give than to receive.**

Here Paul can only rely on oral Tradition as he writes this, because that statement from Jesus appears nowhere in the Gospels.

> 1 Cor. 10:4
> And did all drink the same spiritual drink: for they drank of **that spiritual Rock that followed them:** and that Rock was Christ.

Here again Paul calls to the readers' minds the Jewish Tradition that the rock Moses struck followed them through the wilderness. See Exodus 17:1-17 and Numbers 20:2-13.

> Hebrews 11:37
> They were stoned, **they were sawn asunder,** were tempted, were slain with the sword: they wandered about in sheepskins and goatskins; being destitute, afflicted, tormented;

Again! Only in Jewish Tradition do we find that Isaiah was sawn in half for rebuking wicked King Manasseh. Nowhere in the Bible is it recorded.

> 2 Tim. 3:8
> Now as **Jannes and Jambres withstood Moses,** so do these also resist the truth: men of corrupt minds, reprobate concerning the faith.

Ok, Bible quiz! Who were Jannes and Jambres? All right fine, you can make it open book...still looking? That's because the Bible doesn't say. Once again, Paul reinforces oral Tradition, which tells us they were Pharaoh's magicians.

> Jude 1:9
> **Yet Michael the archangel, when contending with the devil he disputed about the body of Moses,** durst not bring against him a railing accusation, but said, The Lord rebuke thee.

Jude 1:14-15

> **And Enoch also, the seventh from Adam, prophesied of these,** saying, Behold, the Lord cometh with ten thousands of his saints, [15] To execute judgment upon all, and to convince all that are ungodly among them of all their ungodly deeds which they have ungodly committed, and of all their hard speeches which ungodly sinners have spoken against him.

I'm sure you can guess. Although they were mentioned in some apocryphal Old Testament documents, these facts come chiefly from Sacred Tradition. Nowhere are they mentioned in Sacred Scripture. Following the Apostles examples, we discern Sacred Tradition from the God-given authority of the Magisterium and know it as the entire Word of God.

What if Sola Scriptura, the "Bible Alone" Doctrine, is Unbiblical?

> Matthew 28:20
> Teaching them to observe **all things whatsoever** I have commanded you: and, lo, I am with you alway, even unto the end of the world. Amen.

Christ taught and preached for years. And he wants every last thing he's commanded to be handed down. The Apostles did this strictly by oral Tradition for at least several years.

> John 20:30
> And **many other signs truly did Jesus in the presence of his disciples, which are not written** in this book:

> John 21:25
> And there are also many other things which Jesus did, the which, if they should be written every one, I suppose that **even the world itself could not contain the books that should be written.** Amen.

John says that no amount of writing could contain Christ's teaching ministry.

> Luke 1:1-4
> Forasmuch as many have taken in hand to set forth in order a declaration of those things which are most surely believed among us, [2] Even as they delivered them unto us, which from the beginning were eyewitnesses, and ministers of the word; [3] It seemed good to me also, having had perfect understanding of all things from the very first, to write unto thee in order, most excellent Theophilus, [4] **That thou mightest know the certainty of those things, wherein thou hast been instructed.**

Luke does not transmit what was already "instructed" (Tradition) into writing (Scripture) in order to criticize it. He commits some of it to paper in order to reaffirm it. And he certainly doesn't write everything that was orally taught, (as some things only appear in other Gospels) nor does he intend to (we already know from what John said that this would be practically impossible).

> Acts 8:30-31
> And Philip ran thither to him, and heard him read the prophet Esaias, and said, Understandest thou what thou readest? [31] And he said, **How can I, except some man should guide me?** And he desired Philip that he would come up and sit with him.

No one can interpret the Bible on his own. The Family of God must act as One mystical Body, with one mind and one voice, for this to take place. Only the visible leadership of God's Family – the bishops united under the pope – has the authority granted by Christ to do that. We all need help understanding the Scriptures since we can't infallibly interpret them on our own.

> 1 Cor. 5:9-11
> **I wrote unto you in an epistle** not to company with fornicators: [10] Yet not altogether with the fornicators of this world, or with the covetous, or extortioners, or with idolaters; for then must ye needs go out of the world. [11] But **now I have written unto you** not to keep company, if any man that is called a brother be a fornicator, or covetous, or an idolater, or a railer, or a drunkard, or an extortioner; with such an one no not to eat.

Paul refers to a previous letter as being just as authoritative as this one. He thus appeals to a source outside of Scripture in order to teach them. Also see Acts 15:1-14. Peter resolves a huge debate regarding the interpretation of Scripture without quoting a single passage.

> Col. 4:16
> And when this epistle is read among you, cause that it be read also in the church of the Laodiceans; and **that ye likewise read the epistle from Laodicea.**

Again Paul turns to authority outside the Bible – this time to instruct the Colossians in God's Word.

> *1 Thes. 3:10*
> *Night and day praying exceedingly that we might see your face, and might **perfect that which is lacking in your faith***

How can something be lacking if they have the Scriptures? Unless the Scriptures aren't the entire Word of God.

> 2 Peter 1:20
> Knowing this first, that **no prophecy of the scripture is of any private interpretation.**

Scripture is a matter of public interpretation, not private. Otherwise there would be thousands upon thousands of ecclesial groups, with more being started up or breaking off every day. Oh, wait.

> 2 Peter 3:16
> As also in all his epistles, speaking in them of these things; **in which are some things hard to be understood, which they that are unlearned and unstable wrest, as they do also the other scriptures, unto their own destruction.**

Christ cares about his Family and gave the Church the ability to infallibly interpret the entire Word of God; Scripture and Tradition. He does this by means of the authority he granted to the Apostles, with Peter as their leader, and to their successors for all generations to come. That is the only way the unity of the One, Holy, Catholic, and Apostolic Church could have been preserved. It is also why Protestantism continues to splinter.

> 1 Samuel 3:1-9
> **And the child Samuel ministered unto the Lord** before Eli. And **the word of the Lord was precious in**

those days; there was no open vision. [2] And it came to pass at that time, when Eli was laid down in his place, and his eyes began to wax dim, that he could not see; [3] And ere the lamp of God went out in the temple of the Lord, where the ark of God was, and Samuel was laid down to sleep; [4] **That the Lord called Samuel: and he answered, Here am I. [5] And he ran unto Eli, and said, Here am I; for thou calledst me.** And he said, I called not; lie down again. And he went and lay down. [6] **And the Lord called yet again, Samuel. And Samuel arose and went to Eli, and said, Here am I; for thou didst call me.** And he answered, I called not, my son; lie down again. [7] **Now Samuel did not yet know the Lord, neither was the word of the Lord yet revealed unto him. [8] And the Lord called Samuel again the third time. And he arose and went to Eli, and said, Here am I; for thou didst call me. And Eli perceived that the Lord had called the child.** [9] Therefore Eli said unto Samuel, Go, lie down: and it shall be, if he call thee, that thou shalt say, Speak, Lord; for thy servant heareth. So Samuel went and lay down in his place.

Samuel was not a prophet yet, so he didn't "know the Lord" or get new revelation of God's Word. But he did serve the Lord and was a faithful Jew. So why couldn't he discern the very Word of God from a normal man's? God's Word – even his spoken Word – is not always self attesting. Proponents of *sola scriptura* must acknowledge that knowing what books are Scriptural is vital to salvation; unfortunately, there is no table of contents in Scripture. From the very start, people of this invented doctrine must look outside of the Bible in order to figure out what *is* the Bible!

> 2 Tim. 3:14
> But continue **thou in the things which thou hast learned and hast been assured of, knowing of whom thou hast learned them**

> 2 Tim. 3:16-17
> All scripture is given by inspiration of God, and is **profitable** for doctrine, for reproof, for correction, for

instruction in righteousness: [17] That the man of God **may be perfect, thoroughly furnished unto all good works**.

The strongest passage *sola scriptura* may rely on is 2 Timothy 3:16-17. But there are two critical flaws. First, two verses prior in verse 14, Paul exhorts Timothy in the oral Tradition that he already had transmitted to him. Second, nowhere in the verse is *sole* authority of the Bible declared. The key word is "profitable". Nobody argues that Scripture is inerrant, inspired by God, and useful for doctrinal instruction. But does "profitable" mean "exclusive"? Of course not.

> James 1:4
> But let patience have her perfect work, that ye **may be perfect** and **entire, wanting nothing.**

Here, patience is given the same effects as Scripture in 2 Tim. 3:16-17. Does that mean that we live "by *patience* alone"?

> Titus 3:8
> This is a faithful saying, and these things I will that thou affirm constantly, that they which have believed in God might be careful to **maintain good works.** These things are good and **profitable** unto men.

If profitable means "exclusive", then our faith is based exclusively on good works!

> 2 Tim. 2:19-21
> Nevertheless the foundation of God standeth sure, having this seal, The Lord knoweth them that are his. And, Let every one that nameth the name of Christ **depart from iniquity.** [20] But in a great house there are not only vessels of gold and of silver, but also of wood and of earth; and some to honour, and some to dishonour. [21] **If a man therefore purge himself from these,** he shall be a vessel unto honour, sanctified, and meet for the master's use, and **prepared unto every good work.**

It seems we also get similar blessings if we depart from iniquity.

> Col. 4:12
> Epaphras, who is one of you, a servant of Christ, saluteth you, always labouring fervently for you in prayers, **that ye may stand perfect and complete** in all the will of God.

Or perhaps our faith should be based on "other people's prayers alone", so that we'll achieve the same results of 2 Timothy 3:16-17. Obviously that passage does not declare the disastrous doctrine of *sola scriptura*. Nor does any other passage in the Bible, precisely because it is an unbiblical concept.

What if Protestant Bibles Remove Portions of God's Word?

>Baruch 3:29
>**Who has gone up to the heavens** and taken her,
>**or brought her down** from the clouds?

>John 3:13
>And **no man hath ascended up to heaven, but he that came down** from heaven, even the Son of man which is in heaven.

Before John wrote about what he saw, it was prophesied in Baruch.

>1 Maccabees 4:59
>Then Judas and his brothers and the entire congregation of Israel decreed **that the days of the dedication of the altar should be observed** with joy and gladness on the anniversary every year for eight days, from the twenty-fifth day of the month Chislev.

>John 10:22
>And it was at Jerusalem **the feast of the dedication**, and it was winter.

The feast day mentioned in John does not have its origin in Exodus or Deuteronomy, but in Maccabees.

>Sirach 35:12
>For he is a God of justice,
>**who knows no favorites.**

>Romans 2:11
>For there is **no respect of persons with God.**

>Wisdom 13:1
>For all men were by nature foolish who were in ignorance of God,
>and who **from the good things seen did not succeed in knowing him who is,**
>and from studying the works did not discern the artisan;

Romans 1:20
For **the invisible things of him from the creation of the world are clearly seen, being understood by the things that are made**, even his eternal power and Godhead; so that they are without excuse:

Wisdom 15:7
For **truly the potter, laboriously working the soft earth, molds for our service each several article: Both the vessels that serve for clean purposes and their opposites, all alike;**
As to what shall be the use of each vessel of either class the worker in clay is the judge.

Romans 9:21
Hath not the potter power over the clay, of the same lump **to make one vessel unto honour, and another unto dishonour?**

Wisdom 19:7
The cloud overshadowed their camp; and out of what had before been water, dry land was seen emerging:
Out of the Red Sea an unimpeded road, and a grassy plain out of the mighty flood.

1 Cor. 10:1
Moreover, brethren, I would not that ye should be ignorant, how that **all our fathers were under the cloud, and all passed through the sea;**

Baruch 4:7
For you provoked your Maker **with sacrifices to demons, to no-gods**

1 Cor. 10:20
But I say, that the things which the Gentiles sacrifice, **they sacrifice to devils, and not to God**: and I would not that ye should have fellowship with devils.

These passages of Paul were all influenced by the preceding passages from books that Protestant Bibles reject. In some cases, Paul's information could only have come from the Deuterocanonicals.

> 2 Maccabees 12:43-46
> He then **took up a collection among all his soldiers, amounting to two thousand silver drachmas, which he sent to Jerusalem** to provide for an expiatory sacrifice. In doing this he acted in a very excellent and noble way, inasmuch as he had the resurrection of the dead in view; **for if he were not expecting the fallen to rise again, it would have been useless and foolish to pray for them in death.**
> But if he did this with a view to the splendid reward that awaits those who had gone to rest in godliness, it was a holy and pious thought.
> Thus he made atonement for the dead that **they might be freed from this sin**.
>
> 1 Cor. 15:29
> Else **what shall they do which are baptized for the dead, if the dead rise not at all?** why are they then baptized for the dead?

The passage from Maccabees illuminates the passage from the letter to Corinth. Only in Catholic theology (namely the doctrines of purgatory and indulgences – see also 1 Corinthians 3:10-15) does 1 Corinthians 15:29 make sense.

> Wisdom 18:14-15 (NJB)
> **When peaceful silence lay over all,**
> **and night had run the half of her swift course,**
>   **down from the heavens, from the royal throne, leapt your all-powerful Word**
> like a pitiless warrior into the heart of a land doomed to destruction.
> **Carrying your unambiguous command like a sharp sword…**
>
> Hebrews 4:12
>   For **the word of God is quick, and powerful, and sharper than any two-edged sword**, piercing even to the dividing asunder of soul and spirit, and of the joints and

marrow, and is a discerner of the thoughts and intents of the heart.

Not only do we see Paul borrowing a metaphor from Wisdom, but the passage from which he borrowed it contains a wonderful prophecy of Christ's Nativity.

> Tobit 12:12-15
> So you must know that when you and Sarah were at prayer, **it was I who offered your supplications before the glory of the Lord and who read them; so too when you were burying the dead.**
> When you did not hesitate to get up and leave the table to go and bury a dead man, I was sent to test your faith, and at the same time God sent me to heal you and your daughter-in-law Sarah.
> **I am Raphael, one of the seven angels who stand ever ready to enter the presence of the glory of the Lord.**

> Rev. 1:4
> John to the seven churches which are in Asia: Grace be unto you, and peace, from him which is, and which was, and which is to come; **and from the seven spirits which are before his throne**

> Rev. 8:3-4
> And **another angel came and stood at the altar, having a golden censer; and there was given unto him much incense, that he should offer it with the prayers of all saints** upon the golden altar which was before the throne. And the smoke of the incense, which came with **the prayers of the saints, ascended up before God out of the angel's hand.**

I remember running into Revelations 1:4 a long time ago and wondering what "the seven spirits" referred to. I found competing explanations – some even claiming the seven spirits were the Holy Spirit! But Tobit clears that (and the intercession of angels) up quite nicely.

> 1 Cor. 7:12

But to the rest **speak I, not the Lord**: If any brother hath a wife that believeth not, and she be pleased to dwell with him, let him not put her away.

1 Cor. 7:40
But she is happier if she so abide, after my judgment: and **I think** also that I have the Spirit of God.

Some Protestants argue that since the authors of 2 Maccabees and Sirach begin by expressing uncertainty about their writing abilities, the books must not be inspired. But in these passages we see Paul expressing the same kind of uncertainty! Let's also not forget that the authors of Scripture didn't necessarily know that what they wrote would one day be regarded as such.

Wisdom 2:12-21
"Let us beset **the Just One**, because he is obnoxious to us; he sets himself against our doings,
Reproaches us for transgressions of the law
and charges us with violations of our training.
He professes to have knowledge of God
and styles himself a child of the LORD.
To us he is the censure of our thoughts;
merely to see him is a hardship for us,
Because his life is not like other men's,
and different are his ways.
He judges us debased;
he holds aloof from our paths as from things impure.
He calls blest the destiny of the just
and boasts that God is his Father.
Let us see whether his words be true;
let us find out what will happen to him.
For if the just one be **the Son of God**, he will defend him
and deliver him from the hand of his foes.
With revilement and torture let us put him to the test
that we may have proof of his gentleness
and try his patience.
Let us condemn him to a shameful death;
for according to his own words, God will take care of him."
These were their thoughts, but they erred;
for their wickedness blinded them...

Matthew 27:43
He trusted in God; let him deliver him now, if he will have him: for he said, I am the Son of God.

The prophecy from Wisdom clearly refers to the Messiah and the Pharisees. In fact, next to Isaiah 53, this is probably the most obvious, striking, and irrefutable prophecy concerning Christ.

Honor your Fathers! *The Elders Cry Out*

"You shall not waver with regard to your decisions. **Do not be someone who stretches out his hands to receive but withdraws them when it comes to giving [Sir. 4:31]***"*

- *Didache* 4:5 (A.D. 70)

"Since, therefore, [Christ] was about to be manifested and to suffer in the flesh, his suffering was foreshown. For the prophet speaks against evil, 'Woe to their soul, because they have counseled an evil counsel against themselves' [Is. 3:9], saying, **'Let us bind the righteous man because he is displeasing to us'** *[Wis. 2:12]."*

- *Letter of Barnabas* 6:7 (A.D. 74)

"By the word of his might [God] established all things, and by his word he can overthrow them. **'Who shall say to him, "What have you done?" or who shall resist the power of his strength?'** *[Wis. 12:12]"*

- Clement of Rome, *Letter to the Corinthians* 27:5 (A.D. 80)

"Follow the bishop, all of you, as Jesus Christ follows his Father, and the presbyterium as the Apostles. As for the deacons, **respect them as the Law of God. Let no one do anything with reference to the Church without the bishop.** *Only that Eucharist may be regarded as legitimate which is celebrated with the bishop or his delegate presiding. Where the bishop is, there let the community be, just as* **where Jesus Christ is, there is the Catholic Church***."*

- Ignatius of Antioch, *Epistle to the Symyrnaens* 8 (A.D. 110)

"As I said before, the Church, having received **this preaching and this faith***, although she is disseminated throughout the whole world,* **yet guarded it***, as if she occupied but one house. She*

likewise believes these things just as if she had but one soul and one and the same heart; and harmoniously she proclaims them and teaches them and hands them down, as if she possessed but one mouth. **For, while the languages of the world are diverse, nevertheless, the authority of the Tradition is one and the same"**

- Irenaeus, *Against Heresies* 1:10:2 (A.D. 189)

"Let them show the origins of their churches, let them unroll the list of their bishops, through a succession coming down from the very beginning that their first bishop had his authority and predecessor someone from among the number of Apostles or apostolic men and, further, that he did not stray from the Apostles. In this way the apostolic churches present their earliest records. The church of Smyrna, for example, records that **Polycarp was named by John**; the Romans, that **Clement was ordained by Peter**. In just the same way, the other churches show who were made bishops by the Apostles and who **transmitted the apostolic seed to them.** Let the heretics invent something like that."

- Tertullian, *The Prescription Against Heretics 32* (A.D. 200)

"For those are slothful who, having it in their power to provide themselves with proper proofs for the divine Scriptures from the Scriptures themselves, **select only what contributes to their own pleasures.** And those have a craving for glory who voluntarily evade, by arguments of a diverse sort, the things delivered by the blessed apostles and teachers, which are wedded to inspired words; **opposing the Divine Tradition by human teachings, in order to establish the heresy."**

- Clement of Alexandria, *Stromata, 7:16* (A.D. 202)

"Well, they preserving the Tradition of the blessed doctrine derived directly from the holy apostles, Peter, James, John, and

Paul, the sons receiving it from the father (but few were like the fathers), **came by God's will to us also to deposit those ancestral and apostolic seeds.** *And well I know that they will exult; I do not mean delighted with this tribute, but solely on account of the preservation of the truth, according as they delivered it. For such a sketch as this, will, I think, be agreeable to a soul desirous of preserving from loss the blessed Tradition"*

- Clement of Alexandria, *Miscellanies* 1:1 (A.D. 208)

"The Church's preaching has been handed down through an orderly succession from the Apostles and remains in the Church until the present. *That alone is to be believed as the truth which in no way departs from ecclesiastical and apostolic Tradition."*

- Origen, *First Principles* 1,2 (A.D. 230)

"When heretics show us the canonical Scriptures, in which every Christian believes and trusts, they seem to be saying: 'Lo, he is in the inner rooms [the word of truth] ' (Matt 24.6). But **we must not believe them, nor leave the original Tradition of the Church, nor believe otherwise than we have been taught by the succession in the Church of God."**

- Origen, *Homilies on Matthew, Homily 46, PG 13:1667* (A.D. 254)

"But after him (the devil) and with him are all inventors of unlawful heresies, **who indeed refer to the Scriptures, but do not hold such opinions as the saints have handed down**, *and receiving them as the traditions of men, err, because they do not rightly know them nor their power"*

- Athanasius, *Festal Letter 2* (A.D. 350)

*"Wherefore keep yourselves all the more untainted by them, and **observe the Traditions of the Fathers, and chiefly the holy faith in our Lord Jesus Christ, which you have learned from the Scripture**, and of which you have often been put in mind by me."*

- Anthony of Egypt, *Vita S. Antoni* 89 (A.D. 350)

*"...For **they dissent from each other**, and, **whereas they have revolted from their Fathers, are not of one and the same mind**, but float about with various and discordant changes"*

- Athanasius, *De Synodis* 13 (A.D. 359).

*"What **Scripture** says is very true, 'As for a fool he changeth as the moon'[**Sirach 27:11**].*

- Basil the Great, *Hexaemeron* 6:10 (A.D. 370)

*"[T]he **Scripture** tells us, 'into the malicious soul Wisdom cannot come'[**Wisdom 1:4**]."*

- Gregory of Nyssa, *On Virginity* 15 (A.D. 371)

*"Of the dogmas and messages preserved in the Church, **some we possess from written teaching and others we receive from the Tradition of the apostles**, handed on to us in mystery. In respect to piety, both are of the same force. No one will contradict any of these, no one, at any rate, who is even moderately versed in matters ecclesiastical. Indeed, **were we to try to reject unwritten customs as having no great authority, we would unwittingly injure the gospel in its vitals**; or rather, we would reduce [Christian] message to a mere term"*

- Basil the Great, *The Holy Spirit* 27:66 (A.D. 375).

*"It is needful also to make use of Tradition, for **not everything can be gotten from sacred Scripture**. The holy apostles handed down some things in the scriptures, other things in Tradition"*

- Epiphanius of Salamis, *Medicine Chest Against All Heresies* 61:6 (A.D. 375)

*"It suffices for proof of our statement that **we have a Tradition coming down from the Fathers**, an inheritance as it were, **by succession from the Apostles** through the saints who came after them."*

- Gregory of Nyssa, *Against Eunomius* 4:6 (A.D. 384)

*"[Paul commands,] 'Therefore, brethren, stand fast and **hold the traditions** which you have been taught, **whether by word or by our letter**' [2 Thess. 2:15]. From this **it is clear that they did not hand down everything by letter, but there is much also that was not written**. Like that which was written, the unwritten too is worthy of belief. **So let us regard the Tradition of the Church also as worthy of belief.** Is it a Tradition? Seek no further"*

- John Chrysostom, *Homilies on Second Thessalonians* (A.D. 402)

*"What sin have I committed in **following the judgment of the churches**? But when I repeat what **the Jews say against the Story of Susanna and the Hymn of the Three Children, and the fables of Bel and the Dragon**, which are not contained in the Hebrew Bible, the man who makes this a charge against me proves himself to be a fool and a slanderer; for **I explained not what I thought but what they commonly say against us.**"*

- Jerome, *Against Rufinus* 11:33 (A.D. 402)

*"[D]oes not the **scripture** say: 'Burden not thyself above thy power'[**Sirach 13:2**]?"*

- Jerome, *To Eustochium* Epistle 108 (A.D. 404)

*"I have often then inquired earnestly and attentively of very many men eminent for sanctity and learning, **how and by what sure and so to speak universal rule I may be able to distinguish the truth of Catholic faith from the falsehood of heretical depravity;** and I have always, and in almost every instance, received an answer to this effect: That whether I or any one else should wish to detect the frauds and avoid the snares of heretics as they rise, and to continue sound and complete in the Catholic faith, we must, the Lord helping, fortify our own belief in two ways; **first, by the authority of the Divine Law, and then, by the Tradition of the Catholic Church.**"*

- Vincent of Lerins, *Commonitory of the Antiquity and Universality of the Catholic Faith 2:4 (A.D. 434)*

What is the Role of Mary?
Why does Mary play such a big role in Catholicism? Doesn't it detract from Jesus?

Just the Facts, Please! *Dispelling Ignorance*

CATECHISM OF THE CATHOLIC CHURCH

508 From among the descendants of Eve, God chose the Virgin Mary to be the mother of his Son. "Full of grace", Mary is "the most excellent fruit of redemption" (SC 103): from the first instant of her conception, she was totally preserved from the stain of original sin and she remained pure from all personal sin throughout her life.

509 **Mary is truly "Mother of God"** since she is the mother of the eternal Son of God made man, who is God himself.

510 **Mary "remained a virgin in conceiving her Son, a virgin in giving birth to him, a virgin in carrying him, a virgin in nursing him at her breast, always a virgin"** (St. Augustine, Serm. 186, 1: PL 38, 999): with her whole being she is "the handmaid of the Lord" (Lk 1:38).

511 **The Virgin Mary "co-operated through free faith and obedience in human salvation"** (LG 56). She uttered her yes "in the name of all human nature" (St. Thomas Aquinas, S Th III, 30, 1). By her obedience she became the new Eve, mother of the living.

974 **The Most Blessed Virgin Mary, when the course of her earthly life was completed, was taken up body and soul into the glory of heaven**, where she already shares in the glory of her Son's Resurrection, anticipating the resurrection of all members of his Body.

975 **"We believe that the Holy Mother of God, the new Eve, Mother of the Church, continues in heaven to exercise her

maternal role on behalf of the members of Christ" (Paul VI, CPG # 15).

As a former Protestant, I am keenly aware of the paranoia surrounding the Marian doctrines of the Catholic Church. I remember that when the name of Christ's mother was spoken out loud, it usually sent up red flags. Recalling that now, I wonder at how I didn't question the origin of those concerns. They certainly weren't from God! Why would he be afraid I hear the name of his mother? Nevertheless, if there is something in you that wants to skip this portion of my letter altogether, I suggest that you first read the historical grounds (in *Honor Your Fathers*, a few pages ahead) for Catholic beliefs regarding Mary. The ancient quotes I've provided should at least dispel the notions that Marian doctrines have been progressively "invented" since the Middle Ages. Be sure to note that the first seven of these quotes were written before Christianity was legalized. And all but the last one (provided to counter the argument that the Assumption of Mary was invented in the 20th century) originated before the Fall of Rome, 476 A.D. being the most conservative date.

There! Now that's settled. I just wanted to make sure you felt as comfortable as possible before proceeding. I know how unsettling the topic of Mary may be. Awhile ago, for instance, I was chatting with my mother-in-law (an Evangelical Protestant) and Mary came up. She mentioned that thinking about Mary felt like a distraction from Jesus. "None of that stuff matters," she said, with a wave of the hand and an agitated look on her face. "All that matters is Jesus." Well. She's right, when you get down to it. God didn't have to create the world. He certainly doesn't have to put up with it. My mother-in-law's answer would suffice if we were talking about the Creator on these most basic terms. Except of course, that He did and He does. Our God *cares.* He reveals Himself as Father, Son, and Holy Spirit. Our God is *personal.* He chose to forfeit His very Word rather than be separated from His children. If that doesn't say we *matter*, nothing does!

So, since it's obvious that God cares, is personal, and assigns worth to a creation that he didn't *need* to create, it is important to examine *why* he created in the first place. Let's start from the beginning. If God, being Triune, always had perfect fellowship and glory within himself, then *why create the angels*? Furthermore, why "distract" the angels from their worship by creating man and a tangible universe? Further still, why did God give man the capacity to *enjoy* all the animals, the heavens, and the physical pleasures of this world – especially since God knew these things might inevitably be worshiped? First God distracts the *angels* by creating man, and then God distracts *man* by placing him on a planet full of biological wonder! If that isn't enough, we have to handle the problem of woman. Why the need for a spouse if God is *already* your companion, walking and talking with you in the cool of the day?

    The logic can take us further. God made us in his image. He reveals that image as "Father, Son, and Holy Spirit". The Spirit is the only Person of God that allows for any ambiguity regarding gender, yet is still consistently referenced as a "he" in Scripture. And when the Son of God took on flesh, it was as a man, not a woman. So it would seem that God's image – humanly speaking – would be that of a father, a son, and the love shared between them. A question arises: where does a mother fit into this picture?

    Why did God create woman in the first place? Man could have been asexual. God could have created him in any way he wanted. Adam's companionship could have taken the form of a bunch of male friends. Why a woman? God didn't need to create *man* to begin with. So why even further "distract" from God by creating *woman*? Wouldn't she just get in the way of Adam's personal fellowship with the Father?

    Of course not! The more art the artist creates, the more glory is bestowed on him. That's because the more you praise the art, the more you praise the one who created it. Indeed, the greatest insult you could pay an artist is to ignore his work altogether. When Adam looked at Eve, do you think God was displeased that Adam's face had turned away? That Adam, an unnecessary work of art himself, marveled at this new work of art and expressed immense devotion to it? Clearly, all the more glory was heaped onto God because of Adam's wife. Perhaps God had his *own* mother in mind when he created woman.

We know God intends a mother and a father for every family. That is the very heart of the arguments defending "Traditional" family values (when Protestants refer to "traditional family values", they may not be aware that they refer to Sacred Tradition – the Sacrament of Marriage). Read some of the vast literature that groups like *Focus on the Family* provide on the necessity and glory of motherhood. Then take a moment to stop and think of what implications that information must have on the fact that *God* wanted a mother.

So we can see that Mary isn't a distraction *from*, but rather an attraction *to*, God. The only reason we think about Mary is because of whose mother she is. In fact, the more we think about Mary, the more we think about God! All Marian doctrines are entirely Christocentric. The Bible goes so far as to say that her soul *magnifies* the Lord (Luke 1:46)! In this context, Catholics contend that Mary has a special importance that all the other saints lack.

We can return to a comparison with Eve to illustrate this ancient Catholic belief. Eve is very important. She disobeyed God and by her, sin and death entered into the world. She surrendered to the serpent hanging on a tree and trampled God's Word under foot. Mary is even more important. She obeyed God and by her, righteousness and life entered into the world. She surrendered to God's Word, hanging on a tree, and trampled the serpent under foot. So you can see that not only do we learn lessons from saints, but we are affected by them as well. Catholics believe Mary's life affects us more than all the rest because she is God's artistic *masterpiece*.

> ## *Luke 1:46*
> *"And Mary said, 'my soul doth magnify the Lord'…"*

The first thing that needs to be cleared out of everyone's head is the myth that Catholics "worship" Mary in the sense that they worship God. Mary is a creature, meaning she was created by God for his glory and purposes. What Catholics *would* be willing to say is that, so far as creation goes, Mary is the Creator's greatest work of art. We believe this because of what Mary carried within her womb. Coming from Mary's body and blood alone was God, growing and living from within her.

Recall the Ark of the Covenant in the Old Testament, dear brother. Remember how perfect it had to be? How elaborate and holy? How exasperatingly long-winded God was in his building instructions? And why so detailed? Why so holy? Why so perfect? *Because that holy thing would hold the two tablets God had engraved with his own hand – his Word.* And this would serve as his Glory's resting place, where his Spirit would dwell. The ark was so holy, in fact that anyone who touched it irreverently would die. If such holiness, beauty, and perfection were necessitated for God's written Word, how much more for God Himself! Mary carried within her own body the very Person of the Word!

The second thing to be taken into consideration is that all the honor and blessing the Church pays to Mary is practiced precisely because of the infinitely greater honor and blessing due to her Son, God, Himself! If Christ is the source of our life and God is his Father, then by virtue of the Incarnation, within the Family, Mary is our spiritual Mother. If Christ is our King, then within the Kingdom his mother must be our Queen. Remember that the king's mother in any kingdom is the queen-mother, by title and authority. And in God's Word and Law, we see both examples of a queen-mother's role and a command to honor our mother (see Psalm 45:9, 1 Kings 2:17-20, Neh. 2:6). Would Mary receive any less from Jesus? Jesus is Himself the Word! So we begin to see all Marian devotion within the context of Jesus.

Lastly the facts must establish that we believe Mary needed Jesus to save her from her sins. Mary rejoiced in God her Savior. But having already demonstrated that the reverent devotion given to Mary takes place within the context of Jesus, we must turn to that context again to show *how* Mary was saved. In so doing, we see that *a)* if Mary was God's Mother, God would fulfill his own Word by honoring and blessing her as best he could and *b)* if Mary was to be the Ark of the Covenant, born with the egg that would one day develop into Jesus, she would need to be perfectly holy (obviously this wouldn't be necessary for Mary's mother since Mary is merely the Ark).

Now that we have reestablished such a context, we must ask ourselves if anything is impossible with God. I know that you'll say "no" with me! So, just as God created Eve without sin, he created Mary without sin. And like Eve, Mary had the choice to reject God's will. But unlike Eve, whose action brought sin and death into the world, Mary's obedience brought righteousness and life into the world! God saved her at conception and Mary never fell. This is what makes her God's masterpiece.

These three areas were necessary to demonstrate the importance the ancient Church leaders put on Mary's perpetual virginity and her assumption into Heaven. I remember going to my family's Baptist church as a child and hearing a sermon about the Ark of the Covenant. The pastor explained that the Ark was set apart, sacred for God's own use. It couldn't be used as a coffee stand or a storage bin. Why?

Because God specially designed the Ark for his own glory. His Word would dwell inside of it and his glory would overshadow it. I'm sure it would have caused that old pastor to do a double-take if someone said the Ark *really* belonged to the persons chosen to guard or carry it – that they could do with it as they pleased. What was most interesting to me at the time is how he closed his lesson. "We don't really know what happened to it," he began, "but many feel it was assumed into heaven." Years later, I made a connection. If he was ok with those ideas in relation to the Ark of the Old Covenant, why was he so opposed to those ideas in relation to the Ark of the New Covenant? It was almost as if some unseen force was restraining his heart and mind.

It's important to note that Catholics don't ignore Scripture about Jesus' "brothers", nor do we believe that Mary *ascended* into

Heaven. Ancient histories and commentaries on Mary's life hold that she was consecrated to God for the temple as a virgin, although we don't know it for a fact. If the stories are true, at a young age (as was a practice) she was given a care-taker husband, who was an elderly widower named Joseph.

Since Joseph already had grown children from his previous marriage, Jesus did indeed have half-brothers in legality. We know from scripture that at least James and Joseph – both called "brothers" of Jesus (Mark 6:3) – were actually his cousins (Mark 15:47, Matt 27:56). Is this a biblical error? No, it's just that the word "cousin" was used interchangeably with "brother" in Greek because in Hebrew and Aramaic there is no word for "cousin"! Instead, *adelphoi* is used, broadly meaning "kinsmen". So even if the early manuscripts claiming Joseph to have had sons from a prior marriage are wrong, it could easily be that the references to the Lord's *brothers* are actually speaking of his *cousins*.

And finally, Mary's Assumption means God took her, body and soul, up to Heaven a lot earlier than most of us will experience. Jesus *ascended* to Heaven, meaning he did so by his own power. Mary, like Elijah, Enoch, and possibly others before her, was *assumed*. It's interesting that our earliest historical reference to Mary's Assumption is a feast day dedicated to it and a manuscript from the fourth century – the same century that the Divinity of the Holy Spirit was defined.

So why does the Church so stubbornly insist on the truth of this bit of Sacred Tradition? Because whereas Christ's Ascension is primarily connected to our redemption, Mary's Assumption is primarily connected to our *hope* in Christ's work! Mary is part of the Church, which is the Bride of Christ. When Christ ascended, as the Groom, he took Mary up into resurrected glory to symbolically give all of us the assurance that the whole Bride – we, the Church – will one day join him.

It is fitting that the body that gave life and nourishment to God should not be left to rot and decay. I'm sure the Apostles figured as much when they saw her empty tomb. All at once they must have felt thankfulness for confirmation of their mother's role in their lives and joy in knowing God's grace and power. Although this dogma may unfortunately reveal those who do not faithfully submit to Church authority, it also brings a very real advantage to those Christians who do trust in papal infallibility. Like the Apostles before us we may see in the Assumption of Mary not only confirmation of the Church's destiny but also confirmation that Mary is the mightiest aide in our walk with Christ. It is an appropriate conclusion to her life and role on earth and an appropriate prelude to her life and role in Heaven. In short, it is logical; it makes sense.

    Regardless of differences of opinion about the Blessed Mother's life, what a wonderful example of God's grace from beginning to end! Mary and all of her dogmas are vital to our continuing sense and experience of rebirth in Christianity. And consider this point: everything that the Church claims Mary experienced and experiences (sinless perfection, spiritual parenthood, co-mediation with Christ through prayer, an assumed and glorified body, and a crown in Heaven) is what every other Christian by faith also hopes to experience. The Church teaches that Mary's experience of these things was and is far greater and more blessed than ours because she was and is God's Mother, according to eternally pre-destined *grace alone* – and only because of Christ! Mary is a perfect portrait of what the Church will one day become and what God intends us to be now.

    The facts are, the Church believes Mary is worthy of more honor than any other mother since she is the Mother of God, and because of this, God chose to honor her by creating her as a new Eve, without sin, and by assuming her glorified body into heaven. She is also consequently the spiritual Mother of all those Christ is brother of and the Queen-Mother of all whom Christ is King of. This is logically demanded of those who take God to be their Father through Christ as their brother and king. Since access to such faith in our Heavenly Family rests solely on the Incarnation, my stance may be firm: *you cannot take God to be your Father unless you take Mary to be your Mother.*

This perspective has deepened my understanding of rebirth in Christ. I no longer tolerate myself as a sinful son of the original Eve, who said "No" to God. Rather, I resolve myself by God's grace to be a son of Mary; the second Eve, who said "Yes" to God. This gives me a tangible sense of the family and heritage into which I am born.

God's Word tells us to honor our mother. How much more would God's Word incarnate honor *his* mother than we honor *ours*? And aren't we supposed to imitate Christ? The reason we bless Mary, imitate her, and turn to her in practice is because in the Bible, Mary foretells it and Christ calls "the disciple he loves" to take her in to be his Mom! Dear brother, if you can even see Church teaching on Mary as *possibly* being true, wouldn't you think that Satan wants people to doubt it? Her love and prayers may make the difference between souls that don't care and souls that, in imitation of her, surrender totally to Christ.

If you have any further doubts, you need only look through the lens of Christian history. All of the greatest saints – those who exhibited the most intimate and ecstatic relationships with Christ – were deeply devoted to our Blessed Mother. The fruit of Marian devotion is always a closer relationship to her only begotten Son. As you search the scriptures, ask yourself whether or not Marian doctrines are at least *compatible* with God's Word. If it fits and it's historical, pray against any attempt from the Enemy to keep you from the fullness of truth. As you begin to study the information I've provided you from Scripture and Tradition, ask God to remove any blinders or biases you may be carrying with you – and that the Holy Spirit will give you discernment!

Scripture Speaks! *What the Bible Says*

What if Mary is the Ark of the Covenant?

Exodus 25:11-21
    And thou shalt overlay [the ark] with pure gold, within and without shalt thou overlay it, and shalt make upon it a crown of gold round about. [12] And thou shalt cast four rings of gold for it, and put them in the four corners thereof; and two rings shall be in the one side of it, and two rings in the other side of it. [13] And thou shalt make staves of shittim wood, and overlay them with gold. [14] And thou shalt put the staves into the rings by the sides of the ark, that the ark may be borne with them. [15] The staves shall be in the rings of the ark: they shall not be taken from it. [16] And thou shalt put into the ark the testimony which I shall give thee. [17] **And thou shalt make a mercy seat of pure gold**: two cubits and a half shall be the length thereof, and a cubit and a half the breadth thereof. [18] And thou shalt make two cherubims of gold, of beaten work shalt thou make them, in the two ends of the mercy seat. [19] And make one cherub on the one end, and the other cherub on the other end: even of the mercy seat shall ye make the cherubims on the two ends thereof. [20] And the cherubim shall stretch forth their wings on high, covering the mercy seat with their wings, and their faces shall look one to another; toward the mercy seat shall the faces of the cherubims be. [21] And thou shalt put the mercy seat above upon the ark; **and in the ark thou shalt put the testimony that I shall give thee.**

As you can see, the Ark of the Covenant required exquisite detail – God gave perfect instructions for a perfect container for his perfect Word.

1 Chron. 13:9-10
    And when they came unto the threshing floor of Chidon, Uzza put forth his hand to hold the ark; for the oxen stumbled. [10] **And the anger of the Lord was**

kindled against Uzza, and he smote him, because he put his hand to the ark: and there he died before God.

The Ark was so holy because of what it represented and contained that God struck down all those who didn't treat it with reverence.

> 1 Chron. 15:1-16:43
> And David made him houses in the city of David, **and prepared a place for the ark of God, and pitched for it a tent.** [2] Then David said, None ought to carry the ark of God but the Levites: for them hath the Lord chosen to carry the ark of God, and to minister unto him for ever. [3] And David gathered all Israel together to Jerusalem, to bring up the ark of the Lord unto his place, which he had prepared for it…[12]And said unto them, Ye are the chief of the fathers of the Levites: **sanctify yourselves**, both ye and your brethren, that ye may bring up the ark of the Lord God of Israel unto the place that I have prepared for it. [13] For because ye did it not at the first, the Lord our God made a breach upon us, for that we sought him not after the due order. [14] So the priests and the Levites sanctified themselves to bring up the ark of the Lord God of Israel. [15] And the children of the Levites bare the ark of God upon their shoulders with the staves thereon, as Moses commanded according to the word of the Lord. [16] **And David spake to the chief of the Levites to appoint their brethren to be the singers with instruments of music, psalteries and harps and cymbals, sounding, by lifting up the voice with joy** … [19] So the singers, Heman, Asaph, and Ethan, were appointed to sound with cymbals of brass; [20] And Zechariah, and Aziel, and Shemiramoth, and Jehiel, and Unni, and Eliab, and Maaseiah, and Benaiah, with psalteries on Alamoth; [21] And Mattithiah, and Elipheleh, and Mikneiah, and Obed-edom, and Jeiel, and Azaziah, with harps on the Sheminith to excel. [22] And Chenaniah, chief of the Levites, was for song: he instructed about the song, because he was skilful. [23] And Berechiah and Elkanah were doorkeepers for the ark. [24] And Shebaniah, and Jehoshaphat, and Nethaneel, and Amasai, and Zechariah, and Benaiah, and Eliezer, **the**

> **priests, did blow with the trumpets before the ark of God**: and Obed-edom and Jehiah were doorkeepers for the ark...[29] And it came to pass, as the ark of the covenant of the Lord came to the city of David, that Michal the daughter of Saul looking out at a window **saw king David dancing** and playing: and she despised him in her heart.
>
> [16:1] **So they brought the ark of God, and set it in the midst of the tent that David had pitched for it: and they offered burnt sacrifices and peace offerings before God.** [2] And when David had made an end of offering the burnt offerings and the peace offerings, he blessed the people in the name of the Lord. [3] **And he dealt to every one of Israel, both man and woman, to every one a loaf of bread, and a good piece of flesh, and a flagon of wine.**
>
> [4] And he appointed certain of the Levites **to minister before the ark** of the Lord, and to record, and to thank and praise the Lord God of Israel...
>
> [37] So he left there before the ark of the covenant of the Lord Asaph and his brethren, **to minister before the ark continually, as every day's work required**...

Look at the joy...the exaltation...the devotion paid to God through his Ark! Now let's look at some peculiar similarities between the Ark and Mary:

> Luke 1:39
> **And Mary arose** in those days, **and went** into the hill country with haste, **into a city of Judah;**

> 2 Samuel 6:2
> **And David arose, and went** with all the people that were with him from Baale **of Judah, to bring up from thence the ark of God**, whose name is called by the name of the Lord of hosts that dwelleth between the cherubims.

What's so interesting? Well, other than the fact that God chose to inspire the records of these two events with strikingly similar grammar and vocabulary, we see that Mary went to the hill country of Judah after becoming pregnant. And where did David go to retrieve the Ark? Baale, a city in the hill country of Judah.

> Luke 1:41
> And it came to pass, that**, when Elisabeth heard the salutation of Mary, the babe leaped in her womb**; and Elisabeth was filled with the Holy Ghost:

> 2 Samuel 6:16
> **And as the ark of the Lord came into the city of David**, Michal Saul's daughter looked through a window, and saw king **David leaping and dancing before the Lord**; and she despised him in her heart.

> Luke 1:44
> For, lo, as soon as the voice of **thy** salutation sounded in mine ears, **the babe leaped in my womb for joy**.

When the Ark came to him, David leapt for joy. John the Baptist did the same thing when Mary came to him. Again, the grammar and vocabulary were inspired in very similar ways.

> Luke 1:43
> And **whence is this to me, that the mother of my Lord should come to me?**

> 2 Samuel 6:9
> And David was afraid of the Lord that day, and said, **How shall the ark of the Lord come to me?**

These passages speak for themselves, I think. The correlation is undeniable. Luke *had* to realize the connection of what he was writing to the passage in Samuel!

> Luke 1:56
> **And Mary abode with her about three months**, and returned to her own house.

> 2 Samuel 6:11

> **And the ark of the Lord continued in the house of Obed-edom the Gittite three months**: and the Lord blessed Obed-edom, and all his household.

Just keeps getting more interesting, huh? Do you think God's trying to get us to notice something? Now let's see if Revelation can clear things up a bit…

> Rev. 11:19
> And the temple of God was opened in heaven, and **there was seen in his temple the ark of his testament**: and there were lightnings, and voices, and thunderings, and an earthquake, and great hail.

This was a monumental passage for Jewish converts of the time – the Ark had been missing for six centuries. For John to mention it out of nowhere would strike an onslaught of excitement, questions, and praise; but they also knew well that there was a new covenant and a new Ark. So they were not surprised at all to read the verses immediately following:

> Rev. 12:1-17
> And there appeared a great wonder in heaven; **a woman clothed with the sun, and the moon under her feet, and upon her head a crown of twelve stars:** [2] And she being with child cried, travailing in birth, and pained to be delivered. [3] And there appeared another wonder in heaven; and behold a great red dragon, having seven heads and ten horns, and seven crowns upon his heads. [4] And his tail drew the third part of the stars of heaven, and did cast them to the earth: and **the dragon stood before the woman which was ready to be delivered, for to devour her child as soon as it was born.** [5] And **she brought forth a man child, who was to rule all nations with a rod of iron: and her child was caught up unto God, and to his throne.** [6] **And the woman fled into the wilderness, where she hath a place prepared of God, that they should feed her there a thousand two hundred and threescore days**… [17] And the dragon was wroth with the woman, and went to make war with **the remnant of her seed, which keep the**

commandments of God, and have the testimony of Jesus Christ.

This passage most obviously refers to Mary, who is so royally honored in Heaven because her Son is the King of Heaven. Herod, like the dragon, wanted to kill the Infant Jesus as soon as he was born. But when Christ, who was prophesied to "rule all nations with a rod of iron" (see Psalm 2:9, Rev. 2:27; 19:15) was born, God warned the Holy Family to flee to the wilderness (Egypt) where He would take care of them for a time. Some people say that the woman's birth pangs prove she was under the curse of the Fall – but there are many passages in scripture where birth pangs are mentioned metaphorically or to emphasize a point (see Isa. 66:7, Gal. 4:19, Rom. 8:22, Jer. 13:21, Micah 4:9-10).

The passage can also double to refer to the Church or Israel. But although these interpretations wouldn't have eluded John's contemporary readers, the most immediately clear interpretation is to see Mary, Queen-Mother of Heaven by virtue of her Son, the King of Heaven. To further emphasize that point, we see in verse 17 that she is Mother not only of Jesus, but also *all* Christians! Mary *is* the Ark of the Covenant.

What if Mary was Immaculately Conceived?

Luke 1:28-31
    And the angel came in unto her, and said, **Hail, [Full-of-Grace], the Lord is with thee**: blessed art thou among women. [29] And when she saw him, she was troubled at his saying, and cast in her mind what manner of salutation this should be. [30] And the angel said unto her, Fear not, Mary: for **thou hast found favour with God**. [31] And, behold, thou shalt conceive **in thy womb, and bring forth** a son, and shalt call his name Jesus.

The angel addressed Mary as "Kecharitomene" – and this rendered the Greek for "full of Grace" into a name: "Full-of-Grace". Not only that, but the Greek suggests *perfection* of Grace. Kecharitomene is a perfect passive participle, indicating continuance of a perfectly accomplished action. Some translate Kecharitomene (a pretty sounding name when you practice saying it) to be "highly favored one" but that translation just doesn't do the Greek justice. How much grace is God *capable* of giving? The amount is probably equivalent to how much He is *capable* of honoring His Mother…so what does grace do?

Romans 3:24
    Being **justified freely by his grace** through the redemption that is in Christ Jesus:

Titus 3:7
    That being **justified by his grace**, we should be **made heirs** according to the hope of **eternal life**.

Well, for one, it saves us…

Titus 2:11-12
    For **the grace of God that bringeth salvation** hath appeared to all men, [12] **Teaching us that, denying ungodliness and worldly lusts, we should live soberly, righteously, and godly,** in this present world;

Romans 6:14

> For **sin shall not have dominion over you**: for ye are not under the law, but under **grace**.

> 2 Cor. 9:8
> And God is able to make **all grace** abound toward you; that ye, always having all sufficiency in all things, may **abound to every good work**

…and it propels us toward righteousness and away from sin! So if Mary had been full of grace – absolutely full of grace, in fact, warranting a heavenly name – when Gabriel so royally greeted her, could there have ever been a time when there was any room left for sin or damnation?

> Acts 6:8
> And Stephen, **full of faith and power**, did great wonders and miracles among the people.

Some Bible translations use the phrase "full of grace" when this passage describes Stephen. But the Greek here is just that: a momentary description. The word used is "charitos", which neither renders "charitoo" as a *perfect passive participle*, nor (more importantly) as a *name* – something that connotes one's very being.

> 1 John 3:6, 9
> **Whosoever abideth in him sinneth not**: whosoever sinneth hath not **seen** him, neither **known** him…Whosoever is **born of God** doth not commit sin; for his seed remaineth in him: and **he cannot sin**, because he is born of God.

Here, God's Word specifically connects one's aptitude to sin with one's relationship with Christ. The greater the relationship with Christ, the less the relationship with Satan. Who saw Jesus more than anyone else? Who knew Jesus better than anyone else? Whose heart did Jesus abide in more than anyone else? A person would have to be conscious of either irrationality or self-deception if he or she named anyone other than Christ's own Mother.

Furthermore, being "born of God" through (and because of) Christ is exactly what Catholics argue for when speaking of Mary's Immaculate Conception. The difference is that while all other Christians are born of God through Baptism and Confirmation (the Holy Spirit) by hands of other Christians, Mary was born of God at conception by the hand of God himself!

> Zeph. 3:14-17
> Sing, **O daughter of Zion**; shout, O Israel; be glad and rejoice with all the heart, O daughter of Jerusalem. [15] **The Lord hath taken away thy judgments, he hath cast out thine enemy:** the king of Israel, even **the Lord, is in the midst of thee**: thou shalt not see evil any more. [16] In that day it shall be said to Jerusalem, Fear thou not: and to Zion, Let not thine hands be slack. [17] The Lord thy God in the midst of thee is mighty; he will save, he will rejoice over thee with joy; he will rest in his love, he will joy over thee with singing.

This gleam of prophecy can and has been understood to refer to Mary as well as Israel. God was in Mary's midst. Her judgments were taken away because Holiness Himself would be connected to her; growing within her and feeding off her. God saved her from the stain of Original Sin at conception for this purpose.

> Romans 3:23
> For **all** have sinned, and come short of the glory of God;

In making the connection that Mary is the Ark of the New Covenant, we see that God would create her in a fashion after the original Ark. If the old Ark had to be perfect in order to house God's written Word, how much more so the new Ark, which would spawn, nourish, and give birth to the incarnated Person of the Word? How holy would this thing have to be in order for God to *grow out of her*? To *feed from* and be *connected to* her? Further, how much would God honor His Mother? To the best of His ability? The Church teaches that God created Mary like He created Eve – without original sin, but with the capacity for it if she so chose. Her parents gave birth to what appeared to be a normal baby girl, but God's *grace* saved her from sin at conception. So what do Catholics do with Romans 3:23?

> Romans 11:26
> And so **all** Israel shall be saved: as it is written, There shall come out of Sion the Deliverer, and shall turn away ungodliness from Jacob

Well, Paul says *all* Israel will be saved, here. So all Israelites are Christians, huh? That's quite a news bulletin…

> Romans 15:14
> And I myself also am persuaded of you, my brethren, that ye also are full of goodness, filled with **all** knowledge, able also to admonish one another.

Is Paul saying the Romans are omniscient, here?

> 1 Cor. 1:5
> That in every thing **ye are enriched by him**, in **all** utterance, and in **all** knowledge

What about here? Could it be that this is hyperbole or common Hebrew idiom?

> Romans 3:10-12
> As it is written, There is none righteous, no, not one: [11] There is none that understandeth, there is none that seeketh after God. [12] They are all gone out of the way, they are together become unprofitable; **there is none that doeth good, no, not one.**

Here, Paul quotes this Psalm:

> Psalm 14:2-3

> The Lord looked down from heaven upon the children of men, to see if there were any that did understand, and seek God. [3] They are all gone aside, they are all together become filthy: **there is none that doeth good, no, not one.**

And yet in the very next Psalm, David talks about people who *are* righteous and good:

> Psalm 15:2
> He that **walketh uprightly, and worketh righteousness,** and speaketh the truth in his heart.

Is it possible that David and Paul are trying to emphasize humility towards the grace of God? That they don't literally mean that everyone throughout all time has sinned anymore than Jesus meant for us to cut off our hands if they offend us? Are they allowed to use such exaggerated expressions as speaking devices? The use of hyperbole is consistent with the rest of Scripture, as well as the language of the time.

Logically, it's *impossible* to apply Romans 3:23 absolutely, since Jesus, infants, and the mentally challenged are some pretty big exceptions. Catholics only argue for one more exception: Mary. Whereas God cleans the rest of us off *after* we've been conceived in (and subsequently born into) the mud-pit of original sin, he *prevented* his Mother from being conceived in the mud to begin with. However, it was up to her to continue to cooperate with his saving grace; she had to respond to it with living faith. We (Mary included) are always undeserving of salvation in the same way that creatures don't deserve to be created. We owe both our first and second birth to God's grace alone.

> Genesis 3:15
> And I will put **enmity** between thee and **the woman,** and between thy seed and **her seed**; it shall bruise thy head, and thou shalt bruise his heel.

God saved Eve from sin upon her creation. However, she failed to cooperate with God's saving grace. When God rebukes the "serpent" for tempting Eve, he promises a Messiah, born of a virgin. Furthermore, he equates the same enmity between Christ and Satan with that between Mary and Satan. Mary was saved from the stain of original sin upon her conception and unlike Eve, continued to cooperate with God's grace throughout her life.

What if the Immaculate Mary, the Second Eve, has Always Been Essential to God's Plan?

> Genesis 3:15
> And I will put enmity between thee and **the Woman**, and between thy seed and **her seed**; it shall bruise thy head, and thou shalt bruise his heel.

> Revelations 12:4
> the Dragon stood before **the Woman** which was ready to be delivered, for to devour **her child** as soon as it was born.

Notice that the Bible opens and closes with a Woman fighting a Serpent. Interesting, isn't it? And who ever heard of a *woman* having "seed"? Oh, right…the Virgin birth.

> Jeremiah 1:5
> Before I formed thee in the belly I knew thee; and **before thou camest forth out of the womb I sanctified thee**, and I ordained thee a prophet unto the nations.

This verse shows that God sets people apart for special purposes before they are born – sometimes He even *sanctifies* them from birth. That's exactly what the Church teaches about Mary. In fact, many people see this as another prophecy of the Immaculate Conception.

> John 19:26-27
> When Jesus therefore saw his mother, and the disciple standing by, whom he loved, he saith unto his mother, **Woman, behold thy son!** [27] Then saith he to the disciple, **Behold thy mother!** And from that hour that disciple took her unto his own home.

> Rev. 12:17
> And the Dragon was wroth with **the Woman**, and went to make war with the remnant of **her seed, which keep the commandments of God, and have the testimony of Jesus Christ.**

Today, mainstream Christianity puts a great deal of time, money, and effort into the defense of the "Traditional" family. We hold as sacred God's intention for children to have both a father *and* a mother. Well, we also know that God intends us to be a Family. So if God is our heavenly Father, who is our heavenly *Mother*? These passages are very interesting. The first one contains some of the last few words of Christ before he dies. His words from the cross are critical and universally important for obvious reasons. What then might be the significance these verses? What portion of God's eternal plan might be fulfilled here, that these words are engraved in Sacred Scripture?

What if the Blessed Virgin Mary Remained a Virgin Her Whole Life?

>Ezekiel 44:2
>Then said the Lord unto me; This gate shall be shut, it shall not be opened, **and no man shall enter in by it; because the Lord, the God of Israel, hath entered in by it,** therefore it shall be shut.

Without being too graphic here, what (or whose) gate did Christ enter into the world by? This sounds a little more than prophetic here, don't you think?

>Luke 1:31
>And, behold, thou **shalt conceive in thy womb, and bring forth a son**, and shalt call his name Jesus.

>Luke 1:34
>Then said Mary unto the angel, **How shall this be,** seeing I know not a man?

What's interesting here is that Gabriel is using future tense here and yet Mary, betrothed to Joseph, finds it odd that she might get pregnant in the future. If, on the other hand, she had taken a vow of lifelong virginity and Joseph was an elderly care-taker husband (as other extra-biblical historic documents relate) then her question makes perfect sense.

>John 19:26-27
>When Jesus therefore saw his mother, and the disciple standing by, whom he loved, he saith unto his mother, **Woman, behold thy son!** [27] Then saith he to the disciple, **Behold thy mother!** And **from that hour that disciple took her unto his own home.**

It would be unthinkable for Jesus to turn his mother over to a friend if she had other sons, wouldn't it?

>Mark 6:3

> Is not this the carpenter, **the** son of Mary, the brother of James, and Joses, and of Juda, and Simon? and are not his sisters here with us? And they were offended at him.

Why is Jesus referred to as *the* son of Mary instead of *a* son, if James and the others were his biological brothers?

> John 19:25
> Now there stood by the cross of Jesus his mother, and **his mother's sister, Mary the wife of Cleophas**, and Mary Magdalene.

Pay attention here. Mary, the wife of Clopas (Cleophas) is the Blessed Virgin's *sister*. Keep that in mind for the next couple of verses…

> Matthew 27:61
> And there was Mary Magdalene, and **the other Mary**, sitting over against the sepulchre.

Matthew even refers to Clopas' wife as "the other Mary" (cf. Matt 28:1).

> Matthew 27:56
> Among which was Mary Magdalene, and **Mary the mother of James and Joses,** and the mother of Zebedee's children.

> Mark 15:47
> And Mary Magdalene and **Mary the mother of Joses** beheld where he was laid.

Wait – I thought Joses (Joseph) and James were the *brothers* of Jesus? What's going on here?

> Mark 6:3
> Is not this the carpenter, the son of Mary, **the brother of James, and Joses,** and of Juda, and Simon? and are not his sisters here with us? And they were offended at him.

Sure enough, the Bible's doing it again! We just learned that James and Joseph were the *cousins* of Jesus by the "other" Mary. So why does the Bible refer to them as Jesus' brothers? In the language of the time (Aramaic), there was no word for "cousin" because in the culture, all your kinsmen were regarded as immediate family. In Greek, the words were used interchangeably for the same reason. Kinsmen for family, "brothers" and "sisters" alike.

> Genesis 29:15
> And Laban said unto Jacob, Because **thou art my brother**, shouldest thou therefore serve me for nought? tell me, what shall thy wages be?

We see the same principle applied to the Old Testament. Laban is Jacob's cousin, yet he calls him his brother. Why? Because all your *kinsmen* are your "brothers and sisters". The perpetual virginity of Mary along with this explanation of Jesus' brethren fits the better context of the Bible.

> Matthew 1:25
> And **knew her not till she had brought forth her firstborn son**: and he called his name Jesus.

If you really try to grasp at straws, you might use this passage to attack Mary's virginity because of the words "until" and "firstborn"…

> Matthew 28:20
> Teaching them to observe all things whatsoever I have commanded you: and, lo, I am with you alway, **even unto** the end of the world. Amen.

> 2 Samuel 6:23
> Therefore Michal the daughter of Saul had no child **unto the day of her death**.

…but there are many, many, places where "until" or one of its variations are used in Scripture as a way of emphasizing something of *permanence* (cf. Luke 20:43)

> Exodus 13:2
> Sanctify unto me all **the firstborn, whatsoever openeth the womb** among the children of Israel, both of man and of beast: it is mine.

Here, we discover that "firstborn" is a status, not an implication of future children (cf. Exodus 34:20). If it is a necessary article of the faith that Jesus Christ was his Father's only begotten Son, would it make any less sense that he was also his *Mother's* only begotten Son?

What if the Mother of God was Assumed by Him into Heaven?

> Matthew 27:52-53
> And the graves were opened; and many bodies of the saints which slept arose, [53] And came out of the graves after his resurrection, and went into the holy city, and appeared unto many.

Where did these saints go? They had experienced the resurrection and it is only appointed to man *once* to die...so are they still around? Or is there precedence in the Bible for someone being assumed into Heaven?

> Hebrews 11:5
> By faith Enoch **was translated that he should not see death; and was not found, because God had translated him:** for before his translation he had this testimony, that he pleased God.

> Genesis 5:24
> And Enoch walked with God: **and he was not; for God took him.**

Well, there's good, old, Enoch...

> 2 Kings 2:1
> And it came to pass, **when the Lord would take up Elijah into heaven by a whirlwind**, that Elijah went with Elisha from Gilgal.

> 2 Kings 2:11
> And it came to pass, as they still went on, and talked, that, behold, there appeared a chariot of fire, and horses of fire, and parted them both asunder; **and Elijah went up by a whirlwind into heaven.**

...and good, old, Elijah!

> Psalm 132:8
> Arise, O Lord, into thy rest; **thou, and the Ark of thy strength.**

It's interesting that this verse is cited by many Protestants as a prophecy of Christ's Ascension into Heaven. If it is such a prophecy, then it also pertains to his Ark: Mary.

> Psalm 16:10
> For thou wilt not leave my soul in hell; **neither wilt thou suffer thine Holy One to see corruption.**

God wouldn't allow his Son to see corruption…what of his Holy Mother? Death and bodily decay are the consequences of sin. If Mary was sinless, then her passing would mean immediate bodily glorification at the end of her earthly life. If God was able (certainly) and he loved and honored the Mother he specially created for Himself (of course), do you think He would do any less for her than he had for Enoch, Elijah, and many others? Obviously, this can't be used as "proof" of the assumption. But does it at least illustrate how the doctrine is *compatible* with Scripture? Even more so, don't these passages suggest the doctrine to be *logical*? Well, if the assumption of Mary is compatible with Scripture, is logical, and fairly historical, why should it cause such a fuss among Protestants?

Honor your Fathers! *The Elders Cry Out*

"He became man by the Virgin, **in order that the disobedience which proceeded from the serpent might receive its destruction in the same manner in which it derived its origin.** *For Eve, who was a virgin and undefiled, having conceived the word of the serpent, brought forth disobedience and death. But the Virgin Mary received faith and joy, when the angel Gabriel announced the good tidings to her that the Spirit of the Lord would come upon her, and the power of the Highest would overshadow her: wherefore also the Holy Thing begotten of her is the Son of God; and she replied, 'Be it unto me according to thy word.'* **And by her has He been born**, *to whom we have proved so many Scriptures refer, and by whom God destroys both the serpent and those angels and men who are like him; but works deliverance from death to those who repent of their wickedness and believe upon Him."*

- Justin Martyr, *Dialogue with Trypho*, 100 (A.D. 155).

"For as Eve was seduced by the word of an angel to flee from God, having rebelled against His Word, so Mary by the word of an angel received the glad tidings that she would bear God by obeying his Word. The former was seduced to disobey God, but the latter was persuaded to obey God, so that the Virgin Mary might become **the advocate** *of the virgin Eve.* **As the human race was subjected to death through a virgin, so it was saved by a virgin.**"

- Irenaeus, *Against Heresies*, V:19,1 (A.D. 180)

"But the Lord Christ, **the fruit of the Virgin**, *did not pronounce the breasts of women blessed, nor selected them to give nourishment; but when the kind and loving Father had rained down the Word, Himself became spiritual nourishment to the good. O mystic marvel! The universal Father is one, and one the universal Word; and the Holy Spirit is one and the same everywhere,* **and one is the only Virgin Mother. I love to call her**

the Church. This mother, when alone, had not milk, because alone she was not a woman. But she is once virgin and mother-- pure as a virgin, loving as a mother. And calling her children to her, she nurses them with holy milk, viz., with the Word for childhood. Therefore she had not milk; for the milk was this child fair and comely, the body of Christ, which nourishes by the Word the young brood, which the Lord Himself brought forth in throes of the flesh, which the Lord Himself swathed in His precious blood."

- Clement of Alexandria, *The Instructor*, I:6 (A.D.202)

"Accordingly, **a virgin did conceive and bear 'Emmanuel, God with us.'**...But the whole of this new birth was prefigured, as was the case in all other instances, in ancient type, **the Lord being born as man by a dispensation in which a virgin was the medium.** ...For it was while Eve was yet a virgin, that the ensnaring word had crept into her ear which was to build the edifice of death. **Into a virgin's soul, in like manner, must be introduced that Word of God which was to raise the fabric of life; so that what had been reduced to ruin by this sex, might by the selfsame sex be recovered to salvation.** As Eve had believed the serpent, so Mary believed the angel. **The delinquency which the one occasioned by believing, the other by believing effaced....**"

- Tertullian, *Flesh of Christ*, 17 (A.D. 212)

"This Virgin Mother of the Only-begotten of God is called Mary, worthy of God, **immaculate of the immaculate**, one of the one."

- Origen, *Homily* 1 (A.D. 244)

"...the brethren of Jesus were sons of Joseph by a former wife, whom he married before Mary. Now those who say so wish to preserve the honor of Mary in virginity to the end, so that body of hers which was appointed to minister to the Word...might not know intercourse with a man after the Holy Spirit came into her and the *power from on high overshadowed her. And **I think it in harmony with reason that Jesus was the firstfruit among men of the purity which consists in chastity, and Mary was among women. For it were not pious to ascribe to any other than to her the firstfruit of virginity**"*

- Origen, *Commentary on Matthew* 2:17 (A.D. 248)

*"**We fly to your patronage** [or: 'under your mercy we take refuge'],*
O Holy Mother of God.
Despise not our petitions
in our necessities,
but deliver us from all danger,
O ever glorious and blessed Virgin."

- Anonymous, *Sub Tuum Praesidium*, Papyrus from John Rylands Library (~A.D. 250 or earlier)

*"After this, we receive the doctrine of the resurrection from the dead, of which Jesus Christ our Lord became the first-fruits; **Who bore a Body, in truth, not in semblance, derived from Mary the mother of God** in the fullness of time sojourning among the race, for the remission of sins: who was crucified and died, yet for all this suffered no diminution of His Godhead."*

- Alexander of Alexandria, *Epistle to Alexander*, 12 (A.D. 324)

*"Many, my beloved, are the true testimonies concerning Christ. The Father bears witness from heaven of His Son: the Holy Ghost bears witness, descending bodily in likeness of a dove: the Archangel Gabriel bears witness, bringing good tidings to **Mary: the Virgin Mother of God bears witness**: the blessed place of the manger bears witness."*

- Cyril of Jerusalem, *Catechetical Lectures* (A.D. 350).

*"Therefore let those who deny that the Son is from the Father by nature and proper to His Essence, deny also that **He took true human flesh of Mary Ever-Virgin**; for in neither case had it been of profit to us men, whether the Word were not true and naturally Son of God, or the flesh not true which He assumed."*

- Athanasius, *Orations against the Arians*, (A.D. 362)

*"'And when he had taken her, he knew her not, till she had brought forth her first-born Son.' **He hath here used the word till,' not that thou shouldest suspect that afterwards he did know her, but to inform thee that before the birth the Virgin was wholly untouched by man. But why then, it may be said, hath he used the word, till'? Because it is usual in Scripture often to do this, and to use this expression without reference to limited times.** For so with respect to the ark likewise, it is said, The raven returned not till the earth was dried up.' And yet it did not return even after that time. And when discoursing also of God, the Scripture saith, From age until age Thou art,' not as fixing limits in this case. And again when it is preaching the Gospel beforehand, and saying, In his days shall righteousness flourish, and abundance of peace, till the moon be taken away,' it doth not set a limit to this fair part of creation. So then here likewise, it uses the word "till," to make certain what was before the birth, but **as to what follows, it leaves thee to make the inference.**"*

- John Chrysostom, *Gospel of Matthew* (A.D. 370).

*"Thou alone **and thy Mother are in all things fair**, there is no flaw in thee and **no stain in thy Mother.**"*

- Ephraem, *Nisibene Hymns*, 27:8 (A.D. 370)

*"O noble Virgin, truly **you are greater than any other greatness**. For who is your equal in greatness, O dwelling place of God the Word? **To whom among all creatures shall I compare you, O Virgin?** You are greater than them all O Covenant, **clothed with purity instead of gold!** You are the Ark in which is found the golden vessel containing the true manna, that is, the flesh in which divinity resides."*

- Athanasius, *Homily of the Papyrus of Turin*, 71:216 (ante AD 373)

*"**If** the Holy Virgin had died and was buried, her falling asleep would have been **surrounded with honour, death would have found her pure, and her crown would have been a virginal one**...**Had** she been martyred according to what is written: 'Thine own soul a sword shall pierce', then **she would shine gloriously** among the martyrs, and **her holy body would have been declared blessed**; for by her, did light come to the world."*

- Epiphanius, *Panarion* 78:23 (A.D. 377)

*"If anyone does not believe that Holy **Mary is the Mother of God**, he is severed from the Godhead."*

- Gregory of Nazianzus, *To Cledonius*, 101 (A.D. 382)

*"Mary, a Virgin not only undefiled but a Virgin **whom Grace has made inviolate, free of every stain of sin**."*

- Ambrose, *Sermon* 22:30 (A.D. 388)

*"We **must except** the Holy Virgin Mary, concerning whom **I wish to raise no question when it touches the subject of sins**, out of honour to the Lord; for **from Him we know what abundance of grace for overcoming sin in every particular was conferred upon her who had the merit to conceive and bear Him** who*

undoubtedly had no sin."

- Augustine, *Nature and Grace* (A.D.415)

"**Hail, Mary,** you are the most precious creature in the whole world; hail, Mary, **uncorrupt dove**; hail, Mary, inextinguishable lamp; for from you was born the Sun of justice...**through you, every faithful soul achieves salvation**."

- Cyril of Alexandria, *Homily 11* at Ephesus (A.D. 431)

"A virgin, ***innocent, spotless, free of all defect, untouched, unsullied, holy in soul and body,*** *like a lily sprouting among thorns."*

- Theodotus of Ancrya, *Homily* VI:11(A.D. 446)

"The Apostles took up her body on a bier and placed it in a tomb; and they guarded it, expecting the Lord to come. ***And behold, again the Lord stood by them; and the holy body having been received, He commanded that it be taken in a cloud into paradise: where now, rejoined to the soul, [Mary] rejoices with the Lord's chosen ones...***"

- Gregory of Tours, *Eight Books of Miracles*, 1:4 (~A.D. 575-593)

What is the Communion of the Saints?

Isn't prayer supposed to be directed to God alone? After all, he is the only mediator. Besides, the saints in heaven can't hear us, anyway.

Just the Facts, Please! *Dispelling Ignorance*

CATECHISM OF THE CATHOLIC CHURCH

956 "**Being more closely united to Christ, those who dwell in heaven fix the whole Church more firmly in holiness.... They do not cease to intercede with the Father for us**, as they proffer the merits which they acquired on earth through the one mediator between God and men, Christ Jesus.... So by their fraternal concern is our weakness greatly helped.

957 "**It is not merely by the title of example that we cherish the memory of those in heaven; we seek, rather, that by this devotion to the exercise of fraternal charity the union of the whole Church in the Spirit may be strengthened. Exactly as Christian communion among our fellow pilgrims brings us closer to Christ, so our communion with the saints joins us to Christ**, from whom as from its fountain and head issues all grace, and the life of the People of God itself"[496]:

959 "**For if we continue to love one another and to join in praising the Most Holy Trinity - all of us who are sons of God and form one family in Christ** - we will be faithful to the deepest vocation of the Church."[499]

960 **The Church is a "communion of saints": this expression refers first to the "holy things" (sancta), above all the Eucharist**, by which "the unity of believers, who form one body in Christ, is both represented and brought about" (LG 3).

961 **The term "communion of saints" refers also to the communion of "holy persons"** (sancti) in Christ who "died for all," so that what each one does or suffers in and for Christ bears fruit for all.

962 "**We believe in the communion of all the faithful of Christ, those who are pilgrims on earth, the dead who are

> **being purified, and the blessed in heaven, all together forming one Church;** and we believe that in this communion, the merciful love of God and his saints is always [attentive] to our prayers" (Paul VI, CPG # 30).

A good friend of mine once told me that his conversion to Christianity took place under the sad circumstances of his mother's passing. She had cancer. He said that the suffering he saw her undergo tore away at his soul. He wanted there to be meaning to his pain and some sense of hope. God opened his heart through the experience and he found what he was looking for in Christ Jesus.

My own dad passed away from cancer last October. I know the pain my friend went through. And just as God used that pain in his life, so he also did in mine. I was already Christian, but I was deeply immersed in my studies of Catholicism. The decision to become Catholic had already been made. And something wonderful occurred as my dad slipped from this world. As I held his hand on the hospital bed and watched him take his last breaths, tears started to flow – but hope began to overflow. I knew that through my faith, I was one with the Lord on earth. Thus, I was also one with those who were with the Lord in Purgatory and Heaven (unlike most Protestant impressions, Purgatory is not a "second chance area" between Heaven and Hell – it is the experience of personal purification that a Christian's soul undergoes in the transition from Earth to Heaven). The Holy Spirit bridged a gap between heaven and earth and through Him I had access to the City of God. What a wonderful hope! I can talk to my dad through the Holy Spirit because he is alive in Christ!

I know there are many Protestants that feel uncomfortable with this teaching. But do you have loved ones that have passed away? Have you ever wished that they were still around? To love and talk to? My guess is there may be many saints in heaven that feel the same way about the loved ones on earth who are ignoring them. Not that it would detract from their own perfect communion with God, of course. But look at it this way: many people leave flowers at the gravesites of their loved ones. A similar thing is going on when a Catholic lays flowers or some other token of love at the base of a saint's image.

There is one blessed difference, however. We Catholics can bow our heads in prayer in communion with the saints – the very family of God! It must be considered that Catholics, both Western and Eastern Orthodox, believe that not only can people in Heaven *perceive* us on Earth but that they can and do constantly *pray* for us as well. This has been historically held as a firm position through all the years of the New Covenant.

And not just the Catholics, but the Jews as well! Even if you do not regard the book of Maccabees as the Early Church did (canonical – the inspired Word of God), it still sheds light on the historical beliefs, customs, and general practices of our spiritual ancestors, the Jews. The intercession of saints in Heaven is illumined in 2 Maccabees 15:13-16 (NAB), *"Then in the same way another man appeared, distinguished by his white hair and dignity, and with an air about him of extraordinary, majestic authority. Onias then said of him, 'This is God's prophet Jeremiah, who loves his brethren and fervently prays for his people and their holy city.' Stretching out his right hand, Jeremiah presented a gold sword to Judas. As he gave it to him he said, 'Accept this holy sword as a gift from God; with it you shall crush your adversaries.'"*

Of course, Jeremiah had passed into eternal life long before this. Now, whether or not you agree that these events are historical you may at least appreciate that this demonstrates Hebrews did not find a problem with this doctrine. More evidence of this early held belief is found in Matt. 27:47-49 and Mark 15:35-36, where the people mistakenly interpret Christ's groaning words for a call to Heaven for Elijah's intercession. They don't take that as proof that Jesus was indeed a blasphemer. Instead, they wait to see if Elijah appears!

But wait…there's more: Not just the historical, ancient, branches of Catholic Christianity and not just the Jews; but to at least some degree, the Protestant Reformers as well. In the reference to his commentary on the Magnificat, Martin Luther wrote, "May the tender mother of God herself *procure for me* the Spirit of wisdom profitably and thoroughly to expound this song of hers." Luther here admits some trust in a heavenly saint's ability to intercede for him through prayer (in this case, Mary), even if he discounted the practice. Most of the neglect Protestants give toward their departed brethren in heaven is due to an inherited paranoia of becoming "too Catholic". Unfortunately, this causes them to miss out on *such* a vital part of the Christian life.

A particularly emphasized aspect of my old Protestant church was to find and regularly attend a small group. What a great idea! It is so very important to cultivate deep relationships with our brothers and sisters in Christ. We share our struggles with them, our sorrows, our fears, and our joys. And why? Because they are our family. They're here for us. We are connected as members of the Body of Christ – a very mystical and mysterious aspect of our Faith.

> *If we are so mystically joined, and there is only one Body of Christ, then why has a belief arisen that saints in heaven don't intercede for us?*

Together, we make up the One Body; the Bride of Christ. And through the redemptive incarnation of Christ, the Holy Spirit breaks through the barriers of time and space, allowing us to approach "the city of the living God, the heavenly Jerusalem, an innumerable company of angels, the general assembly and church of the firstborn, God the Judge of all, and to the spirits of just men made perfect" (Heb. 12:22-23). If we are so mystically joined, and there is only one Body of Christ, then why has a belief arisen that saints in heaven don't intercede for us? For the same reason small groups are important, and in the same way, cultivating devotions and relationships with the *entire* Family of God is a miraculous blessing!

And think of this: unlike our earthly brothers and sisters in Christ, those Family members in Heaven see as God sees – know as he knows – since they have been perfected in total union with the Trinity (1 Corinthians 13:12, 2 Corinthians 5:1-10). They always know just what to pray for – what you really need. And you don't have to worry about whether or not they have "time" to pray for you. Since Heaven is where God's infinite totality dwells, we know it is not confined to time and space. Thus, those who dwell with God in Heaven also exist outside of time and space. This means that at any given moment of Earth's "time", a saint in Heaven has literally all of *eternity* to pray for any specific request by any individual (without necessitating omniscience or omnipresence).

    James 5:16 tells us that the prayer of a righteous person is very powerful. But righteous people here on Earth are hard to come by – and if you find one, chances are he or she is already busy praying for *other* people. Heaven, on the other hand, has no shortage of righteous people. In fact, *everyone* in Heaven is righteous. Thank God for the intercession of Christ and the Holy Spirit, whose work grants access to all the host of heaven! Now, when we put our requests before the Father, we approach him with all the support and love of his complete and united Family. The Holy Spirit, our Counselor, acts as the Great Living Channel through which the rivers of prayer travel up to God; emptying out into the sea of the Father's infinite love for his children. What a wonderful love, joy, strength, encouragement, and peace!

Scripture Speaks! *What the Bible Says*

What if Christians are Co-Heirs, Co-Mediators, and Co-Redeemers through, with, and in Christ?

> John 10:11-16
> **I am the good shepherd**: the good shepherd giveth his life for the sheep. [12] But he that is an hireling, and not the shepherd, whose own the sheep are not, seeth the wolf coming, and leaveth the sheep, and fleeth: and the wolf catcheth them, and scattereth the sheep. [13] The hireling fleeth, because he is an hireling, and careth not for the sheep. [14] I am the good shepherd, and know my sheep, and am known of mine. [15] As the Father knoweth me, even so know I the Father: and I lay down my life for the sheep. [16] And other sheep I have, which are not of this fold: them also I must bring, and they shall hear my voice; and there shall be one fold, and one shepherd.

Jesus is the true Shepherd...

> John 21:15-17
> So when they had dined, Jesus saith to Simon Peter, Simon, son of Jonas, lovest thou me more than these? He saith unto him, Yea, Lord; thou knowest that I love thee. **He saith unto him, Feed my lambs.** [16] He saith to him again the second time, Simon, son of Jonas, lovest thou me? He saith unto him, Yea, Lord; thou knowest that I love thee. **He saith unto him, Feed my sheep.** [17] He saith unto him the third time, Simon, son of Jonas, lovest thou me? Peter was grieved because he said unto him the third time, Lovest thou me? And he said unto him, Lord, thou knowest all things; thou knowest that I love thee. **Jesus saith unto him, Feed my sheep.**

...yet he assigns lesser shepherds to take care of his sheep. Likewise God is the True Judge of all peoples...

> Matthew 19:28

And Jesus said unto them, Verily I say unto you, That ye which have followed me, in the regeneration when the Son of man shall sit in the throne of his glory, **ye also shall sit upon twelve thrones, judging the twelve tribes of Israel.**

1 Cor. 6:2-3
Do ye not know that the saints shall judge the world? and if the world shall be judged by you, are ye unworthy to judge the smallest matters? [3] **Know ye not that we shall judge angels?** how much more things that pertain to this life?

Rev. 20:4
And I saw thrones, and they sat upon them, and judgment was given unto them: and I saw the souls of them that were beheaded for the witness of Jesus, and for the word of God, and which had not worshipped the beast, neither his image, neither had received his mark upon their foreheads, or in their hands; and they lived and reigned with Christ a thousand years.

…yet he assigns lesser judges to take care of his kingdom.

1 Cor. 9:22
To the weak became I as weak, that I might gain the weak: I am made all things to all men, that **I might by all means save** some.

Ephes. 3:2
If ye have heard of the dispensation of the grace of God which is **given me to youward**:

1 Tim. 4:16
Take heed unto thyself, and unto the doctrine; continue in them: for in doing this **thou shalt both save thyself, and them that hear thee**.

1 Cor. 3:9
For we are **labourers together with God**: ye are God's husbandry, ye are God's building.

2 Cor. 6:1

> We then, **as workers together with him**, beseech you also that ye receive not the grace of God in vain.

We also see here further evidence that God deigns that we work with him in mediation and redemption, although God is the True Mediator and Redeemer.

What if the Church Remained United as One Body of Christ on Earth, in Purgatory, and Heaven?

> Ephes. 3:14-15
> For this cause I bow my knees unto the Father of our Lord Jesus Christ, [15] Of whom the whole family **in heaven and** earth is named

God makes certain we know we are One Family under One Name – a unity which transcends earthly death for those who are eternally alive, both in Heaven and Earth.

> Col. 1:24
> Who now rejoice in my sufferings for you, and fill up that which is behind of the afflictions of Christ in my flesh **for his body's sake, which is the church**:

> 1 Cor. 15:29
> Else what shall they do **which are baptized for the dead**, if the dead rise not at all? **why are they then baptized for the dead?**

We are all connected; "one" through union with the Church. When one suffers on behalf of another (e.g. "baptisms" of prayer, abstinence, almsgiving, or fasting), the whole Church benefits. The Church is one Body, connected between Earth, Purgatory, and Heaven. We are a vast number of cells working together as one organism. Christ is not divided!

> 2 Tim. 1:16-18
> The Lord give mercy **unto the house of** Onesiphorus; for he oft refreshed me, and was not ashamed of my chain: [17] But, when he was in Rome, he sought me out very diligently, and found me. [18] **The Lord grant unto him that he may find mercy of the Lord in that day:** and in how many things he ministered unto me at Ephesus, thou knowest very well.

Most theologians take this passage at face value; that Paul is eulogizing Onesiphorus, who appears to have died. He prays for

Onesiphorus's family and then for Onesiphorus himself. Regardless of whether Onesiphorus was alive on Earth, in Purgatory, or in Heaven, the point is the connection he still had with Paul. Onesiphorus is separated from Paul, but no matter the distance, he still exists in the same Body; Christ connects us all.

What if God Wants All the Members of His Body to Intercede for One Another?

> James 5:16
> Confess your faults one to another, and **pray one for another**, that ye may be healed. The effectual fervent prayer of **a righteous man availeth much**.

Here God commands us to be fervent intercessors and mediators for each other. We also see that the closer the person is to God, the more powerful their intercession is.

> Luke 18:1-8
> And he spake a parable unto them to this end, **that men ought always to pray, and not to faint**; [2] Saying, "There was in a city a judge, which feared not God, neither regarded man: [3] And there was a widow in that city; and she came unto him, saying, 'Avenge me of mine adversary.' [4] And he would not for a while: but afterward he said within himself, 'Though I fear not God, nor regard man; [5] **Yet because this widow troubleth me, I will avenge her, lest by her continual coming she weary me.**" [6] And the Lord said, **"Hear what the unjust judge saith. [7] And shall not God avenge his own elect, which cry day and night unto him, though he bear long with them? [8] I tell you that he will avenge them speedily.** Nevertheless when the Son of man cometh, shall he find faith on the earth?"

Our Lord outlined the proper spirit of prayer. Prayer is to be disciplined, faithful, and persistent. Many Protestants are uncomfortable with this passage, feeling it to be "too Catholic". But our God wants the Family to be in continual prayer for one another.

> John 2:3
> And when they wanted wine, **the mother of Jesus saith unto him**, They have no wine.

Like the persistent widow, though the Judge may appear not to enjoy hearing our pleas, he will nonetheless respond to them. Here, Mary is an example of this parable. Jesus knew the wine was gone. But he waits for his Mother's intercession and only then responds to the problem.

What if Christians Didn't Truly Die?

> 1 Samuel 28:12-15
> And when the woman saw Samuel, she cried with a loud voice: and the woman spake to Saul, saying, Why hast thou deceived me? for thou art Saul. [13] And the king said unto her, Be not afraid: for what sawest thou? And the woman said unto Saul, **I saw gods ascending out of the earth.** [14] And he said unto her, What form is he of? And she said, **An old man cometh up; and he is covered with a mantle. And Saul perceived that it was Samuel, and he stooped with his face to the ground, and bowed himself.**
> [15] And Samuel said to Saul, **Why hast thou disquieted me, to bring me up?** And Saul answered, I am sore distressed; for the Philistines make war against me, and God is departed from me, and answereth me no more, neither by prophets, nor by dreams: therefore I have called thee, that thou mayest make known unto me what I shall do.

Here, we see that though the saints pass away, their spirits are more alive than ever. Communion with the dead (necromancy) is forbidden but we see here that since Samuel is alive, he is able to dialogue – something which catches the witch, who is used to dealing with the souls of the lost (the truly dead), off guard.

> Jeremiah 15:1
> Then said the Lord unto me, "**Though Moses and Samuel stood before me**, yet my mind could not be toward this people: cast them out of my sight, and let them go forth."

Here God, who is Truth itself and can neither deceive nor be deceived, suggests that Moses and Samuel dwell with him – and that they are truly alive and well. Not only that, but the passage at least hints that they may hypothetically intercede on behalf of their friends, family, and nation.

> Matthew 17:1-3

> And after six days Jesus taketh Peter, James, and John his brother, and bringeth them up into an high mountain apart, [2] And was transfigured before them: and his face did shine as the sun, and his raiment was white as the light. [3] And, behold, **there appeared unto them Moses and Elias talking with him**.

Here, we see that in Heaven, the kind fellowship that was in the Garden of Eden is restored. Moses and Elijah enjoy a casual conversation with God in the cool of the day! If they could pray for others on earth…how much more so in Heaven?

What if the Saints in Heaven are like Angels?

Matthew 22:30
For in the resurrection they neither marry, nor are given in marriage, but **are as the angels of God in heaven**.

Pay attention to this verse; for God says that in Heaven, we are like angels. So what are angels like?

Luke 15:10
Likewise, I say unto you, there is **joy in the presence of the angels** of God over one sinner that repenteth.

…Well, for one, they are aware of any souls drawing near to God and able to celebrate it in a grand fashion!

1 Cor. 4:9
For I think that God hath set forth us the apostles last, as it were appointed to death: for we are **made a spectacle** unto the world, and **to angels**, and to men.

…Just as they can perceive the entire lives of souls still on earth.

Psalm 34:7
The angel of the Lord **encampeth round about them** that fear him, and **delivereth them.**

Psalm 91:11-12
For **he shall give his angels charge over thee, to keep thee in all thy ways.** [12] They shall bear thee up in their hands, lest thou dash thy foot against a stone.

Matthew 18:10
Take heed that ye despise not one of these little ones; for I say unto you, that **in heaven their angels do always behold the face of my Father** which is in heaven.

Hebrews 1:13-14
But to which of **the angels** said he at any times, 'Sit on my right hand, until I make thine enemies thy footstool?'

> [14] **Are they not all ministering spirits, sent forth to minister for them who shall be heirs of salvation?**

Angels guard us, keep watch over us, and minister to us in the presence of the Holy Spirit…

> Rev. 8:3-4
> And **another angel came and stood at the altar**, having a golden censer; and there was given unto him much incense, that **he should offer it with the prayers of all saints** upon the golden altar which was before the throne. [4] And the smoke of the incense, which came with **the prayers of the saints, ascended up before God out of the angel's hand.**

…and the angels even offer up our prayers to God! If we are like the angels in Heaven, but with more – not any less – grace and power, what might these passages suggest our heavenly activities include?

What if Interaction between Heaven and Earth is Possible?

> Matthew 27:50-53
> Jesus, when he had cried again with a loud voice, yielded up the ghost. [51] And, behold, the veil of the temple was rent in twain from the top to the bottom; and the earth did quake, and the rocks rent; [52] And the graves were opened; and **many bodies of the saints which slept arose, [53] And came out of the graves after his resurrection, and went into the holy city, and appeared unto many.**

This is interaction between the living on earth and the living in Heaven at the highest degree! Truly, the members of Christ's Body are never cut off from each other!

> Rev. 5:8
> And when he had taken the book, the four beasts and four and twenty elders fell down before the Lamb, having every one of them harps, and golden vials full of odours, which are **the prayers of saints**.

Even when there aren't apparitions of the saints communicating with us, we can take heart in that they are busily offering up our prayers to God.

> Psalm 35:17
> **Lord, how long** wilt thou look on? rescue my soul from their destructions, my darling from the lions.

Here we read David's heart breaking prayer to God about the distress of earthly life...

> Rev. 6:9-10
> And when he had opened the fifth seal, I saw under the altar the souls of them that were slain for the word of God, and for the testimony which they held: [10] And they cried with a loud voice, saying, **How long, O Lord**, holy and true, dost thou not judge and avenge our blood on them that dwell on the earth?

…and here we see the martyrs in Heaven echoing that prayer.

What if the Church is Never Divided and there Exists Communion of All Saints?

> Hebrews 12:1
> Wherefore seeing **we also are compassed about with so great a cloud of witnesses**, let us lay aside every weight, and the sin which doth so easily beset us, and let us run with patience the race that is set before us

God reveals to us that there is an enormous "cloud" of witnesses to our lives and actions – both the good and the bad – but what is the context of this?

> Hebrews 12:22-24
> But ye are come unto mount Sion, **and unto the city** of the living God, **the heavenly Jerusalem**, and **to an innumerable company of angels**, [23] To the general assembly and church of the firstborn, which are written in heaven, and to God the Judge of all, **and to the spirits of just men made perfect,** [24] And to Jesus the mediator of the new covenant, and to the blood of sprinkling, that speaketh better things than that of Abel.

God says that cloud includes all the host of Heaven! We may not only come to God with our prayers, praises, joys, and struggles – but just as on earth, we may come to any or all of our departed brothers and sisters, and even the angels! All by the power of the Holy Spirit through the mediation of Jesus Christ's redemptive Incarnation, which broke the barrier between Heaven and Earth.

> Hebrews 12:28
> Wherefore we **receiving a kingdom** which cannot be moved, let us have grace, whereby we may serve God acceptably with reverence and godly fear

Paul, inspired by God, gives final clarification in a summary by reminding us that we don't just receive the Heavenly

King, but the entire heavenly kingdom. Dear Brother, let's not waste such a gift and opportunity for family communion.

> Proverbs 15:29
> The Lord is far from the wicked: but he heareth the prayer of **the righteous.**

The more righteous the person who prays, the more that prayer avails the beneficiary. Logically then, the prayers of those who are perfected in Love by Grace in Heaven have the most powerful prayers.

> Psalm 148:1-2
> Praise ye the Lord. Praise ye the Lord from the heavens: praise him in the heights. [2] **Praise ye him, all his angels: praise ye him, all his hosts.**

No wonder David could in confident joy call the entire host of Heaven into praise of God!

Honor your Fathers! *The Elders Cry Out*

"[The Shepherd said:] 'But those who are weak and slothful in prayer, hesitate to ask anything from the Lord; but the Lord is full of compassion, and gives without fail to all who ask him. But you, [Hermas,] **having been strengthened by the holy angel** *[you saw],* **and having obtained from him such intercession***, and not being slothful, why do not you ask of the Lord understanding, and receive it from him?'"*

- Hermas, *The Shepherd of Hermas* 3:5:4 (A.D. 80).

"In this way is he [the true Christian] always pure for prayer. He also prays in the society of angels, as being already of angelic rank, and he is never out of their holy keeping; **and though he pray alone, he has the choir of the saints standing with him** *[in prayer]"*

- Clement of Alexandria, *Miscellanies* 7:12 (A.D. 208).

"As often as the anniversary comes round, we make **offerings for the dead** *as birthday honors."*

- Tertullian, *The Crown, 3* (A.D. 211)

"But not the high priest [Christ] alone prays for those who pray sincerely, but **also the angels . . . as also the souls of the saints who have already fallen asleep***"*

- Origen, *Prayer* 11 (A.D. 233)

"Let us remember one another in concord and unanimity. Let us **on both sides** *always pray for one another. Let us relieve burdens and afflictions by mutual love,* **that if one of us, by the swiftness of divine condescension, shall go hence first, our love may continue**

in the presence of the Lord, and our prayers for our brethren and sisters not cease in the presence of the Father's mercy."

- Cyprian of Carthage, *Epistles* 56:5 (A.D. 253)

*"Then we commemorate also those who have fallen asleep before us, first Patriarchs, Prophets, Apostles, Martyrs, **that at their prayers and intercessions God would receive our petition.**"*

- Cyril of Jerusalem, *Catechetical Lectures*, 23:9 (A.D. 350).

*"Thus might you console us; but what of the flock? Would you first promise the oversight and leadership of yourself, a man under whose wings we all would gladly repose, and for whose words we thirst more eagerly than men suffering from thirst for the purest fountain? Secondly, persuade us that the good shepherd who laid down his life for the sheep has not even now left us; but is present, and tends and guides, and knows his own, and is known of his own, and, **though bodily invisible, is spiritually recognized,** and defends his flock against the wolves, and allows no one to climb over into the fold as a robber and traitor; to pervert and steal away, by the voice of strangers, souls under the fair guidance of the truth. **Aye, I am well assured that his intercession is of more avail now than was his instruction in former days, since he is closer to God**, now that he has shaken off his bodily fetters, and freed his mind from the clay which obscured it, and holds intercourse naked with the nakedness of the prime and purest Mind; being promoted, if it be not rash to say so, to the rank and confidence of an angel."*

- John Chrysostom, *On the Death of his Father, Oration* 18:4 (A.D. 374)

*"Only may that power come upon us which **strengthens weakness, through the prayers of [St. Paul]** who made his own strength perfect in bodily weakness."*

- Gregory of Nyssa, *Against Eunomius*, 1:1(A.D. 380)

*"But God forbid that any in this fair assembly should appear there suffering such things! but **by the prayers of the holy fathers,** correcting all our offences, and having shown forth the abundant fruit of virtue, may we depart hence with much confidence."*

- John Chrysostom, *On Statues*, Homily 6:19 (A.D. 387)

*"A Christian people celebrate together in religious solemnity the memorials of the martyrs, both to encourage their being imitated and **so that it can share in their merits and be aided by their prayers.**"*

- Augustine, *Against Faustus the Manichean* (A.D. 400)

*"For you say that the souls of Apostles and martyrs have their abode either in the bosom of Abraham, or in the place of refreshment, or under the altar of God, and that they cannot leave their own tombs, and be present there they will…And while the devil and the demons wander through the whole world, and with only too great speed present themselves everywhere; are martyrs, after the shedding of their blood, to be kept out of sight shut up in a coffin, from whence they cannot escape? You say, in your pamphlet, that so long as we are alive we can pray for one another; but once we die, the prayer of no person for another can be heard, and all the more because the martyrs, though they cry for the avenging of their blood, have never been able to obtain their request. **If Apostles and martyrs while still in the body can pray for others, when they ought still to be anxious for themselves, how much more must they do so when once they have won their crowns, overcome, and triumphed?** A single man, Moses, oft wins pardon from God for six hundred thousand armed men; and Stephen, the follower of his Lord and the first Christian martyr, entreats pardon for his persecutors; **and when once they have entered on their life with Christ, shall they have less power***

than before? *The Apostle Paul says that two hundred and seventy-six souls were given to him in the ship;* **and when, after his dissolution, he has begun to be with Christ, must he shut his mouth, and be unable to say a word for those who throughout the whole world have believed in his Gospel? Shall Vigilantius the live dog be better than Paul the dead lion?** *I should be right in saying so after Ecclesiastes, if I admitted that Paul is dead in spirit.* **The truth is that the saints are not called dead,** *but are said to be asleep. Wherefore Lazarus, who was about to rise again, is said to have slept. And the Apostle forbids the Thessalonians to be sorry for those who were asleep."*

- Jerome, *Against Vigilantius*, 6 (A.D. 406)

What is the Mass?

Isn't the Mass full of pagan origins? How can it be a sacrifice when Jesus was only sacrificed once for all? Aren't the bread and wine merely symbols?

Just the Facts, Please! *Dispelling Ignorance*

CATECHISM OF THE CATHOLIC CHURCH

1407 The Eucharist is the heart and the summit of the Church's life, for in it Christ associates his Church and all her members with his sacrifice of praise and thanksgiving offered once for all on the cross to his Father; by this sacrifice he pours out the graces of salvation on his Body which is the Church.

1408 The Eucharistic celebration always includes: the proclamation of the Word of God; thanksgiving to God the Father for all his benefits, above all the gift of his Son; the consecration of bread and wine; and participation in the liturgical banquet by receiving the Lord's body and blood. These elements constitute one single act of worship.

1409 The Eucharist is the memorial of Christ's Passover, that is, of the work of salvation accomplished by the life, death, and resurrection of Christ, a work made present by the liturgical action.

1410 It is Christ himself, the eternal high priest of the New Covenant who, acting through the ministry of the priests, offers the Eucharistic sacrifice. And it is the same Christ, really present under the species of bread and wine, who is the offering of the Eucharistic sacrifice.

1413 By the consecration the transubstantiation of the bread and wine into the Body and Blood of Christ is brought about. Under the consecrated species of bread and wine Christ himself, living and glorious, is present in a true, real, and substantial manner: his Body and his Blood, with his soul and his divinity (cf. Council of Trent: DS 1640; 1651).

1419 Having passed from this world to the Father, Christ gives us in the Eucharist the pledge of glory with him.

> Participation in the Holy Sacrifice identifies us with his Heart, sustains our strength along the pilgrimage of this life, makes us long for eternal life, and unites us even now to the Church in heaven, the Blessed Virgin Mary, and all the saints.

The Mass is the heart of the Church. Why? Because in the Mass, the Family of God is made most fully known. God wants total communion with humanity. As soon as the Fall took place, God immediately busied Himself with the restoration of fellowship man had lost with Him. We see the progressive development of a complex system of commands and regulations in the Old Testament, revealed by the direct instruction of God so that man best may come to know Him. As more was revealed, previous methods of discerning that relationship were understood with greater clarity. The reason for this is that only in retrospect could God's people really understand what God was preparing them for: deeper, heavenly realities. He did this through the use of symbols and types. Everything pointed to God. The common theme was sacrifice – eventually the whole cultural and theological world of Israel revolved around one sacrifice in particular; that of the Passover.

If the greater context and meaning of these things are only understood in their fulfillment, then the atonement made by Jesus on the cross must be intimately connected to the Passover. Only when the Paschal Lamb was consumed was the Passover complete – only then was atonement fully realized. It makes sense then, that when Jesus stopped short while celebrating the Last Supper (which took place in the context of the "seder meal" of the Passover) and only consummated it with the final drink of wine on the cross, he could cry out "It is finished!" His sacrifice was and is connected to the Last Supper – communion with Him is totally achieved when the sacrificed Lamb of the Passover is eaten.

That's the chief reason blood wasn't allowed as drink in the Old Testament; the sacrifices of the Old Covenant were merely *types* and *shadows* of their ultimate fulfillment. There was no cause to partake in the life (the blood) of an animal. God's people were not to be in communion with a *lamb*. They were to be in communion with *God*! And that's why it was only after God came down to man that His blood alone – his life – could be consumed. Thusly Peter can boldly pronounce that we are partakers of the Divine Nature (2 Pet. 1:4), having become one Flesh and one Body with God. This can only occur during what Catholics call the Eucharist.

    The word "Eucharist" means thanksgiving. That's because every time Christ's sacrifice is offered in the Eucharist, it is a "love feast" of thanks and praise. Now, don't understand this in the wrong way. The Church believes that Christ was sacrificed "once for all" and there is no longer a need for the priests of Moses to offer endless numbers of lambs. Instead, the priests of Christ offer one Lamb, under the appearance of bread and wine. Neither are we re-crucifying Christ.

    Remember that although the crucifixion happened *within* time, it also *transcends* time, so that anyone today can benefit from it. In a similar way, when the bread and wine are consecrated by the priest (that is, Christ through the priest says, "This is my Body" and "This is my Blood), they are no longer bread and wine. They have not been transformed (their physics and appearance remain the same), but they have been *transubstantiated* (their metaphysics and substance have been changed).

> ***Jesus is come in the flesh among us! What could be greater?***

By the Word of God, they have become the Body, Blood, Soul, and Divinity of Jesus Christ – in other words the *fullness* of God incarnate – while he hung there on that cross. That one sacrifice transcends time and space to be present wherever it is sacrificially offered in the Eucharist. This happens at the Mass.

    It's called Mass because the word "mass" comes from the Latin, "missa", which loosely means "the sending". Why is that significant? Because every time you go to Mass and receive the Eucharist, you are consummating both your relationship with Christ (by becoming one flesh with Him) and your Passover sacrifice (consuming the lamb is the final and vital step) – so you are fully equipped with a renewed Covenant and the Grace that comes with it! You're ready to spread the Word, share the Good News, serve others in love, and praise God for all the blessings He's given you. You are *sent!*

But why all those "bells and whistles", so to speak? Why all the ritual? The extra devotions and disciplines? Because they help draw us in to the presence of God. They are signs of our respect and love for him. Beyond that, these signs are communal; so they help bring the Family together! Greeting and blessing one another, hearing God's Word and praising Him for it, sharing a meal that bonds us together, singing…these are all Family activities! The Mass is a heavenly Family reunion in which all the angels and saints join us in prayer, praise, and thanksgiving. But more than that, the incarnated Jesus is come in the flesh among us! What could be greater?

Scripture Speaks! *What the Bible Says*

What if the Eucharist is Necessary to Fulfill Scripture?

> Genesis 14:18
> And Melchizedek king of Salem brought forth **bread and wine: and he was the priest** of the most high God.

Our first presentation of a priest in Scripture is one who offers bread and wine, pronouncing blessings.

> Psalm 110:4
> The Lord hath sworn, and will not repent, **Thou art a priest for ever after the order of Melchizedek.**

If Christ is a priest like Melchizedek, then what would he offer with blessings?

> Malachi 1:11
> For from **the rising of the sun even unto the going down of the same my name shall be great among the Gentiles; and in every place incense shall be offered unto my name, and a pure offering**: for my name shall be great among the heathen, saith the Lord of hosts.

How is this prophecy fulfilled, today? What Church is globally situated, populating every continent, comprised mostly of Gentiles, and offering incense and a pure offering usually several times a day?

> Exodus 12:43-45
> And the Lord said unto Moses and Aaron, This is the ordinance of the passover: **There shall no stranger eat thereof:** [44] But every man's servant that is bought for money, when thou hast circumcised him, then shall he eat thereof. [45] **A foreigner and an hired servant shall not eat thereof.**

> Ezekiel 44:9

> Thus saith the Lord God; **No stranger, uncircumcised in heart, nor uncircumcised in flesh, shall enter into my sanctuary,** of any stranger that is among the children of Israel.

Here we see that one must be a member of the *visible Family* of God's Covenant in order to receive and consume the Passover lamb. In what Church is this command fulfilled and obeyed with the Lamb of God?

> Exodus 24:9-11
> Then went up Moses, and Aaron, Nadab, and Abihu, and seventy of the elders of Israel: [10] And they saw the God of Israel: and there was under his feet as it were a paved work of a sapphire stone, and as it were the body of heaven in his clearness. [11] And upon the nobles of the children of Israel he laid not his hand: **also they saw God, and did eat and drink.**

We see this Covenant consummated with a supper in the presence of God. How is the New Covenant consummated? And how is it as "in the presence of God" as this?

> Exodus 29:33
> And **they shall eat those things wherewith the atonement was made**, to consecrate and to sanctify them: but a stranger shall not eat thereof, because they are holy.

If Christ made our atonement, how must we fulfill this passage?

> Leviticus 7:15
> And **the flesh of the sacrifice** of his peace **offerings for thanksgiving** shall be **eaten the same day that it is offered**; he shall not leave any of it until the morning.

Communion with God isn't completed until the flesh of the sacrifice is consumed. Coincidentally, "Eucharist" comes from the Greek word "eukaristia" which means "thanksgiving".

Hebrews 13:15
> By him therefore let us offer the **sacrifice of praise** to God continually, that is, **the fruit of our lips giving thanks** to his name.

If the New Covenant must fulfill the Old, then to what does this refer?

Leviticus 7:12-15
> If he **offer it for a thanksgiving**, then he shall offer with the **sacrifice of thanksgiving** unleavened cakes mingled with oil, and **unleavened wafers** anointed with oil, and cakes mingled with oil, of fine flour, fried. [13] Besides the cakes, he shall offer for his offering leavened bread with the **sacrifice of thanksgiving** of his peace offerings. [14] And of it he shall offer one out of the whole oblation for an heave offering unto the Lord, and it shall be the priest's that sprinkleth the blood of the peace offerings. [15] **And the flesh of the sacrifice of his peace offerings for thanksgiving shall be eaten the same day that it is offered**; he shall not leave any of it until the morning.

Leviticus 22:29-30
> And **when ye will offer a sacrifice of thanksgiving** unto the Lord, offer it at your own will. [30] On **the same day it shall be eaten up**; ye shall leave none of it until the morrow: I am the Lord.

We see it refers again to wafers of bread having some kind of connection to a sacrificed lamb, which must be eaten – in the Old Covenant. Rabbinic tradition says that this offering, the "todah", will never cease. So what is the connection between the sacrifice of thanksgiving and the New Covenant if not the Eucharist?

What if Christ is the Passover Lamb and Must Fulfill the Law?

Matthew 26:2
Ye know that after two days **is the feast of the Passover**, and **the Son of man is betrayed to be crucified.**

Mark 14:12
And the first day of unleavened bread, when they killed the Passover, his disciples said unto him, **Where wilt thou that we go and prepare that thou mayest eat the Passover?**

Luke 22:7
Then came **the day of unleavened bread**, when **the Passover** must be killed.

John 1:29
The next day John seeth Jesus coming unto him, and saith, **Behold the Lamb of God**, which taketh away the sin of the world.

John 1:36
And looking upon Jesus as he walked, he saith, **Behold the Lamb of God!**

Acts 8:32
The place of the scripture which he read was this, **He was led as a sheep to the slaughter;** and like a lamb dumb before his shearer, so opened he not his mouth:

1 Peter 1:19
But with the precious blood of Christ, **as of a lamb without blemish** and without spot:

The crucifixion of Christ is clearly seen to be the new Passover.

Exodus 12:8
And they **shall eat the flesh in that night**, roast with fire, and unleavened bread; and with bitter herbs they shall eat it.

Exodus 12:11
> And thus **shall ye eat it**; with your loins girded, your shoes on your feet, and your staff in your hand; and ye shall eat it in haste: **it is the Lord's Passover**.

Notice that the Passover Lamb had to be consumed in its entirety. If Christ is our Passover Lamb, the fulfillment of this passage, what are we instructed to do?

Exodus 12:14
> And this day shall be unto you for **a memorial**; and ye shall keep it **a feast** to the Lord throughout your generations; **ye shall keep it a feast by an ordinance for ever**.

Exodus 12:17
> And ye shall **observe the feast of unleavened bread**; for in this selfsame day have I brought your armies out of the land of Egypt: therefore shall ye observe this day in your generations by an ordinance **for ever**.

Exodus 12:24
> And ye shall observe this thing for **an ordinance to thee and to thy sons for ever**.

This "feast" of the lamb; this offering of bread; this Passover memorial; it was to last *forever*. That means the New Covenant may fulfill it – but it has to be kept and reenacted some way.

1 Cor. 5:7
> Purge out therefore the old leaven, that ye may be a new lump, as ye are unleavened. For even **Christ our Passover is sacrificed** for us:

To fulfill the Law, the Passover Lamb has been sacrificed…

1 Cor. 5:8

> Therefore let us **keep the feast**, not with old leaven, neither with the leaven of malice and wickedness; but with the unleavened bread of sincerity and truth.

…and so to fulfill the Law, the Passover Lamb must be eaten, whole.

What if Christ's Flesh is the Manna From Heaven?

Exodus 16:4, 14, 31, 35
Then said the Lord unto Moses, Behold, **I will rain bread from heaven** for you; and the people shall go out and gather a certain rate every day, that I may prove them, whether they will walk in my law, or no.

[14] And when the dew that lay was gone up, behold, upon the face of the wilderness there lay **a small round thing**, as small as the hoar frost on the ground. [15] And when the children of Israel saw it, they said one to another, **It is manna: for they wist not what it was.** And Moses said unto them, **This is the bread which the Lord hath given you to eat.**

[31] And the house of Israel called the name thereof Manna: and **it was like coriander seed, white; and the taste of it was like wafers made with honey.**

[35] And the children of Israel **did eat manna forty years**, until they came to a land inhabited; they did eat manna, until they came unto the borders of the land of Canaan.

Neh. 9:15
And gavest them bread from heaven for their hunger...

John 6:31
Our fathers did eat manna in the desert; as it is written, He gave them **bread from heaven to eat**.

John 6:49
Your fathers **did eat** manna in the wilderness, and are dead.

John 6:50-53
This is the bread which cometh down from heaven, that a man may eat thereof, and not die. [51] **I am the living bread which came down from heaven:** if any man **eat** of this bread, he shall live for ever: and the bread

that I will give **is my flesh**, which I will give for the life of the world.

The manna that came down from heaven was not a symbol or metaphor. It was real, substantial, and had to be eaten. Christ says he is the real manna and that he must be eaten. When does Christ say that he's speaking metaphorically? Do the people listening perceive it as obvious symbolism? What Church most takes the Word of God at face value, here? And where are these passages about white, round, wafers fulfilled?

> 2 Kings 4:40-44
> And there came a man from Baal-shalisha, and brought the man of God bread of the firstfruits, **twenty loaves** of barley, and full ears of corn in the husk thereof. And he said, Give unto the people, that they may eat. [43] And his servitor said, What, **should I set this before an hundred men**? He said again, Give the people, that they may eat: for **thus saith the Lord, They shall eat, and shall leave thereof.** [44] So he set it before them, and **they did eat, and left thereof**, according to the word of the Lord.

Multiplication of the loaves…what does this remind you of? And why would it be important enough to foreshadow in the Old Testament? Who is the true bread from heaven?

> Ezekiel 2:8-10
> But thou, son of man, hear what I say unto thee; Be not thou rebellious like that rebellious house: **open thy mouth, and eat that I give thee.**
> [9] And when I looked, behold, an hand was sent unto me; and, lo, a roll of a book was therein; [10] And he spread it before me; and it was written within and without: and there was written therein lamentations, and mourning, and woe.
>
> Ezekiel 3:1-3
> Moreover he said unto me, **Son of man, eat that thou findest; eat this roll**, and go speak unto the house of Israel. [2] **So I opened my mouth, and he caused me to eat that roll.** [3] And he said unto me, Son of man, cause

thy belly to eat, and fill thy bowels with this roll that I give thee. Then did I eat it; and **it was in my mouth as honey for sweetness**.

A few things worth mentioning, here. First, Ezekiel is commanded to literally and physically eat the Word of God. Does that seem to foreshadow anything to you? Second, he says it tasted like honey. What did the manna from heaven taste like? What is the true manna from heaven?

What if Christ's Blood is the Only Source of Life?

> Leviticus 17:11
> For **the life of the flesh is in the blood**: and I have given it to you upon the altar to make an atonement for your souls: for **it is the blood that maketh an atonement for the soul.**

> Leviticus 17:14
> For it is the life of all flesh; the blood of it is for the life thereof: therefore I said unto the children of Israel, **Ye shall eat the blood of no manner of flesh: for the life of all flesh is the blood thereof**: whosoever eateth it shall be cut off.

> Genesis 9:4-5
> But flesh with the life thereof, which is **the blood thereof, shall ye not eat**. [5] And surely your blood of your lives will I require; at the hand of every beast will I require it, and at the hand of man; at the hand of every man's brother will I require the life of man.

> Deut. 12:16
> Only **ye shall not eat the blood**; ye shall pour it upon the earth as water.

> Deut. 12:23-24
> Only be sure that thou eat not the blood: for the blood is the life; and **thou mayest not eat the life with the flesh.** [24] Thou shalt not eat it; thou shalt pour it upon the earth as water.

Why, under the Old Covenant, could the blood not be consumed (besides sanitary reasons)? Because the life was in it. Why and how were the children of the Old Covenant (before Christ) cut off from the Life? Who is our only source of life? Does he command us to drink from that source? Why did God wait until the incarnation to command us to drink his blood? (see John 6)

What if We Must Eat the Passover Lamb to Consummate our Passover?

> Luke 2:7
> And she brought forth her firstborn son, and wrapped him in swaddling clothes, and laid him **in a manger**; because there was no room for them in the inn.
>
> Luke 2:12
> And this shall be a sign unto you; Ye shall find the babe wrapped in swaddling clothes, **lying in a manger.**

Do you know what a manger is? A feeding trough. When the Lamb of God was born, He was laid in a feeding trough. And in what city? Bethlehem. Bethlehem means "house of bread". When the Passover Lamb was born into this world, it was onto a feeding trough in the house of bread. Think God's trying to tell us something?

What if Christ's One Sacrifice Transcends Time and Space in Order to be Re-Presented in the Eucharist?

> Numbers 10:10
> Also in the day of your gladness, and in your solemn days, and in the beginnings of your months, ye shall blow with the trumpets over your burnt offerings, and over **the sacrifices of your peace offerings; that they may be to you for a memorial** before your God: I am the Lord your God.

We see that a "memorial" doesn't have to mean "symbolism".

> Luke 22:19
> And he took bread, and gave thanks, and brake it, and gave unto them, saying, This **is** my body which is given for you: this do in **remembrance** of me.

In fact, if the author wanted to specify that it was strictly a memorial he could have. There is a Greek word, "mnemosunon" that refers strictly to remembrance, not necessarily a reenactment (see Acts 10:4 as an example where that's used). Instead, Luke chooses to use the word "anamnesis", which refers to a sacrifice. Further, even the word he uses for "do" ("poiein") refers to a sacrifice. Why?

> Hebrews 9:23
> It was therefore necessary that the patterns of things in the heavens should be purified with these; but the heavenly things themselves with better **sacrifices** than these.

This passage teaches us that things foreshadowed in the Old Covenant are better fulfilled in the New. However, why when referring to the sacrificial system of the Old Covenant does the author use the plural form of sacrifice when referring to the New? Christ was sacrificed once for all, he's not re-sacrificed…unless that one sacrifice transcends time and space – which is exactly what the Catholic Church has always taught.

> 1 Cor. 10:17-18
> For we being many are **one bread, and one body**: for we are all partakers of **that one bread.** [18] Behold Israel after the flesh: are not they which **eat of the sacrifices partakers of the altar**?

Far from meat sacrificed to idols, when we partake of the Eucharist, we partake of Christ's sacrifice and become blood-relatives, bonded together by the Body of Christ.

> 1 Cor. 10:21
> Ye cannot drink the cup of the Lord, and the cup of devils: ye cannot be partakers of **the Lord's table**, and of the table of devils.

Paul here refers to the Eucharistic feast as being an altar of sacrifice. How can we be sure? The Jews unmistakably connected the phrase "table of the Lord" with the altar upon which a sacrifice was made…

> Leviticus 24:6
> And thou shalt set them in two rows, six on a row, upon the pure **table before the Lord**.

> Ezekiel 41:22
> The altar of wood was three cubits high, and the length thereof two cubits; and the corners thereof, and the length thereof, and the walls thereof, were of wood: and he said unto me, This is **the table that is before the Lord**.

> Malachi 1:7
> Ye offer polluted bread upon mine altar; and ye say, Wherein have we polluted thee? In that ye say, **The table of the Lord** is contemptible.

…and would have immediately understood the expression as the altar of the Eucharistic sacrifice.

What if Christ makes it Clear?

> John 6:4
> And the **Passover**, a feast of the Jews, was nigh.

Before Christ launches into the serious proclamations contained in chapter six, notice the immediate context of the situation. When was this taking place? Right before the Passover, when the Paschal lambs were being gathered to be sacrificed and *consumed* only a short time later.

> John 6:33-34
> For **the bread of God is he which cometh down from heaven**, and giveth life unto the world. [34] Then said they unto him, Lord, evermore give us this bread.

The Jews didn't quite grasp what Jesus was saying at first…

> John 6:35
> And Jesus said unto them, **I am the bread** of life: he that cometh to me shall never hunger; and he that believeth on me shall never thirst.

So Jesus clarifies…

> John 6:47
> Verily, verily, I say unto you, He that believeth on me hath everlasting life. [48] **I am that bread of life.**

…repeats himself, emphasizing the need for faith…

> John 6:49-51
> Your fathers did **eat manna** in the wilderness, and are dead. [50] This is the bread which cometh down from heaven, that **a man may eat thereof**, and not die.

...and clarifies again, this time using a story they all know. The manna that came down from heaven for Israelites was real – *substantial* – and they ate it and lived off of it. You can imagine some eyebrows, furrowing in confusion.

> John 6:51
> **I am the living bread** which came down from heaven: if any man **eat** of this bread, he shall live for ever: and **the bread that I will give is my flesh**, which I will give for the life of the world.

Yet Jesus reiterates the connection again, making it even clearer. Then he restates that the bread is his flesh, eliminating any possible doubt as to what he's trying to say.

> John 6:52
> The Jews therefore strove among themselves, saying, **How** can this man give us his **flesh to eat**?

"Ok," we can imagine them saying, "That's it. The guy's a loon." They knew perfectly well that Christ wasn't speaking metaphorically, anymore. He actually expected them to have the child-like faith necessary to believe that his literal, physical, flesh-and-blood self could be consumed?

> John 6:53
> Then Jesus said unto them, **Verily, verily**, I say unto you, Except ye **eat the flesh** of the Son of man, **and drink his blood**, ye have no life in you.

Apparently so. "Truly, truly," he says, adamant he get the fact engraved in their heads. He repeats himself again...

> John 6:54
> Whoso **eateth my flesh, and drinketh my blood**, hath eternal life; and I will raise him up at the last day.

...and again...

> John 6:55
> For **my flesh is meat indeed, and my blood is drink indeed.**

…and again…

> John 6:56
> He that **eateth my flesh, and drinketh my blood,** dwelleth in me, and I in him.

…and again…

> John 6:57
> As the living Father hath sent me, and I live by the Father: so he that **eateth me,** even he shall live by me.

…and again…

> John 6:58
> This is that bread which came down from heaven: not as your fathers did eat manna, and are dead: **he that eateth of this bread shall live for ever.**

…and again. If you want to dig really deep, I suggest you look up his words in the Greek. Throughout his speech, he uses progressively more graphic vocabulary to describe the consumption of his flesh. Finally, he recaps with the same connection to the real, tangible, manna that the Israelites had to physically consume.

> John 6:60
> Many therefore of his disciples, when they had heard this, said, **This is an hard saying**; who can hear it?

Those disciples knew exactly what Jesus meant. It certainly wasn't like referring to himself as "the door" – not only was the use and meaning of that metaphor obvious, but to compare it to this he would have to have said something like, "I am the door; he that doesn't receive splinters from my wood will not enter heaven!" No, this time he couldn't be clearer. He had never repeated himself so much. He had never gone through such painstaking efforts to drive the point home... nor had he corrected what would have been a fatal misunderstanding, as he did in other instances, such as this:

> Matthew 16:5-12
> And when his disciples were come to the other side, they had forgotten to take bread. Then Jesus said unto them, Take heed and beware of the leaven of the Pharisees and of the Sadducees. [7] And they reasoned among themselves, saying, It is because we have taken no bread. [8] Which **when Jesus perceived, he said unto them, O ye of little faith, why reason ye among yourselves, because ye have brought no bread?** [9] Do ye not yet understand, neither remember the five loaves of the five thousand, and how many baskets ye took up? [10] Neither the seven loaves of the four thousand, and how many baskets ye took up? [11] **How is it that ye do not understand that I spake it not to you concerning bread,** that ye should beware of the leaven of the Pharisees and of the Sadducees? [12] **Then understood they how that he bade them** not beware of the leaven of bread, but of the doctrine of the Pharisees and of the Sadducees.

When they got it wrong, Jesus told them.

> John 6:61
> When Jesus knew in himself that his disciples murmured at it, he said unto them, **Doth this offend you?**

Instead, he sees they understood it correctly, yet are having a hard time buying it.

> John 6:63-65
> It is the **spirit** that quickeneth; the **flesh** profiteth nothing: **the words that I speak unto you, they are spirit, and they are life.** [64] But there are some of you **that believe not.** For Jesus knew from the beginning who they were that believed not, and who should betray him. [65] And he

said, Therefore said I unto you, that no man can come unto me, **except it were given unto him of my Father**.

So he chastises them! Faith in God trumps human understanding any day. Only by the help of the Father can a person have such childlike faith. Our meager brains (the flesh) certainly can't figure it out – because it's something *of God* (the Holy Spirit). Jesus used similar language to say this in another passage:

> John 8:15-16
> **Ye judge after the flesh**; I judge no man. [16] And yet if I judge, my judgment is true: for I am not alone, but I and the Father that sent me.

Here again Christ rebukes those who try to limit God's ways to the confines of human understanding. And guess what?

> John **6:66**
> From that time many of his disciples went back, **and walked no more with him**.

…They got the message loud and clear. There was no room for error, here. Christ was not speaking in parables, riddles, or metaphors. He was perfectly clear. And they just didn't have the faith to apprehend it. Does Jesus stop them? Does he take this opportune moment to explain the physics and metaphysics of transubstantiation? And how with God all things are possible?

> John 6:67
> Then said Jesus unto the twelve, **Will ye also go away?**

No. Sorrowful, disappointed, frustrated; he turns to his disciples and asks the simple, desperate, question of whether or not they'll abandon Him too.

> John 6:68-69
> Then Simon Peter answered him, Lord, to whom shall we go? **thou hast the words of eternal life.** [69] And we

> believe and are sure that thou art that Christ, the Son of the living God.

At least they got it. If the Word of God speaks it, it's Truth.

> 1 Cor. 10:16
> The cup of blessing which we bless, is it not the communion of **the blood of Christ**? The bread which we break, is it not the communion of **the body of Christ**?

Paul certainly grasped this! His questions read almost rhetorically, as if he's stating the obvious to those who take it for granted.

> 1 Cor. 11:27
> Wherefore whosoever shall eat this bread, and drink this cup of the Lord, unworthily, **shall be guilty of the body and blood of the Lord**.

> 1 Cor. 11:29
> For he that eateth and drinketh unworthily, eateth and drinketh damnation to himself, **not discerning the Lord's body**.

He leaves no room for question, here. How can you answer for the body and blood of someone (tantamount to serious murder) if all you've profaned is a symbol? No, in the Holy Eucharist we must discern the whole Paschal Lamb; Body, Blood, Soul, and Divinity.

> Matthew 26:26-28
> And as they were eating, Jesus took bread, and blessed it, and brake it, and gave it to the disciples, and said, Take, eat; this **is** my **body**. [27] And he took the cup, and gave thanks, and gave it to them, saying, Drink ye all of it; [28] For this **is** my **blood of the new testament**, which is shed for many for the remission of sins.

> Mark 14:22

> And as they did eat, Jesus took bread, and blessed, and brake it, and gave to them, and said, Take, eat: this **is** my **body**.

> Mark 14:24
> And he said unto them, This is my **blood of the new testament**, which is shed for many.

> Luke 22:19-20
> And he took bread, and gave thanks, and brake it, and gave unto them, saying, This **is** my **body** which is given for you: this do in remembrance of me. [20] Likewise also the cup after supper, saying, This cup **is** the new testament in my **blood**, which is shed for you.

Finally, let's not ignore the plain fact that in gospel accounts of the Last Supper, the incarnated Word of God declared "this *is* my body", "this *is* my blood"! Then he plainly instructs us to remember what he did at that supper and repeat it. Why has there ever been room for doubt? There wasn't, for so very many centuries…but as the history of heresy has shown, anything that *can* be twisted in Scripture eventually *is*.

> Exodus 24:8
> And Moses took the blood, and sprinkled it on the people, and said, Behold **the blood of the covenant**, which the Lord hath made with you concerning all these words.

In fact, the language Jesus chose even refers directly to the language of the Law. The blood of the Covenant must be real, and the life must be in it, or the sacrifice and consumption of the Passover Lamb is utterly meaningless.

What if the Celebration of the Mass is Understood in Scripture?

> Acts 2:42
> And they continued stedfastly in the apostles' **doctrine** and **fellowship**, and in **breaking of bread**, and in **prayers**.

Here we have the rubric for the entire Mass! The Liturgy of the Word (doctrine) with greetings and intercessions (fellowship) and the Liturgy of the Eucharist (the breaking of bread) with prayers of praise and thanksgiving.

> Matthew 6:11
> Give us this day **our daily bread**.

Ever wondered if there might be a little bit more of a specific meaning to this line of the Lord's Prayer?

> Matthew 19:6
> Wherefore they are no more twain, but **one flesh**. What therefore God hath joined together, let not man put asunder.

If Christ is married to the Church, when does he become one flesh with her?

> Ephes. 1:22-23
> And hath put all things under his feet, and gave him to be the head over all things to the church, [23] **Which is his body**, the fulness of him that filleth all in all.

> Ephes. 5:30-32
> For we are members of his body, **of his flesh**, and of his bones. [31] For this cause shall a man leave his father and mother, and shall be joined unto his wife, and they two shall be one flesh. [32] **This is a great mystery: but I speak concerning Christ and the church.**

Christ left his Heavenly Father and his earthly Mother, joined himself to the Church in his life of self-giving love, and then became one flesh with her. But how? Through the Eucharist! (see 1 Cor. 10:17)

> Luke 24:26-31
> Ought not Christ to have suffered these things, and to enter into his glory? [27] And beginning at Moses and all the prophets, **he expounded unto them in all the scriptures the things concerning himself.** [28] And they drew nigh unto the village, whither they went: and he made as though he would have gone further. [29] But they constrained him, saying, Abide with us: for it is toward evening, and the day is far spent. And he went in to tarry with them. [30] And it came to pass, **as he sat at meat with them, he took bread, and blessed it, and brake, and gave to them. [31] And their eyes were opened, and they knew him;** and he vanished out of their sight.

Again we see the structure for the Mass; the Liturgy of the Word followed by the Liturgy of the Eucharist. Also notice that it wasn't until Christ consecrated the bread as his body that they perceived his presence. And as soon as they knew him in what was once the bread, he vanished.

> 2 Peter 1:4
> Whereby are given unto us exceeding great and precious promises: that by these **ye might be partakers of the divine nature**, having escaped the corruption that is in the world through lust.

How can we truly partake of the Divine Nature unless we receive the Body, Blood, Soul, and Divinity of Christ into our bodies? The Eucharist makes this exceedingly great and precious promise a reality!

What if Elements of the Mass are in Revelations?

> Rev. 1:10
> I was in the Spirit on **the Lord's day**, and heard behind me a great voice, as of a trumpet,

First we notice that John witnesses the Divine Liturgy on a Sunday.

> Rev. 1:12
> And I turned to see the voice that spake with me. And being turned, I saw **seven golden candlesticks;**

> Rev. 2:5
> Remember therefore from whence thou art fallen, and repent, and do the first works; or else I will come unto thee quickly, and **will remove thy candlestick out of his place**, except thou repent.

Just as in the heavenly Liturgy, the Church uses candles at Mass. The candles also serve to symbolically remind us of Christ, who is the Light of the world.

> Rev. 1:13
> And in the midst of the seven candlesticks one like unto the Son of man, **clothed with a garment down to the foot**, and girt about the paps with **a golden girdle**.

On earth, before Christ returns, priests clothe themselves with proper vestments because they stand in his place.

> Rev. 2:5
> **Remember therefore from whence thou art fallen, and repent, and do the first works**; or else I will come unto thee quickly, and will remove thy candlestick out of his place, except thou repent.

This is echoed in the Penitential Rite of the Mass, during which we call to mind both our sins and God's mercy.

Rev. 2:17
> He that hath an ear, let him hear what the Spirit saith unto the churches; To him that overcometh will I give to **eat of the hidden manna**, and will give him a white stone, and in the stone a new name written, which no man knoweth saving he that receiveth it.

In the heavenly Liturgy, manna is distributed. On earth, the true manna from heaven, Jesus Christ, is distributed under the appearance of bread.

Rev. 4:8
> And the four beasts had each of them six wings about him; and they were full of eyes within: and they rest not day and night, saying, **Holy, holy, holy, Lord God Almighty, which was, and is, and is to come.**

This is the exact same chant of praise the Church echoes back to heaven from earth at every Mass (c.f. Isaiah 6:3).

Rev. 5:8
> And when he had taken the book, the four beasts and four and **twenty elders fell down before the Lamb, having every one of them harps, and golden vials full of odours, which are the prayers of saints.**

Rev. 6:9-11
> And when he had opened the fifth seal, I saw **under the altar the souls of them that were slain for the word of God**, and for the testimony which they held: [10] And **they cried with a loud voice, saying, How long, O Lord, holy and true, dost thou not judge and avenge our blood on them that dwell on the earth?** [11] And white robes were given unto every one of them; and it was said unto them, that they should rest yet for a little season, until their fellowservants also and their brethren, that should be killed as they were, should be fulfilled.

Rev. 8:3-4
> And **another angel came** and stood at **the altar, having a golden censer; and there was given unto him much incense, that he should offer it with the prayers**

of all saints upon the golden altar which was before the throne. **[4] And the smoke of the incense, which came with the prayers of the saints, ascended up before God out of the angel's hand.**

The heavenly Liturgy emphasizes the intercession of angels and saints the same way the Mass does. Also notice the use of incense. And in Rev. 6:9, see how the martyrs are under the alter? Every permanent altar the Eucharist is sacrificed on has relics of a martyr or saint under or inside it.

> Rev. 7:3
> Saying, Hurt not the earth, neither the sea, nor the trees, till we have **sealed the servants of our God in their foreheads.**
>
> Rev. 14:1
> And I looked, and, lo, a Lamb stood on the mount Sion, and with him an hundred forty and four thousand, having **his Father's name written in their foreheads.**
>
> Rev. 22:4
> And they shall see his face; and **his name shall be in their foreheads.**

Several times during the Mass you'll see people making the sign of the cross either solely on their foreheads or starting there and continuing over their body. When they do this, they pronounce the Name of the Father, Son, and Holy Spirit.

> Rev. 7:9
> After this I beheld, and, lo, a great multitude, which no man could number, of **all nations, and kindreds, and people, and tongues, stood before the throne, and before the Lamb,** clothed with white robes, and palms in their hands;
>
> Rev. 14:6
> And I saw another angel fly in the midst of heaven, having the everlasting gospel to preach unto them that

dwell on the earth, **and to every nation, and kindred, and tongue, and people,**

Sounds like a Catholic (Universal, Global) Church to me!

Rev. 14:4
These are they which were not defiled with women; **for they are virgins. These are they which follow the Lamb whithersoever he goeth.** These were redeemed from among men, being the firstfruits unto God and to the Lamb.

Consecrated celibates have a place in heaven, just as the priests on earth.

Rev. 12:1-5
And there appeared a great wonder in heaven; **a woman clothed with the sun, and the moon under her feet, and upon her head a crown of twelve stars**: [2] And she being with child cried, travailing in birth, and pained to be delivered. [3] And there appeared another wonder in heaven; and behold a great red dragon, having seven heads and ten horns, and seven crowns upon his heads. [4] And his tail drew the third part of the stars of heaven, and did cast them to the earth: and the dragon stood before the woman which was ready to be delivered, for to devour her child as soon as it was born. [5] And **she brought forth a man child, who was to rule all nations with a rod of iron: and her child was caught up unto God, and to his throne.**

The heavenly Liturgy puts emphasis on Mary because she is God's specially created Mother and the Ark of the Covenant.

Rev. 12:7
And there was war in heaven: **Michael and his angels fought against the dragon**; and the dragon fought and his angels,

Before or after many Masses, the Church places emphasis on Her protection by Michael the Archangel.

> Rev. 19:9
> And he saith unto me, Write, Blessed are they which are called unto **the marriage supper of the Lamb**. And he saith unto me, These are the true sayings of God.

As we've already seen, we become one flesh with Christ through the Eucharist, our "marriage supper", which takes place at every Mass.

> Rev. 2:7
> He that hath an ear, let him hear what the Spirit saith unto the churches; To him that overcometh will I give to **eat of the tree of life**, which is in the midst of the paradise of God.

> Rev. 22:14
> Blessed are they that do his commandments, that they may have right to **the tree of life**, and may enter in through the gates into the city.

When Christ was hung on a tree, that tree became the tree of life. And that sacrifice of our Passover Lamb – the fruit of that tree – can only be consumed in the Eucharist.

Honor your Fathers! *The Elders Cry Out*

*"Assemble on the Lord's Day, and **break bread and offer the Eucharist**; but first make confession of your faults, so that your **sacrifice** may be a pure one. Anyone who has a difference with his fellow is not to take part with you until he has been reconciled, so as to **avoid any profanation of your sacrifice** [Matt. 5:23–24]. For this is the offering of which the Lord has said, 'Everywhere and always bring me a sacrifice that is undefiled, for I am a great king, says the Lord, and my name is the wonder of nations' [Mal. 1:11, 14]"*

- Teaching of the Twelve Apostles, *Didache* 14 (A.D. 70)

*"Our sin will not be small if we eject from the episcopate those who blamelessly and holily have **offered its sacrifices**. Blessed are those presbyters who have already finished their course, and who have obtained a fruitful and perfect release"*

- Pope Clement I, *Letter to the Corinthians* 44:4–5 (A.D. 80)

*"**Make certain, therefore, that you all observe one common Eucharist; for there is but one Body of our Lord Jesus Christ, and but one cup of union with his Blood, and one single altar of sacrifice**—even as there is also but one bishop, with his clergy and my own fellow servitors, the deacons. This will ensure that all your doings are in full accord with the will of God"*

- Ignatius of Antioch, *Letter to the Philadelphians* 4 (A.D. 110)

*"I have no taste for corruptible food nor for the pleasures of this life. **I desire the bread of God, which is the flesh of Jesus Christ**, who was of the seed of David; **and for drink I desire his blood**, which is love incorruptible"*

- Ignatius of Antioch, *Letter to the Romans* 7:3 (A.D. 110)

"Take note of those who hold heterodox opinions on the grace of Jesus Christ which has come to us, and see how contrary their opinions are to the mind of God. . . . **They abstain from the Eucharist and from prayer because they do not confess that the Eucharist is the flesh of our Savior Jesus Christ, flesh which suffered for our sins** *and which that Father, in his goodness, raised up again.* **They who deny the gift of God are perishing in their disputes**"

- Ignatius of Antioch, *Letter to the Smyrnaeans* 6:2–7:1 (A.D. 110)

"We call this food Eucharist, and no one else is permitted to partake of it, except one who believes our teaching to be true and who has been washed in the washing which is for the remission of sins and for regeneration and is thereby living as Christ enjoined. For not as common bread nor common drink do we receive these; but since Jesus Christ our Savior was made incarnate by the word of God and had both flesh and blood for our salvation, **so too, as we have been taught, the food which has been made into the Eucharist by the Eucharistic prayer set down by him, and by the change of which our blood and flesh is nurtured, is both the flesh and the blood of that incarnated Jesus**"

- Justin Martyr, *First Apology* 66 (A.D. 151)

"**God speaks by the mouth of Malachi**, *one of the twelve [minor prophets], as I said before,* **about the sacrifices at that time presented by you**: *'I have no pleasure in you, says the Lord, and I will not accept your sacrifices at your hands; for* **from the rising of the sun to the going down of the same, my name has been glorified among the Gentiles, and in every place incense is offered to my name, and a pure offering**, *for my name is great among the Gentiles . . . [Mal. 1:10–11]. He then speaks of those*

Gentiles, namely us [Christians] **who in every place offer sacrifices to him, that is, the bread of the Eucharist and also the cup of the Eucharist"**

- Justin Martyr, *Dialogue with Trypho the Jew* 41 (A.D. 155)

"He took from among creation that which is bread, and gave thanks, saying, **'This is my body.'** *The cup likewise, which is from among the creation to which we belong, he* **confessed to be his blood. He taught the new sacrifice of the new covenant, of which Malachi, one of the twelve [minor] prophets, had signified beforehand:** *'You do not do my will, says the Lord Almighty, and I will not accept a sacrifice at your hands.* **For from the rising of the sun to its setting my name is glorified among the Gentiles, and in every place incense is offered to my name, and a pure sacrifice;** *for great is my name among the Gentiles, says the Lord Almighty' [Mal. 1:10–11]. By these words he makes it plain that the former people will cease to make offerings to God; but that* **in every place sacrifice will be offered to him, and indeed, a pure one,** *for his name is glorified among the Gentiles"*

- Irenaeus, *Against Heresies* 4:17:5 (A.D. 189)

"If the Lord were from other than the Father, how could he rightly take bread, which is of the same creation as our own, and **confess it to be his body** *and* **affirm that the mixture in the cup is his blood?"**

- Irenaeus, *ibid.*, 4:33–32

"He has declared the cup, a part of creation, to be his own blood, *from which he causes our blood to flow;* **and the bread, a part of creation, he has established as his own body,** *from which he gives increase unto our bodies.* **When, therefore, the mixed cup** *[wine and water]* **and the baked bread receives the Word of God and**

*becomes the Eucharist, the body of Christ, and from these the substance of our flesh is increased and supported, how can they say that the flesh is not capable of receiving the gift of God, which is eternal life—**flesh which is nourished by the body and blood of the Lord, and is in fact a member of him?**"*

- Irenaeus, *ibid.*, 5:2

*"'Eat my flesh,' [Jesus] says, 'and drink my blood.' The Lord supplies us with these intimate nutrients, **he delivers over his flesh and pours out his blood**, and nothing is lacking for the growth of his children"*

- Clement of Alexandria, *The Instructor of Children* 1:6:43:3 (A.D. 191)

*"[T]here is not a soul that can at all procure salvation, except it believe whilst it is in the flesh, so true is it that the flesh is the very condition on which salvation hinges. And since the soul is, in consequence of its salvation, chosen to the service of God, it is the flesh which actually renders it capable of such service. The flesh, indeed, is washed [in baptism], in order that the soul may be cleansed . . . the flesh is shadowed with the imposition of hands [in confirmation], that the soul also may be illuminated by the Spirit; **the flesh feeds** [in the Eucharist] **on the body and blood of Christ, that the soul likewise may be filled with God"***

- Tertullian, *The Resurrection of the Dead* 8 (A.D. 210)

*"'And she [Wisdom] has furnished her table' [Prov. 9:2] . . . refers to his [Christ's] honored and undefiled **body and blood, which day by day are administered and offered sacrificially at the spiritual divine table, as a memorial** of that first and ever-memorable table of the spiritual divine supper [i.e., the Last Supper]"*

- Hippolytus, Fragment from *Commentary on Proverbs* (A.D. 217)

"Formerly there was baptism in an obscure way . . . now, however, in full view, there is regeneration in water and in the Holy Spirit. **Formerly, in an obscure way, there was manna for food; now, however, in full view, there is the true food, the flesh of the Word of God, as he himself says: 'My flesh is true food, and my blood is true drink'** *[John 6:55]"*

- Origen, *Homilies on Numbers* 7:2 (A.D. 248)

"He [Paul] threatens, moreover, the stubborn and forward, and denounces them, saying, 'Whosoever eats the bread or drinks the cup of the Lord unworthily, **is guilty of the body and blood of the Lord'** *[1 Cor. 11:27]. All these warnings being scorned and contemned—[lapsed Christians will often take Communion] before their sin is expiated, before confession has been made of their crime,* **before their conscience has been purged by sacrifice and by the hand of the priest, before the offense of an angry and threatening Lord has been appeased,** *[and so]* **violence is done to his body and blood;** *and they sin now against their Lord more with their hand and mouth than when they denied their Lord"*

- Cyprian of Carthage, *The Lapsed* 15–16 (A.D. 251)

"If Christ Jesus, our Lord and God, is himself the high priest of God the Father; and if he offered himself as a sacrifice to the Father; and if he commanded that this be done in commemoration of himself, **then certainly the priest, who imitates that which Christ did, truly functions in place of Christ***"*

- Cyprian of Carthage, *Letters* 63:14 (A.D. 253)

"It has come to the knowledge of the holy and great synod that, in some districts and cities, the deacons administer the Eucharist to

the presbyters [i.e., priests], **whereas neither canon nor custom permits that they who have no right to offer** *[the Eucharistic sacrifice]* **should give the Body of Christ to them that do offer** *[it]"*

- Council of Nicaea I, Canon 18 (A.D. 325)

"After having spoken thus [at the Last Supper], **the Lord rose up from the place where he had made the Passover and had given his body as food and his blood as drink***, and he went with his disciples to the place where he was to be arrested. But* **he ate of his own body and drank of his own blood,** *while he was pondering on the dead.* **With his own hands the Lord presented his own body to be eaten, and before he was crucified he gave his blood as drink"**

- Aphraahat the Persian Sage, *Treatises* 12:6 (A.D. 340)

"Accept therewith our hallowing too, as we say, 'Holy, holy, holy Lord Sabaoth, heaven and earth is full of your glory.' Heaven is full, and full is the earth, with your magnificent glory, Lord of virtues. Full also is this sacrifice, with your strength and your communion; for to you **we offer this living sacrifice, this unbloody oblation***"*

- Serapion, *Prayer of the Eucharistic Sacrifice* 13:12–16 (A.D. 350)

"The bread and the wine of the Eucharist before the holy invocation of the adorable Trinity were simple bread and wine, **but the invocation having been made, the bread becomes the body of Christ and the wine the blood of Christ***"*

- Cyril of Jerusalem, *Catechetical Lectures* 19:7 (A.D. 350)

*"**Do not, therefore, regard the bread and wine as simply that; for they are, according to the Master's declaration, the body and blood of Christ. Even though the senses suggest to you the other, let faith make you firm. Do not judge in this matter by taste, but be fully assured by the faith,** not doubting that you have been deemed worthy of the body and blood of Christ. . . . [Since you are] fully convinced that the apparent bread is not bread, even though it is sensible to the taste, but the body of Christ, and that the apparent wine is not wine, even though the taste would have it so, . . . partake of that bread as something spiritual, and put a cheerful face on your soul"*

- Cyril of Jerusalem, *ibid.*, 22:6, 9

*"Then, having sanctified ourselves by these spiritual hymns, we beseech the merciful God to send forth his Holy Spirit upon the gifts lying before him, **that he may make the bread the Body of Christ and the wine the Blood of Christ**, for whatsoever the Holy Spirit has touched is surely sanctified and changed. Then, **upon the completion of the spiritual sacrifice, the bloodless worship, over that propitiatory victim** we call upon God for the common peace of the churches, for the welfare of the world, for kings, for soldiers and allies, for the sick, for the afflicted; and in summary, **we all pray and offer this sacrifice for all who are in need**"*

- Cyril of Jerusalem, *ibid.*, 23:7–8 (A.D. 350)

*"Cease not to pray and plead for me when you draw down the Word by your word, **when in an unbloody cutting you cut the Body and Blood of the Lord, using your voice for a sword**"*

- Gregory Nazianzen, *Letter to Amphilochius* 171 (A.D. 383)

"When you see the Lord immolated and lying upon the altar, and the priest bent over that sacrifice praying, and all the people

empurpled by that precious blood, **can you think that you are still among men and on earth? Or are you not lifted up to heaven?"**

- John Chrysostom, *The Priesthood* 3:4:177 (A.D. 387)

"We saw the prince of priests coming to us, we saw and heard him offering his blood for us. We follow, inasmuch as we are able, being priests, and we offer the sacrifice on behalf of the people. Even if we are of but little merit, still, in the sacrifice, we are honorable. **Even if Christ is not now seen as the one who offers the sacrifice, nevertheless it is he himself that is offered in sacrifice here on Earth when the body of Christ is offered. Indeed, to offer himself he is made visible in us, he whose word makes holy the sacrifice that is offered"**

- Ambrose of Milan, *Commentaries on Twelve Psalms of David* 38:25 (A.D. 389)

"Perhaps you may be saying, **'I see something else; how can you assure me that I am receiving the body of Christ?'** *It but remains for us to prove it. And how many are the examples we might use! . . . Christ is in that sacrament, because* **it is the body of Christ"**

- Ambrose of Milan, *The Mysteries* 9:50, 58 (A.D. 390)

"Reverence, therefore, reverence this table, of which we are all communicants! **Christ, slain for us, the sacrificial victim who is placed thereon!"**

- John Chrysostom, *Homilies on Romans* 8:8 (A.D. 391)

" **'The cup of blessing which we bless, is it not communion of the blood of Christ?'** *Very trustworthy and awesomely does he [Paul] say it. For what he is saying is this:* **What is in the cup is that which flowed from his side, and we partake of it.** *He called it a*

cup of blessing because when we hold it in our hands that is how we praise him in song, wondering and astonished at his indescribable gift, blessing him because of his having poured out this very gift so that we might not remain in error; **and not only for his having poured it out, but also for his sharing it with all of us.** *'If therefore you desire blood,' he [the Lord] says, 'do not redden the platform of idols with the slaughter of dumb beasts, but my altar of sacrifice with my blood.' What is more awesome than this? What, pray tell, more tenderly loving?"*

- John Chrysostom, *Homilies on First Corinthians* 24:1(3) (A.D. 392)

"In ancient times, because men were very imperfect, God did not scorn to receive the blood which they were offering . . . to draw them away from those idols; and this very thing again was because of his indescribable, tender affection. But now he has transferred the priestly action to what is most awesome and magnificent. **He has changed the sacrifice itself, and instead of the butchering of dumb beasts, he commands the offering up of himself**"

- John Chrysostom, *ibid.*, 24:2

"What then? **Do we not offer daily? Yes, we offer, but making remembrance of his death; and this remembrance is one and not many.** *How is it one and not many? Because this sacrifice is offered once, like that in the Holy of Holies. This sacrifice is a type of that, and this remembrance a type of that.* **We offer always the same, not one sheep now and another tomorrow, but the same thing always. Thus there is one sacrifice.** *By this reasoning, since the sacrifice is offered everywhere, are there, then, a multiplicity of Christs? By no means! Christ is one everywhere. He is complete here, complete there, one body.* **And just as he is one body and not many though offered everywhere, so too is there one sacrifice**"

- John Chrysostom, *Homilies on Hebrews* 17:3(6) (A.D. 403)

"When [Christ] gave the bread he did not say, 'This is the symbol of my body,' but, 'This is my body.' In the same way, when he gave the cup of his blood he did not say, 'This is the symbol of my blood,' but, 'This is my blood'; for he wanted us to look upon the [Eucharistic elements] after their reception of grace and the coming of the Holy Spirit not according to their nature, **but receive them as they are, the body and blood of our Lord**. We ought . . . not regard [the elements] merely as bread and cup, but as the body and blood of the Lord, into which they were transformed by the descent of the Holy Spirit"

- Theodore of Mopsuestia, *Catechetical Homilies* 5:1 (A.D. 405)

"Christ was carried in his own hands when, referring to his own body, he said, 'This is my body' *[Matt. 26:26]. For he carried that body in his hands"*

- Augustine, *Explanations of the Psalms* 33:1:10 (A.D. 405)

"I promised you [new Christians], who have now been baptized, a sermon in which I would explain the sacrament of the Lord's Table. . . . **That bread which you see on the altar, having been sanctified by the word of God, is the body of Christ. That chalice, or rather, what is in that chalice, having been sanctified by the word of God, is the blood of Christ***"*

- Augustine, *Sermons* 227 (A.D. 411)

*"***What you see is the bread and the chalice; that is what your own eyes report to you. But what your faith obliges you to accept is that the bread is the body of Christ and the chalice is the blood of Christ.** *This has been said very briefly, which may perhaps be sufficient for faith; yet faith does not desire instruction"*

- Augustine, *ibid.*, 272

"In the sacrament he is immolated for the people not only on every Easter Solemnity but on every day; and a man would not be lying if, when asked, he were to reply that Christ is being immolated. For if sacraments had not a likeness to those things of which they are sacraments, they would not be sacraments at all; and they generally take the names of those same things by reason of this likeness"

- Augustine, *Letters* 98:9 (A.D. 412)

"For when he says in another book, which is called Ecclesiastes, 'There is no good for a man except that he should eat and drink' [Eccles. 2:24], **what can he be more credibly understood to say** [prophetically] **than what belongs to the participation of this table which the Mediator of the New Testament himself, the priest after the order of Melchizedek, furnishes with his own body and blood?** For that sacrifice has succeeded all the sacrifices of the Old Testament, which were slain as a shadow of what was to come. . . . **Because, instead of all these sacrifices and oblations, his body is offered and is served up to the partakers of it"**

- Augustine, *The City of God* 17:20 (A.D. 419)

"We will necessarily add this also. Proclaiming the death, according to the flesh, of the only-begotten Son of God, that is Jesus Christ, confessing his resurrection from the dead, and his ascension into heaven, **we offer the unbloody sacrifice in the churches, and so go on to the mystical thanksgivings, and are sanctified, having received his holy flesh and the precious blood of Christ the Savior of us all. And not as common flesh do we receive it; God forbid:** nor as of a man sanctified and associated with the Word according to the unity of worth, or as having a divine indwelling, **but as truly the life-giving and very flesh of the Word himself.** For he is the life according to his nature as God, *and when he became united to his flesh, he made it also to be life-giving"*

- Council of Ephesus, Session 1, *Letter of Cyril to Nestorius* (A.D. 431)

*"Hold most firmly and never doubt in the least that the only-begotten **God the Word himself became flesh [and] offered himself in an odor of sweetness as a sacrifice and victim to God on our behalf**; to whom . . . in the time of the Old Testament animals were sacrificed by the patriarchs and prophets and priests; and to whom now, I mean in the time of the New Testament . . . **the holy Catholic Church does not cease in faith and love to offer throughout all the lands of the world a sacrifice of bread and wine**. In those former sacrifices what would be given us in the future was signified figuratively, but in this sacrifice which has now been given us is shown plainly. **In those former sacrifices it was fore-announced that the Son of God would be killed for the impious, but in the present sacrifice it is announced that he has been killed for the impious**"*

- Fulgentius of Ruspe, *The Rule of Faith* 62 (A.D. 524)

***

My prayer is that in reading the thoughts of the Early Church and the scriptural passages I provided, you'll at least see how the Catholic stance can be reached without Catholics feeling that they're contradicting God's Word. Even if a particular doctrine cannot be conclusively *proved* from the Bible alone (a task Catholics aren't forced to perform since we believe God's Word has been communicated orally, as well as on paper) it can be seen to be *compatible* with the rest of Scripture. And if the context of Scripture *allows* it and the Apostolic Fathers of the Church *believed* it, why is it so hard for Protestants to accept? I suspect that only Satan could be behind such dissent from the historical teaching of the Church – especially given the issues at stake.

> *Satan has been a home wrecker since day one.*

Satan has been a home wrecker since day one. He yearns to break apart God's Family. So it would make sense that he attacks the doctrines that most bond the Family together. If the Family is left without a family tree (apostolic succession) it is left without an identity and without structure. If the Family is left without the Father's whole Word (all of Sacred Scripture and Sacred Tradition) it is left without a clear understanding of how it should function and behave. If the Family is left without a Mother (Mary's role, by virtue of who her Son is and how he's related to us) it is left without its very heart; lacking the physically maternal tenderness that God intends for a family. If the Family is left without total unity (the communion of the saints) it is left without complete relationships; siblings become isolated, and the Body divided. If the Family is left without Supper (the Mass) it is left without the nourishment it needs to survive – God's Word: written, oral, and incarnate – and without the gathering place where regardless of sibling rivalry or quarrels, the Family is of one voice, one mind, and one Spirit. It would be no wonder to me that Satan attacks these things.

Church Authority (the Magisterium), Sacred Tradition (the lived experience of the Apostles), Mary (our Mother and Queen), Communion of the Saints (the prayers and relational ability of our departed brothers and sisters), and the Mass (the Family meal and gathering place) all tie into the intended experience of God's Covenant Family and together present three core answers I've found to the question, "Why be Catholic?": The One, Holy, Catholic, and Apostolic Church contains, exhibits, and grants access to the *whole* Family of God, the *whole* Word of God, and the *whole* means of Grace.

I have 2,000 years worth of brothers and sisters who help me by their prayers and examples and a Mother, crowned above all others as my greatest intercessor.

I have not only the Sacred Scriptures in their entirety, but the lived experience of the ones who wrote them in Sacred Tradition, and the guidance of the Apostles' successors to keep me a well-behaved Family member.

Finally, I have the source and summit of all the Faith in the Eucharist, where Christ is *come in the flesh* and meets me with the Grace of a heavenly, eternal, and beloved Family. There can be no greater grace than this; it is where the sacrifice that redeems us is made complete and it is where the marriage between Christ and his Church is consummated.

There may be many things the Church has done wrong, but that is to be expected. She's contained the most vile and atrocious of sinners from day one. But if the first generation of Christians could stay true to the Apostles in spite of the fact that one of them had betrayed Christ and subsequently committed suicide, then I think future generations can handle anything. Questioning things is fine – there are answers. Look at the Rock-solid defense the Church has on her side. Read some Catholic Apologetics instead of merely buying in to the plethora of anti-Catholic rhetoric that's out there. But before you do, you have to decide how to handle the evangelistic challenges of Catholicism toward any other brand of Christianity.

We are a Church marked by miracles, attested by good works, and proven by survival and growth in every generation since Jesus walked the earth. We hold the only claim to a succession of papal authority traced back to Christ, Himself. We allege wonderful privileges and offerings no other denomination of Christianity can touch. And we contend that in this Church, God's Word is best fulfilled and presented. But most importantly, after reading this letter, where do you think the *Family* fits in? God has not left you orphaned…He does not want you to be alone. There is a loving Family praying earnestly for you to come home and waiting at the door, ready to welcome you in with open arms. Is it worth risking all that?

Embrace the Grace,

Brian Forrest Roberts

THE FOURTH LETTER

Dear Brother,

You know, it's ironic, the way God works. My last obstacle on the path toward Catholicism became my biggest reason for becoming Catholic. I wanted to get my senior pastor's opinions about the Church and why he wasn't Catholic. We met up and eased into the conversation by chatting about the redecoration of his office. Soft lighting. Nice couch. You know.

The reason we were trying to dodge awkwardness was because we both knew what was at stake. If he couldn't convince me that there was a reason I shouldn't be Catholic, I was going to leave his church. I could see that he wasn't approaching the subject lightly. As our conversation turned toward Catholicism, his eyes narrowed. He leaned forward, honestly trying to absorb every word I said. He's good at making you feel important.

After listening to me explain the problems I saw in Protestantism (that by nature it is divisive, that it lacks visible headship and authority, that *sola scriptora* is unbiblical, that it fosters intellectual elitism, is non-historical, that it adds to and removes from the Bible, is invented by man, and encourages individualism) and that among the many virtues I saw in Catholicism were solutions to these problems, he leaned back and prepared for the big question.

"So…why *aren't* you Catholic?" I didn't have to wait long for his answer. He smiled. "Well, I guess there must be a good reason!" We laughed and he began explaining the big issue that prevented his heart from submitting to the Church. "Brian," he started, "There is no perfect church. That's because things are never as black and white as they first appear. In a world full of grey areas, Catholicism consists of too much absolutism."

Wow. I honestly wasn't prepared for that one. If he attacked a doctrine, I could cite biblical support and historical cases that backed it up. Instead, he attacked Catholicism's *attitude*. I had to admit, it certainly seemed he was right. I mean, the Church has more official guide books and documents than it knows what to do with! The Catechism is probably the most popular. Yet in the world, it certainly does *seem* like there's a lot of room for error – a lot of "grey". For the moment, I was stumped.

The Catholic Church certainly is not perfect…and still it strives for perfection. It certainly doesn't know all there is to know…and yet it claims to have the fullness of truth. It certainly doesn't have the best leaders…but it instructs the faithful to be obedient, respectful, and work within the system, anyway. Aren't those impossible goals? It seems like Catholicism has set itself up for failure. Nevertheless, it has persisted and grown for the last *two thousand years*. So what's the secret?

In this world, faith, morality, and justice turn all shades of grey under the diverse and watchful eyes of six billion people. Everyone has his or her own idea of what these three virtues *ought* to be. This is because the eyes of each individual have lenses of bias; developed from a lifetime of personal shortcomings, victimizations, and resentments. We become most focused on the causes of our suffering, neglecting to see the suffering we've caused. And the murky outcome is a polarized culture. A culture full of people who cling to the law so fiercely that they forget the good deeds that make their neighbor feel loved, the world feel peace, and the needy feel accounted for. A culture full of people who strive so hard for love, peace, and provision that the law gets ignored, relativism is encouraged, socialism is idealized, and depravity is actualized.

This line of thinking can be traced back to the origin of humanity, when we first decided what was right and wrong *for ourselves*, in spite of what God had revealed. In this initial act of conscience and consciousness, we presumed to rise up and be like God, knowing the difference between good and evil. And ever since then we've repeated that same mistake, no matter the political, philosophical, or theological party we claim as our own.

We draw a circle around our camp, excluding everyone outside it. In arrogance, supposing ourselves to be like God, we declare that we *know* the absolutes – in stunning black and white – of faith, morality, and justice, naively determining them based on our particular group's convictions about what God has revealed.

The result is oppositional chaos. So how then can we faithfully live in a world full of grey areas and endless interpretations of Scripture?

As Christians, our answer must be through the kingdom of God in Christ's Church. When infinite Spirit humbly took upon finite flesh, a wedding was taking place between God and Man. The Christ fulfilled all of the previous laws and covenants – both their requirements and their curses – while at the same time exercising his divine authority to begin a new one. He did not found a philosophy or religion. He inaugurated a Family; he began a Church.

In a world of grey – of countless denominations in Christianity – we need a visible authority to keep us as close as possible to the proper contemporary interpretation and application of objective, Christian truths. Yet because we are fallible, sinful, creatures, the task is humanly impossible. We are prone to disagree, to squabble over who's right and who's wrong, mutating loving faith into arrogant knowledge. Thus do divorce and broken families, war and broken nations, heresy and broken faith, exist.

If we all only humbled ourselves and became meek in the face of God's Word, loving faith would dominate the evil in this world. Yet although this is the goal to be strived after, it is not realistic. God is no fool. He knows that we would not be able to maintain universal doctrine on our own. Schisms would happen and there would be no way of settling them, since differing interpretations of God's Word spawned them to begin with.

In a foggy world of grey, we need a clearly visible authority.

No, if such oversight of the Church were to be possible it would require no less than the infallible protection of God Himself. And this is just what the Church claims for herself. When the pope, who stands in place of Peter – Christ's visible authority – exercises all his office's power on a matter of faith or morals, God supernaturally prevents falsehood from his lips. In the same way, God protects the faith-related decisions of a general council of

Catholic bishops. Consequently, whenever a dogma is formally defined, it happens because God wanted it to happen, precisely when it happened. Thus could a Church universally condemn heresy, make pleas for further clarification of doctrine, and correctly interpret God's Word.

The Church may have as many wolves as sheep and weeds as wheat – and further, the wicked ones may make bad decisions with terrible consequences – but her teachings on faith and morals will stand forever. What other group of Christians has an unbroken history, traced back to Christ, and has remained firm in her stances on faith and morals? How many Christians still preach that artificial contraception is sinful? How many Christians still believe in Hell? Or that the Holy Spirit is a Person, not an It? What about the indissolubility of marriage? Is gluttony and excess still as bad as it used to be?

Catholic Christianity has existed throughout the ages and stands today as one of the oldest continuous organizations in human history. Remarkably so, in the face of terrible persecutions, poor decisions, and sometimes corrupt leaders. She has served as a Mother, a Teacher, and a Guide through the gloom and foggy sea of "grey areas". As a beacon of light, She has kept watch over all wayfaring spiritual sojourners, illuminating dangers so they might steer clear. As a city set upon a hill, She has maintained a clearly visible presence for all those who might want to know what Christianity *is*. As guardian of the Faith, she has upheld, explored, and further clarified the Word of God along with her condemnation of heresies as they've arisen. This is the Church of Augustine, Jerome, Francis, Aquinas, Theresa, John Paul, and *thousands* more like them. This is the One, Holy, Catholic, and Apostolic Church of Christ.

I decided to come home to the house God built for my Family about one year ago, today (February 23, 2005). Ironically, February is the same month that I came back to Christ in 2002. Both of these life changing decisions took place after a great deal of thought, study, and reflection. This time around, prayer was also vital. Yet the circumstances were similar. I had to remove a blindfold – a paradigm I'd been holding on to – in both cases. It's a scary thing to do, admitting to yourself that you might be wrong. It feels much more comfortable to stay where you are. But ours is a God who calls us to step out of the boat and onto the water, leaving everything behind. This requires an open mind and a heart after Truth.

    Have you ever been frustrated at an agnostic for not getting the proper information from the right sources? After all, it's out there and is easily accessible. Well, for every finger you point, there are three pointing back at you, as they say. If you take issue with what I've said, I challenge you to do the research for yourself. Delve into some *Catholic* apologetics with the fervor you wish an atheist would delve into general apologetics. Pray for discernment from the Holy Spirit without letting your own bias creep in. Pray simply for his will and guidance into Truth, unconditionally. He will protect you.

    This letter is not primarily meant to convince you of anything. It is more so meant to relieve misunderstanding, fear, and anger towards the Catholic Church and *inspire you* to check out a book or two on Catholic apologetics – just to take a refreshing break from the paranoia, the skepticism, and the paradigm. The first Appendix of this book may be a good place to start.

You have nothing to lose and everything to gain!

Don't have time to read anything besides the Bible? Ok. You know, there are plenty of audio books out there; even lectures and all-out sermons on tape or CD. Your local Catholic Church might have some in a library. You can even have some mailed to you for free at the Mary Foundation's website: http://www.catholicity.com/maryfoundation/.

    I may be wrong in this decision. But I have faith I'm right! And because of that Faith I have very high hopes for the future. Whatever the case may be, I know that I can stand before God and honestly say that I did my best to follow His will. In the end, I've chosen to become Catholic because my heart tells me that if I didn't, God would ask *why not*, after I pass away. And if there's a chance – even a glimmer of one – that I'm right, you have nothing to lose and everything to gain by doing your homework on the subject. I so very much hope you will.

In the Name of Father, Son, and Holy Spirit,

Brian Forrest Roberts

AFTERWORD

Me and my pastor, Father Ed Fride

My reconciliation with the Church (first confession) took place on Saturday, March 19th, 2005. I was confirmed one week later, on the 26th during the Easter vigil. Before the close of the vigil I had my first communion. Each of these three experiences could only be compared to two others in my whole life – my baptism and marriage. In each of these moments, there was transforming grace at work. Each time, I thought I had a decent understanding of what was about to happen. But each time, it was only in retrospect that I could fully appreciate what had just occurred. These events were all Sacraments. Words just can't do justice to some things, I guess.

A good friend, Jon, was confirmed right along with me and had a similar experience. Now, I know Jon. He's not a guy that likes to get *too* emotional. Three years of praying, studying the Bible, and doing service-work with him and I had never seen him crack. Well, we hang out just about every other Thursday and he recently wondered out loud to me about how long it'll take before he *doesn't* get misty-eyed at Mass! He knows what's going on. He knows an infinite gift has been offered to him. And he also knows that all he can do in response is fall to his knees and meekly say:

"Holy...Holy...Holy LORD...God of power and might...Heaven and Earth are full of your glory! Hosanna in the highest! Blessed is he who comes in the Name of the LORD. Hosanna in the highest!"

When you face the Real Presence of your Creator – offering the fullness of his Body, Blood, Soul, and Divinity to you – is there any other way to respond? Before I was blessed to enter into full communion with the Church, I often fantasized about traveling back in time to see the Savior. I had a deep longing to know his Real Presence – to touch him and embrace him. At the time, short of a miracle, I knew it was just wishful thinking. Now that miracle has come to me! After all those years of fantasizing, my dreams came true on the night of my confirmation.

I remember – so clearly – walking up before the altar and falling to my knees, *knowing* in my heart what my brain took in on *faith*: that what appeared to be bread before me was no longer bread at all, but Jesus Christ on the cross of so long ago, transcending time and space! "For this cause shall a man leave his father and mother, and shall be joined unto his wife, and they two shall be one flesh," says Paul in his letter to the Ephesians, "this is a great mystery: but I speak concerning Christ and the Church." The wedding feast of the Lamb is here and now – in the Mass!

Before you set these pages down, I want to give a "witness" to what has been one of the most joyous occasions in my life. I've demonstrated my conviction that the Catholic form of Christianity is the most practical, meaningful, biblical, historical, and logical. But I've run into several people who wonder how a Catholic might verbally evangelize a lost soul. I grew up in an atmosphere where a great deal of stress was put on "witnessing", getting non-believers "saved", or "leading people to the Lord" – depending on which expression a person liked to run with. So these letters would feel incomplete if I didn't include such a tract.

First though, I want to emphasize that Catholics much rather win souls by example than by word. We are a Church of the ordinary just as much as we are of the extraordinary. When we hug someone, we hug Christ. When we pick up some trash and toss it away, we clean God's path. When our boss is yelling at us for something we didn't do, we suffer with Jesus before the Sanhedrin. When we do our chores, we personally serve the Holy Spirit. We are a Church of the physical, the mundane. In a word, *ordinary*. And after 2,000 years we've found that the closer we live according to this principle of self-sacrifice for the benefit of others, the more souls are attracted to Christ. Sure, sermons, books, and even those little leaflets come about, certainly helping people. But we like to focus more on living Jesus than preaching Him. You see, if we are living properly, our *lives* become the message.

Nevertheless just as the Ethiopian eunuch asked, "How must I be saved?" there is good reason for old fashioned "altar calls" (an expression that, when you think about it, makes little sense outside of a Catholic context). They tell the story of God's love for us – the meaning of life – and invite us to a meeting point with Him. Catholic Christians don't have to shy away from questions like the eunuch's, should they be asked. We have 2,000 years of reflection to give a pretty solid answer: *surrender your whole life toward God's Word.*

If it were not for God's Word, there would be no Sacred Scripture, no Sacred Tradition, no Incarnation, no Eucharist, and no Church; well, there would be nothing! The Bible says all things were created through Him and their existence is tied up in Him. I personally have come to a deeper relationship with Him through the Catholic Church than I ever thought possible in this earthly life. The real question is *how* has that been accomplished? How do we *fully* surrender our lives to Him? The Catholic Church believes it involves more than a simple one-time prayer and indeed, involves the story of humanity from Creation to the present.

When God created the world, everything was good. The lush world surrounding our ancient parents was vibrant with life. God crowned the physical – the mud, the mush, the saliva, and all the down and dirty – with glory. Everything was good. And we screwed it up. God gives us free choice and the Garden of Eden story shows that when we separate ourselves in any way from His Word, we die. Eve, the mother of the human race, trampled God's Word under foot when she ate of the tree God had prohibited. The action itself was the knowledge of good and evil for humanity, since it was the first evil act. The fruit was the food of death. Somehow this action affected the whole universe. And because of their sin, humanity was barred from the "tree of life".

The immediate image God's Word presents as a solution is to cloth the two humans in animal skin. The flesh of an innocent creature was placed on them. It is the first recorded sacrifice – and it was done by God's own hand. It must have struck Adam and Eve – this act of God, illustrating the suffering and death caused by disharmony with His Way – to have their shame "covered" by the life of a scapegoat. God also offered the two a prophecy of a woman who would give birth to a Savior; a man who would crush the "serpent", the symbol of humanity's Fall. Thus began a series of events in God's progressive revelation that increasingly pointed to that woman and that man to come.

The grandest of these events was the handing down of God's Law. It prescribed a highly disciplined way of life in order to safeguard the people from the effects of sin. The center of this life was the Passover: a commemoration of freedom. In this celebration, God ordered a lamb without blemish to be sacrificed for sins. The sacrifice was not complete until it was eaten. In fact, if a person simply offered the lamb but didn't consume it, the whole thing was void. The person's sin remained. What's more, God ordered this to be a perpetual memorial – it could never be revoked. Some way or another, these Passover commandments had to be fulfilled.

Centuries (and many prophecies) later, a young girl was visited by an angel, who told her that she would become pregnant. This startled the girl, who was a virgin. Although she was engaged, she didn't see how it was possible in the future that she would have a child (likely because she was an avowed virgin and her elderly betrothed was to be a care-taker husband). She must have also wondered at the name the angel called her by: *Full-of-Grace*. But she did indeed conceive and named the baby, Jesus.

Jesus made strong claims; that he was the Son of God, that he was equal and one with God, that he was the Messiah (Savior) promised to Adam and Eve and so many others throughout history. But more than that, he backed these claims up. Miracle after miracle, insight after insight, Jesus proved that he was truly the Christ. He certainly fulfilled all the prophecies that had been made about the Messiah, even if he did so in surprising ways.

What was most surprising was that he didn't perform the Passover as it had been traditionally laid out. He actually *fulfilled* it himself! He offered himself up as a perfect Lamb to be sacrificed and consumed – the Law would not be abolished; it would be fulfilled. In this higher way would God's Word stand forever. God established a New Covenant with the whole world. We must choose to either offer ourselves to God in atonement for our sins or the Lamb he provided, "who takes away the sins of the world". And if we offer the Lamb, we must first believe he is still alive to be offered! Christ rose from the dead and ascended to the Father's right hand in glory, to eternally present himself to God as our Great Advocate. We make this once-for-all sacrifice and offer it to God by consuming Christ's Body, Blood, Soul, and Divinity in the Eucharist, just as we would have to do in the Passover.

We can join in this New Covenant by becoming members of his Church. God's grace does this through the Sacraments he setup. We enter into God and God enters into us through Baptism, the new circumcision, which grafts us into the Mystical Body of Christ. We open ourselves fully to the indwelling of the Holy Spirit when we receive Confirmation. We become one flesh with Christ, consummate, and renew our covenant with him when we consume his Body, Blood, Soul, and Divinity in the Eucharist. Marriage, Holy Orders (the priesthood), Confession, and the Anointing of the Sick are all Sacraments that help us to become living witnesses and examples of Christ at work in the world. All of this is the free gift of God through the Body of Jesus: the One, Holy, Catholic, and Apostolic Church that Christ founded and protects.

Human effort does not achieve these things. They all begin and end with grace. I'll be the first to tell you that I don't deserve my wife. I certainly didn't deserve her hand in marriage. But here we are. And I have faith that we're here for a *reason*. It was God's hand of grace that led us together, not my smooth talk. Baptism wasn't something *I* did. It was something someone *else* did for me! And the person who baptized me wasn't performing the Sacrament for his own benefit – he was merely obeying God. All of the Sacraments operate like this; out of the principle that *grace* saves. If it seems that somehow this feels true to you, you might begin the journey with a simple prayer, asking God to guide you farther into that truth. Follow it up with a visit to your local parish priest – ask about RCIA Inquiry. If you yield an open heart to God, the Holy Spirit will do the rest. He certainly did for me.

God bless you!

Appendix 1: Suggested Reading, Viewing, and Listening

If after reading my letters you feel attracted to the Catholic Church, or at least find yourself more curious about her, I encourage you to do some research on the topics that you have the greatest difficulty understanding.

On Catholicism
- *Catholicism: Christ and the Common Destiny of Man*
  By Henri de Lubac
- *Catholicism for Dummies*
  By John Trigilio
- *The Catholic Sourcebook*
  By Rev. Peter Klein
- *Catholic Christianity*
  By Peter Kreeft

On Church History
- *Triumph – The Power and Glory of the Catholic Church, a 2,000 year History*
  By H.W. Crocker, III
- *One, Holy, Catholic, and Apostolic – The Early Church was the Catholic Church*
  By Kenneth D. Whitehead
- *The Four Witnesses: The Early Church in Her Own Words*
  By Rod Bennett
- *People of God: The History of Catholic Christianity*
  By Anthony E. Gilles
- *Great Heresies*
  By Hilaire Belloc
- *Catholic Martyrs of the Twentieth Century: A Comprehensive World History*
  By Robert Royal

On Church Culture
- *Why Do Catholics Do That? A Guide to the Teachings and Practices of the Catholic Church*
  By Kevin Orlin Johnson, Ph.D.
- *The How-To Book of Catholic Devotions: Everything You Need to Know But No One Ever Taught You*
  By Michael Aquilina
- *Why Do Catholics Genuflect? And Answers to Other Puzzling Questions About the Catholic Church*
  By Al Kresta
- *Catholic Questions, Wise Answers*
  By Michael Daley
- *The Sign of the Cross*
  By Bert Ghezzi
- *The How-To Book of the Mass: Everything You Need to Know But No One Ever Taught You*
  By Michael Dubruiel

On Church Nature
- *A Father Who Keeps His Promises – God's Covenant Love in Scripture*
  By Scott Hahn
- *First Comes Love – Finding Your Family in the Church and the Trinity*
  By Scott Hahn
- *Salvation is From the Jews: The Role of Judaism in Salvation History*
  By Roy H. Schoeman
- *Catholic For a Reason: Scripture and the Mystery of the Family of God*
  By Scott Hahn and Leon J. Suprenant
- *The Salvation Controversy*
  By James Akin

On Church Authority

- *Not by Scripture Alone: A Catholic Critique of the Protestant Doctrine of Sola Scriptura*
  Edited By Robert A. Sungenis
- *Upon This Rock*
  By Stephen Ray
- *Jesus, Peter, & the Keys: A Scriptural Handbook on the Papacy*
  By Scott Butler
- *And On This Rock: Witness of One Land and Two Covenants*
  By Stanley L. Jaki
- *Scripture Alone? 21 Reasons to Reject Sola Scriptura*
  By Joel Peters

On Mary, the Saints, and Communion between Heaven and Earth

- *Any Friend of God's is a Friend of Mine: A Biblical and Historical Explanation of the Catholic Doctrine of the Communion of Saints*
  By Patrick Madrid
- *Hail, Holy Queen – The Mother of God in the Word of God*
  By Scott Hahn
- *Catholic For a Reason II: Scripture and the Mystery of the Mother of God*
  By Scott Hahn and Leon J. Suprenant
- *True Devotion to Mary*
  By Saint Louis de Montfort
- *Queen Mother: A Biblical Theology of Mary's Queenship*
  By Edward Sri
- *Edith Stein: A Biography – The Untold Story of the Philosopher and Mystic Who Lost Her Life in the Death Camps of Auschwitz*
  By Waltraud Herbstrith
- *The Life of Saint Theresa of Avila by Herself*
  By Saint Theresa of Avila

- *Something Beautiful for God – The Classic Account of Mother Teresa's Journey into Compassion*
  By Malcolm Muggeridge
- *Witness to Hope: The Biography of Pope John Paul II*
  By George Weigel
- *The Autobiography of Saint Therese of Lisieux: The Story of a Soul*
  By Saint Therese of Lisieux
- *Lives of the Saints: For Every Day in the Year*
  By Fr. Alban Butler
- *Treasury of Women Saints*
  By Ronda de Sola Chervin

On the Sacraments and the Liturgy
- *The Lamb's Supper: The Mass as Heaven on Earth*
  By Scott Hahn
- *Swear to God: The Promise and Power of the Sacraments*
  By Scott Hahn
- *The Spirit of the Liturgy*
  By Joseph Ratzinger
- *Catholic For a Reason III: Scripture and the Mystery of the Mass*
  By Scott Hahn and Regis J. Flaherty

On the Real Presence
- *Not By Bread Alone – The Biblical and Historical Evidence for the Eucharistic Sacrifice*
  By Robert A. Sungenis
- *The Mass of the Early Christians*
  By Mike Aquilina
- *This Is My Body – An Evangelical Discovers the Real Presence*
  By Mark P. Shea

- *With Us Today: On the Real Presence of Jesus Christ in the Eucharist*
  By John A. Hardon
- *No Wonder They Call it the Real Presence – Lives Changed by Christ in Eucharistic Adoration*
  By David Pearson

On Catholicism in the Bible
- *A Biblical Defense of Catholicism*
  By Dave Armstrong
- *More Biblical Evidence for Catholicism – Companion to A Biblical Defense of Catholicism*
  By Dave Armstrong
- *The Catholic Verses – 95 Bible Passages That Confound Protestants*
  By Dave Armstrong
- *Unabridged Christianity: Biblical Answers to Common Questions About the Roman Catholic Faith*
  By Mario P. Romero

The Whole Word of God
- **Bibles**
  - *Douay-Rheims Haydock Bible*
    Although a bit on the pricey side, if you have the money to spend, this is said to be the finest and most helpful Bible in print. It includes an amazing amount of commentary and resources.
  - *The Catholic Study Bible: New American Bible*
    Presents the best of modern scholarship and contains volumes of additional guides and information for Bible Study, though some question its orthodoxy.
  - *The New Jerusalem Bible – Saints Devotional Edition*
    An enjoyably readable translation that brings the

stories, sermons, and commentary of the Saints to life; also very affordable.
- *The New Catholic Answer Bible*
  This is the Bible I would recommend for most people curious about Catholicism. It contains 88 inserts of Catholic Apologetics, each walking you through the Bible to defend Catholic doctrines.

- **Commentaries**
  - *The Navarre Bible*
    An exhaustively thorough, verse by verse commentary on the Scriptures; multiple volumes. Known widely for its conservative orthodoxy.
  - *The New Jerome Biblical Commentary*
    Not as exhaustive as Navarre's, but it contains a wealth of research. It is scholarly, though some feel it is too liberal.
  - *The International Bible Commentary: A Catholic and Ecumenical Commentary for the Twenty-First Century*
    This commentary is written, as much as is possible, to present the biblical studies, facts, and interpretations that everyone can agree on – without compromising the stances of the Church (meaning some verses might get a "don't go there" treatment.)

- **Church Teaching**
  - *Introduction to the Catechism of the Catholic Church*
    By Cardinal Joseph Ratzinger
  - *The Catechism of the Catholic Church, 2nd Edition*
    By the Catholic Church with the help of the Holy Spirit
  - *Companion to the Catechism of the Catholic Church: A Compendium of Texts Referred to in the*

- *Catechism of the Catholic Church*
  By Ignatius Press
  o *The Compendium of the Catechism of the Catholic Church*
  By the Catholic Church with the help of the Holy Spirit
  o *The Compendium of the Social Doctrine of the Church*
  By the Pontifical Council for Justice and Peace
  o *Fundamentals of Catholic Dogma*
  By Ludwig Ott
  o *The Teachings of the Church Fathers*
  By John R. Willis
  o *An Essay on the Development of Christian Doctrine*
  By John Henry Cardinal Newman
  o *The Code of Canon Law*
  By the Catholic Church
  o *New Commentary on the Code of Canon Law: Study Edition*
  By John P. Beal, James A. Coriden, and Thomas J. Green
  o *The Code in the Hands of the Laity: Canon Law for Everyone*
  By Laurence J. Spiteri
  o *Surprised by Canon Law: 150 Questions Laypeople Ask About Canon Law*
  By Pete Vere and Michael Trueman
  o *Decrees of the Ecumenical Councils*
  By Norman P. Tanner

- **Sacred, Apostolic Tradition**
  o *Faith of Our Fathers*
  By James Cardinal Gibbons
  o *Why is THAT in Tradition*
  By Patrick Madrid

- *The Faith of the Early Fathers (3-volume set)*
  William A. Jurgens
- *By What Authority? An Evangelical Discovers Catholic Tradition*
  By Mark P. Shea
- *Tradition and Traditions*
  By Yves Congar

On Protestant Misunderstandings
- *What Catholics Really Believe – Setting the Record Straight: 52 Answers to Common Misconceptions About the Catholic Faith*
  By Karl Keating
- *Catholicism and Fundamentalism: The Attack on "Romanism" by "Bible Christians"*
  By Karl Keating
- *Letters Between a Catholic and an Evengelical*
  By James G. McCarthy and Fr. John R. Waiss
- *Catholic & Christian: An Explanation of Commonly Misunderstood Catholic Beliefs*
  By Alan Schreck
- *Pope Fiction: Answers to 30 Myths and Misconceptions About the Papacy*
  By Patrick Madrid

On Charismatic Catholicism
- *Christian Initiation and Baptism in the Holy Spirit: Evidence from the First Eight Centuries*
  By Kilian McDonnell & George T. Montague
- *Call to Holiness: Reflections on the Catholic Charismatic Renewal*
  By Paul Josef Cordes
- *Key to Charismatic Renewal in the Catholic Church*
  By Vincent Walsh

- *Fire Within: St. Teresa of Avilla, St. John of the Cross, and the Gospel – On Prayer*
  By Fr. Thomas Dubay

On Catholic Miracles
- *Eucharistic Miracles*
  By Joan Carroll Cruz
- *The Incorruptibles*
  By Joan Carroll Cruz
- *Relics*
  By Joan Carroll Cruz
- *Mysteries Marvels Miracles*
  By Joan Carroll Cruz
- *Padre Pio the Stigmatist*
  By Charles Mortimer Carty
- *A Woman Clothed with the Sun*
  By John J. Delaney

On Contemporary Catholic Issues
- *Life-Giving Love*
  By Kimberly Hahn
- *The Catholic Church at the End of an Age: What is the Spirit Saying?*
  By Ralph Martin
- *Is Jesus Coming Soon? A Catholic Perspective on the Second Coming*
  By Ralph Martin
- *Mass Confusion: The Do's and Don'ts of Catholic Worship*
  By James Akin
- *The Second Spring of the Church in America*
  By George A. Kelly
- *Shaken by Scandals – Catholics Speak Out About Priests' Sexual Abuse*
  By Paul Thigpen

- *Why Catholics Can't Sing – The Culture of Catholicism and the Triumph of Bad Taste*
  By Thomas Day
- *From Scandal to Hope*
  By Fr. Benedict Groeschel
- *Truth And Tolerance: Christian Belief And World Religions*
  By Joseph Cardinal Ratzinger
- *Survivals and New Arrivals: The Old and New Enemies of the Catholic Church*
  By Hilaire Belloc
- *The Rapture Trap: A Catholic Response to "End Times" Fever*
  By Paul Thigpen
- *Will Catholics Be "Left Behind"? A Critique of the Rapture and Today's Prophecy Preachers*
  By Carl E. Olsen
- *The Ratzinger Report: An Exclusive Interview on the State of the Church*
  By Joseph Ratzinger
- *Architects of the Culture of Death*
  By Donald de Marco and Benjamin D. Wiker
- *The Da Vinci Hoax: Exposing the Errors in the Da Vinci Code*
  By Carl E. Olson and Sandra Miesel
- *The Courage to be Catholic: Crisis, Reform, and the Future of the Church*
  By George Weigel

On Conversion

- *Surprised By Truth – 11 Converts give the Biblical and Historical Reasons for Becoming Catholic*
  By Patrick Madrid
- *Born Fundamentalist, Born Again Catholic*
  By David Currie

- *Evangelical Is Not Enough – Worship of God in Liturgy and Sacrament*
  By Thomas Howard
- *Choosing to Be Catholic – For the First Time or Once Again*
  By William J. O'Malley
- *Crossing the Tiber – Evangelical Protestants Discover the Historical Church*
  By Stephen Ray
- *Apologia Pro Vita Sua*
  By John Henry Newman
- *Why Be Catholic?*
  By William J. O'Malley

On Catholic Philosophy
- *The Mystery of the Supernatural*
  By Henri de Lubac
- *Theology of the Body for Beginners – A Basic Introduction to Pope John Paul II's Sexual Revolution*
  By Christopher West
- *The City of God*
  By Saint Augustine
- *A Summa of the Summa: The Essential Philosophical Passages of St Thomas Aquinas' Summa Theologica Edited and Explained for Beginners*
  By Peter Kreeft
- *The Truth of Catholicism: Ten Controversies Explored*
  By George Weigel
- *The Collected Works of G.K. Chesterton (3 Volumes)*
  By G.K. Chesterton

On Catholic Spirituality
- *Scripture Matters: Essays on Reading the Bible From the Heart of the Church*
  By Scott Hahn

- *On Being Catholic*
  By Thomas Howard
- *The How-To Book of the Bible: Everything You Need to Know But No One Ever Taught You*
  Karl A. Schultz
- *Spirit of Catholicism*
  By Karl Adams
- *Splendor in the Ordinary: Your Home as a Holy Place*
  By Thomas Howard
- *Of the Imitation of Christ*
  By Thomas Kempis
- *John Paul II's Book of Mary*
  By Pope John Paul II
- *The Essential Mary Handbook: A Summary of Beliefs, Practices, and Prayers*
  By Judith A. Bauer
- *Introduction to the Devout Life*
  By Saint Francis de Sales
- *Letters to a Young Catholic – The Art of Mentoring*
  By George Weigel
- *The Essential Catholic Handbook: A Summary of Beliefs, Practices, and Prayers*
  By John O'Conner and Redemptorist Pastoral
- *It's My Church and I'll Stay If I Want To – Affirming Catholicism*
  By Lonni Collins Pratt
- *How to Get the Most Out of the Eucharist*
  By Michael Dubruiel

On Catholic Apologetics
- *Apologetics and Catholic Doctrine*
  By Michael Sheehan
- *Search and Rescue: How to Bring Your Family and Friends Into, Or Back Into, the Catholic Church*
  By Patrick Madrid

- *Catholic Controversy: St. Francis de Sales Defense of the Faith*
  St. Francis de Sales
- *Nothing but the Truth*
  By Karl Keating
- *Radio Replies (3 volumes)*
  By Fr. Leslie Rumble and Fr. Charles Carty
- *Nuts and Bolts: A Practical, How-To Guide for Explaining and Defending the Catholic Faith*
  Tim Staples
- *Fundamentals of the Faith – Essays in Christian Apologetics*
  By Peter Kreeft

On Catholic Imagination
- *The Hobbit*
  By J.R.R. Tolkien
- *The Lord of the Rings (3 volumes)*
  By J.R.R. Tolkien
- *Father Brown of the Church of Rome*
  By G.K. Chesterton
- *A Travel Guide to Heaven*
  By Anthony de Stefano
- *Citadel of God*
  By Louis de Wohl
- *A Philadelphia Catholic in King James's Court*
  By Martin de Porres Kennedy
- *The Joyful Begger*
  By Louis de Wohl
- *The Complete Poetry of John Milton*
  By John Milton, edited by John T. Shawcross
- *The Divine Comedy*
  By Dante Alighieri

Videos / DVDs

- *Ultimate Catholic Q & A*
  By Various Speakers
- *Testimony to Truth*
  By Alex Jones and Scott Hahn
- *Footprints of God (series)*
  By Stephen Ray
- *Feast of Faith – The Transforming Power of the Eucharist*
  By Marcellino D'Ambrosio
- *Why Be Catholic?*
  By Patrick Madrid
- *Where is That in the Bible?*
  By Patrick Madrid
- *Reflections on the Mass*
  By Various Speakers
- *No Turning Back – Confessions of a Catholic Priest*
  By Fr. Donald Calloway
- *Interview with an Exorcist*
  Fr. Jose Antonio Fortea
- *The Ratzinger Interview*
  By Cardinal Ratzinger / Pope Benedict XVI

Audio

- *Apologetics for the New Evangelization*
  By Timothy Staples
- *Catholicism Meets Calvary Chapel*
  By Timothy Staples and Jesse Romero
- *Fallen Fathers – Facts and Fallacies*
  By Timothy Staples and Fr. Patrick Brannan
- *St. Paul's Epistle to the Ephesians*
  By Timothy Staples
- *Twisted Scripture – Sola Scriptura Exposed*
  By Timothy Staples
- *The Bible is a Catholic Book*
  By Michael Barber

- *Wisdom of the Saints*
  By Fr. Shannon Collins
- *He Must Reign – the Catholic Church, the Kingdom of Heaven*
  By Scott Hahn, Brant Petrie, Ted Sri, Michael Barber, and Fr. Richard T. Simon
- *Why Be Catholic?*
  By Marcellino D'Ambrosio
- *I'm Not Being Fed*
  By Jeff Cavins
- *What Still Divides Us? A High Powered Protestant/Catholic Debate*
  By Patrick Madrid & Team, Michael Horton & Team
- *Does the Bible Teach Sola Scriptura? A Catholic / Protestant Debate*
  By Patrick Madrid and James White

Software
- *Welcome to the Catholic Church*
  By Harmony Media
- *Catechism of the Catholic Church, Reference Edition*
  By Harmony Media
- *The Early Church Fathers*
  By Harmony Media
- *Catholic Challenge Catechism Computer Game*
  By Divinity Religious Products
- *Catholic Challenge Bible Computer Game*
  By Divinity Religious Products

Websites
- *www.catholic.com*
  The Catholic Answers Apostolate
- *http://home.inreach.com/bstanley/index.htm*
  The Catholic Treasure Chest

- *http://www.scripturecatholic.com/*
  Scripture Catholic
- *http://ic.net/~erasmus/RAZINDEX.HTM*
  Biblical Evidence for Catholicism
- *http://www.liturgyhours.org/*
  The Liturgy of the Hours
- *http://catholicoutlook.com/questions.php*
  Tough Questions for "Bible Christians"
- *http://www.geocities.com/Athens/Troy/6480/solascriptura.html*
  Twenty One Reasons to Reject Sola Scriptura
- *http://www.bringyou.to/apologetics/*
  Evangelical Catholic Apologetics
- *http://www.americancatholictruthsociety.com/*
  American Catholic Truth Society
- *http://www.newadvent.org/*
  New Advent
- *http://biblia.com/jesusbible/types.htm*
  Prophecies and Types of Each Book of the Old Testament Fulfilled in Jesus Christ and His Church – A Total of 1,093
- *http://www.catholic-forum.com/saints/indexsnt.htm*
  Patron Saints Index
- *http://www.getfed.com/*
  Discount Catholic Catalogue
- *http://www.catholicculture.org/sites/sites.cfm*
  Catholic Culture Web Site Reviews
- *http://www.catholic.org/clife/prayers/*
  Catholic Prayers and Beliefs
- *http://www.americancatholic.org/*
  American Catholic
- *http://www.vatican.va/*
  The Holy See
- *http://www.angelfire.com/ms/seanie/forgeries/findex.html*
  Anti-Catholic Forgeries Index

- *http://www.catholic-pages.com/*
  The Catholic Home for Your Browser
- *http://www.catholicexchange.com/*
  Your Faith. Your Life. Your World.
- *http://www.chnetwork.org/*
  The Coming Home Network
- *http://www.catholicmusicnetwork.com/*
  The Catholic Music Network
- *http://www.ewtn.com/*
  Eternal Word Television Network
- *http://www.phatmass.com/*
  Phatmass
- *http://www.peterkreeft.com/home.htm*
  The Official Peter Kreeft Site
- *http://www.catholicnewsagency.com/*
  The Catholic News Agency
- *http://www.vaticanradio.org/*
  Vatican Radio
- *http://www.davidmacd.com/catholic/index2.htm*
  Intro to the Catholic Church For Evangelicals
- *http://www.papalencyclicals.net/all.htm*
  Papal Encyclicals Online
- *http://www.usccb.org/*
  United States Conference of Catholic Bishops
- *http://www.cin.org/*
  The Catholic Information Network
- *http://www.oncecatholic.org/*
  Once Catholic – A Catholic Site for Seekers
- *http://www.catholicfirst.com/*
  Catholic Information Center on the Web
- *http://www.cwnews.com/*
  Catholic World News
- *http://www.catholicoutlook.com/*
  Catholic Outlook – A Protestant's Guide to the Catholic Church

- *http://www.catholic-convert.com/*
  Defenders of the Catholic Faith
- *http://www.east2west.org/*
  Introducing the West to the Treasures of Eastern Catholicism
- *http://www.lifeteen.org/*
  Life Teen – Leading Teens Closer to Christ
- *http://www.wavefactor.com/*
  Next Wave Faithful Online Community
- *http://www.pureloveclub.com/*
  The Pure Love Club
- *http://www.wau.org/*
  The Word Among Us Magazine
- *http://www.aboutcatholics.com/*
  About Catholics
- *http://www.cin.org/users/jgallegos/contents.htm*
  Corunum Catholic Apologetic Webpage

Appendix 2: Fruit of the Family – A Testimony to Truth

Mark 3:23-26
And he called them unto him, and said unto them in parables, How can Satan cast out Satan? And if a kingdom be divided against itself, that kingdom cannot stand. And if a house be divided against itself, that house cannot stand. And if Satan rise up against himself, and be divided, he cannot stand, but hath an end.

(All information gathered from Annuarium Statisticum Ecclesiae 2002 and the United States Conference of Catholic Bishops Office of Media Relations)

Worldwide Statistics

- Number of Baptized Catholics worldwide:
  1,070,315,000 *(growth from 757 million in 1978)*
- Number of Bishops worldwide:
  4,695 *(growth from 3,714 in 1978)*
- Number of Priests (diocesan and religious) worldwide:
  405,058
- Number of Permanent Deacons (diocesan and religious) worldwide:
  30,097 *(growth from 5,562 in 1978)*
- Number of Professed Religious (non-priests, both men and women) worldwide:
  837,760
- Number of Candidates to the Priesthood worldwide:
  113,199 *(growth from 63,882 in 1978)*

United States Statistics

- Number of Catholic Elementary Schools:
  6,853 *(serving 1,892,071 students)*
- Number of Catholic High Schools:
  1,347 *(serving 680,323 students)*
- Number of Catholic Colleges and Universities:
  232 *(serving 747,060 students)*
- Number of Non-Residential Schools for Handicapped Persons:
  83 *(serving 18,179 students)*
- Number of Catholic Hospitals:
  583 *(served 83,898,575 patients in 2004)*
- Number of Catholic Healthcare Centers:
  376 *(served 4,251,107 patients in 2004)*
- Number of Catholic Specialized Homes:
  1,546 *(served 1,412,029 residents in 2004)*
- Number of Catholic Residential Childcare Centers:
  272 *(served 70,886 resident children in 2004)*
- Number of People Served by Catholic Charities in 2002:
  7,134,551 *(served by more than 1,640 Catholic Charities agencies)*
- Number of People Helped by Catholic Community Services in 2002:
  3,312,346 *(social support, education and enrichment, socialization and neighborhood services, health-related services, etc.)*
- Number of People Helped by Catholic Food Services in 2002:
  4,665,445 *(food banks and pantries, soup kitchens, congregate dining, home-delivered meals, etc.)*
- Number of People Helped by Catholic Family Services in 2002:
  1,307,146 *(counseling and mental health, immigration, addiction, refugee, pregnancy, adoption, etc.)*
- Number of People Helped by Catholic Housing Services in 2002:

442,271 *(housing, temporary shelter, supervised living, transitional housing, etc.)*
- Number of People Helped by Catholic Basic Needs Services in 2002:
1,333,425 *(financial assistance, clothing, utilities, prescriptions, etc.)*

Appendix 3: A Word about the Experience of Catholicism

> *"You want to find faith and you do not know the road. You want to be cured of unbelief and you ask for the remedy: learn from those who were once bound like you and who now wager all they have. These are people who know the road you wish to follow, who have been cured of the affliction of which you wish to be cured: follow the way by which they began. They behaved just as if they did believe, taking holy water, having masses said, and so on. This will make you believe quite naturally, and will make you more docile."*
>
> -Blaise Pascal, *Pascal's Pensees*

If you happen to know an atheist, you may well have suggested he *pray* to God even though he doesn't yet *believe* in God. It's like Pascal's suggestion to act into the Faith. You won't know until you try. Whatever may be *said* for Catholicism, it's only by *experience* that you'll truly begin to perceive the Holy Spirit at work in you. So if because of this book you've decided to be open to Catholicism (or even pursue it), the best thing to do is compliment your reading with a lived experience. Here are some resources and ideas you may want to consider in your developing assessment of the Catholic Church:

1. **Go to Mass!** Check out *http://www.masstimes.org/dotNet/* to find information about your nearest parishes. Then check them out! Don't worry, you don't have to miss out on your own church service. Most parishes celebrate Mass daily, so you can attend whenever it fits your schedule. Try to go at least once a week. And don't be afraid to let people there know that you're Protestant. They will most likely be happy to answer any questions you have.

2. **Say the Rosary.** Rosaries are among the first cultural images that pop into people's minds when they hear the

word "Catholic". It might be a good idea to practice the devotion so you can see why it's so popular. Go to *http://www.rosaryarmy.com/default.aspx* to learn about the rosary and how to pray it. If you find yourself on a computer frequently, or have tech savvy, you may also be interested in the *Virtual Rosary*, which can be downloaded for free at *http://www.virtualrosary.org/* .

3. **Pray the Liturgy of the Hours.** Otherwise known as the "Divine Office", the Hours are an ancient way of praying the Psalms in unison with the whole Church at set times throughout the day. There are several variations, the most practical being the *Shorter Christian Prayer* book, which contains only the morning and evening prayers from the Liturgy of the Hours. Another popular option for those who enjoy the Hours is *Magnificat*, a monthly magazine (*http://www.magnificat.com/*).

4. **Visit your Lord, come in the flesh, at Eucharistic Adoration.** Many parishes offer perpetual adoration chapels. Bring your Bible. Meditate on God's Word in the presence of God's Word – your sacrificial Lamb, transcending time and space from the cross to be with you, even until the end of the world. A miracle, right before your eyes, under the appearance of bread! The Blessed Trinity, as Spirit, is present with you everywhere you go. But this side of Heaven, the only place to find the incarnated Son of God in *substantial* form is in the Eucharist.

5. **Go on a pilgrimage.** No matter what city you live in or what country you're from, chances are there is a place of special Catholic significance near you – a shrine, for example. Cemeteries, Cathedrals, Monasteries…all of these holy sites can facilitate a special kind of intimacy with the Holy Spirit. Inspire your imagination, stir your emotions,

provoke your wonder, intrigue your mind, or simply marvel at God's creation by checking out what might be near you. When you do explore your pilgrimage destination, be sure to learn of its history. Again, never be afraid to mention you're a Protestant with a lot of "why" questions. To find a good place for your retreat, try clicking on *http://www.catholiclinks.org/* and scroll down to the tenth topic of the index, "Spiritual Places". Shrines might be the best place to start.

6. **Attend a Catholic home group**. Small, "home" groups are usually centered on fellowship and prayer. They also often include folky, easy to sing worship music (courtesy of any musically talented group member) and a Bible study of some sort. These meetings generally feel more comfortable to Protestants because they're not unlike small groups found in their own places of worship. In fact, Catholics are usually ready to admit that their "separated brethren" (i.e. Protestants) have been by and large ahead of the game when it comes to home groups. Don't be surprised if you're asked for advice on how the group should be run! To find a Catholic home group, phone parishes local to you and ask what they have to offer.

7. **Volunteer at a Catholic charity.** In Catholicism, Charity is the name of the game! Charity is how we carry the Real Presence we receive at Mass out into the world. It's how we bear fruit and witness to hope in Christ. Check out *http://www.catholiccharitiesinfo.org/* to find your local Catholic Charities Agency. Or you can call your local parish priest and ask about volunteering opportunities.

Made in the USA
Middletown, DE
05 August 2016